W9-AUX-626

A compilation of newspaper columns from a small-town newspaper, written by a backwoods philosopher with a sense of humor.

Excerpts

He found a pry-bar over in a corner and jabbed it under Jake's hip and, using a pile of frozen horse manure as a fulcrum, managed to pry him up enough that I could yank the chain out.

With that, he dumped the whole bucket of lemonade on the ground, then threw the bucket at me. "I ain't drikin' no damn water with no damn chaff in it. You go get me some fresh water an' keep it clean."

A coffin was procured from a local undertaker, and Kelley and a large quantity of ice were put into it. There was no use wasting the ice, so the beer was also placed in the coffin to cool.

They are beginning to look more and more appetizing as the spaghetti wears thin. I'm visualizing them as tiny turkeys on tiny platters with their tiny drumsticks sticking up at their sides. They don't look like they'd hold much dressing.

About the Author

I've only lived in the city for six months since I was twelve years old, and with a little luck I never will again. I've always craved country life. I'm almost as bad as Dan'l Boone, who moved every time someone came close enough that he could see the smoke from the neighbor's chimney. The neighbors are closing in, but I still can't see the smoke, so here I'll stay.

I'm eight miles away from the nearest town and it suits me just fine. I like the people and the small town atmosphere, I just don't wanna live there. They have a wonderful small-town newspaper for which I've been writing an almost-weekly column. (We are rather easy-going here.)

To make a living, I make custom-made furniture. I've made a niche in the last few years making rustic, woodsy things that fit well in log cabins. I have a sawmill to make my own lumber, and several ancient vintage tractors and trucks. They, along with some interesting neighbors, provide fodder for my columns, as you'll soon see as you read. Occasionally, I indulge myself by building a log cabin.

I'm in my seventy-fifth year and in good health. I'll continue to write as long as I'm able. Perhaps there will be another book or two.

Dedication

This book is dedicated to Marie "Mimi" Morrison, my soulmate for twenty years. Even when reading my worst columns, she manages to laugh and say, "Oh, that's so good." I couldn't make it without her. She ain't a bad photographer, either.

Credits

Thanks to Mimi Morrison for all the wonderful pictures in this book.

A great big thanks to Kisty Wadsworth for editing ninety columns for me. It was a tremendous amount of work. It was tough, but I managed to keep some of my backwoods accent in spite of her.

I deeply appreciate the help from Mark Hartman, editor of The Logan Daily News, and all the staff. Without their help, there wouldn't be any columns. If I've offended any reader, contact the LDN, not me.

Copyright© 2001 Ed Fassig. Printed and bound in the United States of America. All rights reserved. No part of this book may be reproduced or transmitted in any form or by any means, electronic or mechanical including photocopying, recording, or by an information storage and retrieval system – except by a reviewer who may quote brief passages in a review to be printed in a magazine or newspaper – without permission in writing from the publisher. For information, please contact Backwoods Publishing, 18900 State Route 93S, Logan, Ohio 43138. First Printing 2001.

Printed USA by Easton Printing, Parkersburg, WV

Although the author and publisher have made every effort to ensure the accuracy and completeness of information contained in this book, we assume no responsibility for errors, inaccuracies, omissions, or any inconsistency herein. Any slights of people, places, or organizations are unintentional.

ISBN 0-9709189-0-9

$12.95

Introduction

I started writing in high school English class. My teacher, Miss Cowan, said I had a knack for writing, and she gave me an "A" on every paper. They weren't that good, I'm sure, but she liked me and I could do no wrong. In spite of that, she said I should be a lawyer because I could talk my way out of any situation. I declined on the grounds that I wouldn't go into any profession where I had to wear a necktie. I haven't worn one since, except for wakes and weddings.

In 1995, I applied for the job of weekly columnist at The Logan Daily News in my hometown. I had written a few columns for a weekly paper that died an early death. (Really, it wasn't my fault!) I took those columns to the editor. He glanced at them and said, "They're too long."

I replied that I thought they should be long enough to say what I had to say.

"They're too long," was the reply "But I'll look at 'em and let you know."

When two weeks had passed with no word, I went to see what he thought. When I inquired, the lady at the desk said, "Oh, he retired. Not here any more." Neither, apparently, was my material. Nobody could find it.

A few weeks later I read that there was a new editor who wanted some local writers as columnists. I resolved to try again. I called the lady who ran the defunct paper and she managed to find my old columns on her computer. Armed with these, I went to see the new man. He scanned them quickly and said, "My God, there's exactly what I've been looking for. When can you start?"

And so I was off an running. I had lots of memories from my childhood and youth and the column came easily. These are in chapter one. Later I began to write about daily life here on the home place, which my neighbor dubbed "Fassig's Funny Farm."

After a couple of years, I began to write about the neighbors. Now, every time we are together, they say, "I suppose we'll read about this in the paper."

Though the subject matter is varied, my main thrust is to entertain. I don't take myself too seriously and try to find humor in most situations, although I do get up on the soap box occasionally. I've been accused of having a rather perverse sense of humor, but I think that's better than having no sense of humor, like some of the politicians I write about.

I hope you'll enjoy this book. The "chapters" are arranged according to subject matter and the columns can be read in ten minutes or so and are an easy read, for the most part. Since there is a stopping place every few minutes, you can carry the book with you and read while stopped in traffic or waiting for the bus, or even while milking the cows. Enjoy!

Copyright© 2001 by Edward A. Fassig. All right reserved

Table of Contents

Chapter 1
Them Was the Good Ol' Days

Chapter 2
Fun on the Funny Farm

Chapter 3
History

Chapter 4
The Old Filosifer

Chapter 5
Pure Fantasy

Chapter 6
Travelin' On

Chapter 7
Personal Thoughts

Chapter 8
Nature Notes

Chapter 1
Them Was the Good Ol' Days

Town Characters
July 8, 1995

One of the main differences in the village life of today as compared to when I was growing up fifty to sixty years ago is the lack of what are called town "characters." At least it seems that way. Perhaps I'm just not in the position to notice them.

I was blessed by growing up in a village of some 475 people. It was named Hilliards, Ohio, then. The "s" has since been dropped. Now only the old timers pronounce it. Hilliards had a large population of characters.

One of my favorites was old Jake. I won't tell you his last name because his descendants are still living.

Jake was sort of a handy man. He helped neighbors with such chores as fence building, garden plowing and the like. He worked when he felt like it until he felt like quitting.

He had an old horse and a light wagon that were his sole source of transportation. He hauled his tools in it when he went on jobs. An old German shepherd trotted along beside the wagon. He called the horse and dog both Jake, after himself.

I asked him once why he named them that. He replied, "By God, when I hollar I want everything to come a runnin', an' I named 'em after me so's I could remember what the hell it was."

I first saw the Jakes when I was about twelve years old. We were never close friends, but he always stopped to chat when we saw one another along the road.

Whenever we had a blizzard and school was closed, I'd walk to town and work at the grain elevator. One such storm came late in the year — March, I think, 1945. The roads were closed all week except where we could punch through with the grain trucks. The office got a call from Jake that he needed coal bad. He'd been out for a couple of days and was getting desperate. He ordered one ton. They didn't like to deliver one ton, because it wasn't economical, but they recognized that some people could only afford a ton at a time.

Anyway, they sent me out to Jake's with a great big truck with a tiny ton of coal.

"Dump her right here," said Jake. I wheeled around to where he indicated and dumped it off. I started to pull away, but I was stuck in the snow. There were about ten inches of snow, which was bad enough, but it had been on long enough that the ground had thawed so that I went right through the snow and into the mud. I was really stuck.

I had devised a method of getting out of such situations. I would chain a two-by-four on each wheel so that every time the wheels went around I moved four inches. It was slow, but effective. The problem was there was only one chain on the truck. I asked Jake if he had a chain.

"I believe Jake's layin' on one. If you'll help me, I think we can get it."

That sort of puzzled me because I didn't think it would be that hard to move a horse. We went to the barn. Sure enough, Jake was lying on the chain. The problem was, Jake was deader than a door nail and frozen hard as a rock. We both pulled on the chain, but couldn't budge it.

"Wait a minute; we've got to try sumpin' else," said Jake.

He found a long pry-bar over in the corner. He jabbed it under Jake's hip bone and, using a pile of frozen horse manure as a fulcrum, managed to pry him up enough that I could yank the chain out.

"How long's he been this way?" I asked.

"Oh, a couple of months, I guess," was the reply.

"Gettin' about time to get rid of him, I guess," I said.

"Yeah, I'll have to do sumpin' 'fore he thaws, I reckon," he said.

We went back toward the truck with the chain just as another of our trucks came by. Using all three chains, he managed to pull me out by staying on the driveway.

"Well, come on in and I'll pay you," said Jake.

The door opened into the kitchen. In the very center of the room was a big old round table. It sat in about four inches of dirty water that had frozen into solid ice.

"Watch yourself. Been washing," said Jake.

In a corner sat a ringer-type washer with the drain hose lying on the floor.

"Sink drains froze. Had to run her on the floor. Shoulda drilled a hole under the table first, I s'pose. I didn't think it would be this cold so late. How much do I owe ya?"

I left them there rather sadly. Jake the dog sleeping in the old chair, Jake the man, old, surely feeling his time not far off, and Jake the horse already at peace.

I never saw them again. I went into the Army in the spring and when I got out they were all gone.

I hope they are together again, young and happy.

Ringin' the Sow
July 15, 1995

In 1937, the summer I was ten years old, I spent the entire summer on a farm that belonged to friends of my parents. This experience changed my whole life. From that point on, I viewed everything from the perspective of a farmer. The following is my recollection of that first day on the job.

After chores and breakfast, Mr. Pepper announced that we were going to "ring a sow." It should have been done before, he said, but he needed help, so had put it off until I came. That made me feel a little important. Being a ten-year-old city kid who had only visited the farm at Christmas and Thanksgiving, I wasn't exactly sure what a sow was and had absolutely no idea how to "ring" one.

It didn't take long to find out. He led me to a small outbuilding and climbed a gate across the doorway. I got halfway over the gate. I stopped and did a double-take. In that little twelve-by-twelve building was the biggest pig I had ever seen. She was taller than I was. Mr. Pepper said she weighed about 500 pounds. To me she looked as big as an elephant. He said we were going to put rings in her nose so she wouldn't root in the ground and tear up the pasture.

"Won't that hurt her?" I asked.

"Hell yes, it hurts. That's what keeps her from rootin'. If it didn't hurt she'd go on rootin'," he said.

He took a piece of heavy rope down from a nail, handed me one end through the gate, and fashioned a lasso in the other end. "What I'm gonna do is put this lasso in her mouth and around her snout and

I want you to pull back hard around that gate post and hold her while I put the ring in."

"I don't know if I can," I said. "She's awful big."

"You can if you will," he replied. "Let me tell you what happened to me when I was about your age. We had a neighbor who wanted me to ride a horse he was trying to break. I was afraid because he was a big horse and skittish. The man said he would hold the horse's head with a rope so I had nothing to worry about. Well, I climbed on and he held on. That horse went crazy. He tried to run away, but the man held him back. He tried to rear and throw me, but that man held him down. Finally that horse was wore out and settled down. I climbed down and the man let go of the rope. When he did, his little finger fell to the ground. The horse had torn it right off, but he never let go. After that, whenever he told me he was going to hold something, I knew he meant it. Now, that's what I expect of you," Mr. Pepper said.

Nobody had ever talked to me man to man like that, and I vowed to give it my best.

Mr. Pepper put a little corn in the sow's trough from a bucket that he kept hanging on a peg. As she ate, he scratched her back and talked soothingly to her. "When I holler, you pull as hard as you can on that rope and hold on 'til I tell you to let go," he said to me in the same soothing tones. He worked forward on her until he was scratching her ears and she kept right on eating and grunting quietly. Quick as a flash, he dropped that loop down over her nose, just as she raised her head, and yanked up, pulling the lasso tight. "Pull," he shouted.

I hauled back for all I was worth and that old sow exploded. She started to run, but in that small building there was no place to go but in a circle. As she came toward me, I took up the slack. "Go sideways, around the post," he yelled. I did. That gave me some friction on the rope that was to my advantage. As the sow started the other way, she felt the rope come taunt. The lasso tightened on her snout and she came around facing me and started to back up, dragging me with her a couple of reluctant steps. Her rear end hit the corner of the pen, and she couldn't go any farther, so she just stood there and leaned against the rope. All the time this was going on she was emitting the most ear-splitting scream I had ever heard. It was worse than the fire engines I was used to in the city. There is just nothing that can compare to that noise.

All Mr. Pepper had to do was walk up to her and put in the rings. She just stood there still as a statue and screamed.

The rings are put in by using a special plier-like device that holds them firmly in place. One merely places the ringers, as they are called, over the ridge of cartilage on the hog's nose and squeezes. One side of the ring is sharpened. It goes into the cartilage and curves back out through an eye on the other end of the ring. That's all there is to it. It's no worse than piercing and ear for earrings.

The whole episode took no longer than five minutes, but my arms were trembling by the time he came to the gate and signaled me to let go. The pig's squealing was so loud that I could see Mr. Pepper's mouth move, but couldn't hear him. The second I let loose of the rope, the noise stopped. He shook the rope and it fell clear. The sow walked over to the trough and began to eat as if nothing had happened.

I was amazed. This monumental task was over in minutes and Mr. Pepper wasn't even sweating. I had a lot of respect for a man who could do a job like that so simply and efficiently. My dad would have ranted and raved for hours over it.

He turned to me and said, "By God, Eddie, you did all right. You hung in there like you meant it. I know I can trust you to do your share." I grinned self-consciously, but my chest swelled a bit. And I was just a little disappointed that my little finger didn't fall to the ground when I let go of the rope.

Thrashin' Wheat
August 12, 1995

Mr. Pepper was explaining what we would be doing tomorrow. It was the summer of 1937, the summer I was ten. I was spending the summer with the Peppers, who were friends of my parents.

"Tomorrow we start the thrashin' season at Jim Graham's," Mr. Pepper said. "We'll do chores and a little fixin' up around here first. Ya can't do much with the wheat 'til the dew dries, around 10 a.m."

At the appointed hour, we got into his old '29 Chevy for the mile and a half drive up the gravel road to the Graham farm. I was excited. Mr. Pepper had talked about the thrashin' "ring" ever since we had cut and shocked his wheat a month before, but I still couldn't get it straight in my head what it would be like.

I was really surprised when we arrived. It was like a circus. The drive and barnyard were crowded with teams and wagons. Men were standing around in little knots, laughing and joking. I could tell this was a social event as much as a working event.

In the midst of all the teams and men was an immense piece of machinery attached to another huge machine belching black smoke.

"That red thing is the thrashin' machine and the other is the steam engine that furnishes the power to run it," said Mr. Pepper. "That big belt goes from a pulley on the engine to a pulley on the separator — that's what the thrashin' machine is properly called. When one turns, it turns the other. You'll see in a few minutes. They'll start as soon as they get up steam pressure."

Sure enough, in a few minutes the engine gave off a little "Toot! Toot!" almost like a toy train and the belt began to turn. Things began to shake, chains ran around pulleys, blowers blew and dust flew.

"While he's checking it and greasin' and oilin', we begin loading wagons," he said. "By the way, Graham wants you to be water boy."

"OK, but what do I do?" I replied.

"Just get a bucket and dipper from Mrs. Graham up at the house and make sure every man gets a drink any time he wants one. You'll have to go to the fields, too. The pitchers stay out there, and it's awfully hot out there."

I dutifully went up to the house, where Mrs. Graham gave me a two-and-a-half-gallon porcelain bucket and a dipper and slipped me a handful of cookies on the side. She was a sweet little lady. "Now you be sure to put some ice in each bucket of water. The boys like it cold," she said.

I started on my rounds. I'll tell you, I was in hog heaven. I'd never seen anything so exciting. The separator was in the center, of course. A wagon loaded with sheaves of wheat was pulled up on each side and the drivers would pitch the sheaves onto the conveyor belt, first one then the other, with a natural rhythm that kept the belt filled, all with the heads in first. I don't know for sure what went on inside, but they were beaten, whirled, shaken and generally thrown about and blown upon until the straw came shooting out and was blown onto an ever-growing stack. The grain came out a little chute on the side where a man bagged it and tied the top shut with twine and loaded it on a grain wagon.

The horses paid no attention to the roaring monster at the sides, but quietly switched flies until the wagon was empty. The men worked with precision, keeping up the rhythm hour after hour, all the time shouting back and forth and just having a ball.

Meantime, I continued my rounds. At first, business was slow, but as the day warmed, things picked up and I was kept hopping. The men teased me and ran me around a bit, but it was all in fun and I loved it.

On my third trip after more ice, Mrs. Graham said, "I've got a treat for the boys. I've made some lemonade." Sure enough, she had squeezed about a dozen lemons and sweetened it with plenty of sugar and put in a chunk of ice. It was really good. The lemon pulp floated on top so you could tell it was the real McCoy.

I decided to take this to the field where it was hottest. There were two wagons fairly close together about mid-field. I headed for them. The first two drank gratefully. A burly farmer on the second wagon took the bucket and looked at the lemon pulp. "What's that stuff in the water?"

By now I was getting into the spirit of the day and answered jokingly, "Oh, just a little wheat chaff."

With that, he threw the whole bucket of lemonade on the ground, then threw the bucket at me.

"I ain't drinkin' no damn water with no damn chaff in it. You go get me a fresh bucket of water, and keep it clean!"

That ended my feeble attempt at humor. I went back to the kitchen, tail between my legs. Mrs. Graham said, "My goodness, are you back already? They must have liked it. Well, I'll make some more."

"I'll just take some water now while you're making it." I took the water back to the farmer and I never did give him any lemonade.

About halfway through my next trip, I heard a "toot-toot-toot" from the steam engine. "Lunch time," someone shouted. I was glad. I'd heard about the fabulous thrashin' dinners that were served. I'd also seen seven or eight farm wives in the kitchen preparing it. Each farmer's wife in the ring contributed something toward lunch.

I made my way back to the house. There I met Mr. Pepper, who said, "Eddie, Jim Graham is a grumpy old goat and I'm afraid he won't want to feed you since you're not a working man. I'm sorry, but I think you should walk home for lunch."

My heart sank, and I'm sure my face fell. To be cut out of lunch and the camaraderie that went with it was a cruel blow. I said "OK" and turned and walked to the road. That was all I could say because a huge lump came up in my throat and I couldn't speak without crying.

I was walking down the gravel road kicking stones and trying to swallow that lump in my throat, ignoring the stones that got into my worn-out tennis shoes, when I heard a rumble behind me. I turned and saw a plume of dust being led by a Model A Ford Coupe. The car pulled up beside me and stopped. It was Mr. Graham. "Why ain't you eatin'?" he said.

"Mr. Pepper said I shouldn't eat because I wasn't workin'," I mumbled.

"I thought I seen you workin'?" he asked.

"Well, I guess so."

"Get in," he commanded. I obeyed. The car was dusty and smelled of cigars and cow manure, but it beat walking. I thought he was taking me home. Instead, he turned the car around and headed back.

He strode into the dining room where everyone was sitting down, dragging me in his wake by the shear force of his personality.

"Pepper, feed this boy. How do you expect him to do a man's work without no dinner?" he growled.

Mr. Pepper winked at me. "Better warsh up on the back porch," he said.

I went to the back porch and poured water from the pitcher into a porcelain basin and splashed a little on my face and hair, then searched in vain for a dry spot on the roller towel. I climbed up on the bench so I could see in the cracked mirror and combed my hair with a scraggly old comb with half the teeth missing and scurried back to the dining room.

Well, that was the signal for the wives to take over. They kept my plate full. There was roast pork and roast beef, corn, homemade bread and several other things I can't remember. There were five kinds of pie. It's a wonder the table didn't break down.

The afternoon went quickly and smoothly and we finished all the wheat.

In retrospect, I can say that day was well up there in being one of the happiest days of my life.

A Trumpet in the Land
September 23, 1995

The first time I ever saw my dad in church was when my sister got married. Mom always went, but Dad, never. Since we had no transportation, we went to the nearest church. Our religion changed every time we moved. We attended Church of Christ, Lutheran, Methodist, and some home church that never made it.

Mom liked to go to church just to get away from him once in a while, and we went rather than stay home alone with him.

Dad went through different phases. For a while, he was a Rosecrucion, whatever that was. He got books and literature which he read occasionally. That wore off pretty soon. Then someone talked him into going to a "trumpet meeting." We were never sure what a trumpet meeting was, but we were sure it was some kind of magic or cult. He would tell of meeting people who had died, and of strange lights and sounds. Mom didn't give it much credence. I think she suspected he was fooling around, and I suspect now that she was right.

Anyhow, every Thursday night he put on his brown pin-striped suit, tie and Fedora hat — the very essence of what the well-dressed Al Capone would wear — and went out and didn't return until late. He would regale us at supper next evening with tales of the spirits that had appeared.

One night, he came home with his own trumpet. He'd bought it from the charleton who had organized the trumpet meetings. It cost seventeen dollars. Mom was furious. She didn't often complain, but this thing pushed the right button. In 1934, the depths of the Depression, seventeen dollars was more than a week's pay. That we were barely getting by so that he could buy a trumpet to talk to dead guys was more than she could take.

Dad said it was well worth it because the dead people might be able to tell him something worth a lot of money.

"Bull feathers," was the reply.

To placate her, Dad said that since he had his own trumpet, he could have his own seance and we'd have one and we could see for ourselves what it would do. He even let us see the trumpet. It was nothing but a sort of a funnel. It looked like a megaphone made of cheap tin or aluminum. I'm sure you could have bought something similar in a hardware store for fifty cents. It was in a really tacky looking fake leather case. I thought it was really a gyp except that it had magic powers.

So we began to anticipate a trumpet meeting. One of my mother's friends was staying with us at the time. She was an English lady my mother had known in England before she immigrated here. There was an English colony of sorts in Columbus at the time, and they kept in touch. Mrs. Taylor was her name. She had no home and made her living "staying" with people, supposedly in exchange for help around the house. She never really did any work except make quilts and hooked rugs and crocheted things. She was nice and she was funny and she kept us entertained, so she usually stayed two or three months at a time.

She was a spunky old gal and didn't take any of my dad's crap. When he got to blowing off, she'd just say, "Arthur, thee can just stoof it oop thy backside," and he'd stomp out. Many's the time I heard him tell Mom, "One of these days I'm gonna throw that old woman out on her backside," but he never did. I think secretly he admired her spunk. The rest of us slunk around with our tails between our legs like whipped pups when he was around, but she stood up and spit in his eye. I think he liked that.

The next night was chosen as the date of the big trumpet meeting. We gathered in what we called the alcove. It was a small room next to the dining room with a curtain over a double doorway. It had no windows and it really got dark in there, which should be good for ghosts, since you couldn't see them in the daylight. I was torn between skepticism and fear, leaning more toward fear as the time got nearer. Being seven years old at the time, I didn't know exactly what to expect.

Finally, my dad assembled us in a circle in the alcove and turned off the lights. The trusty trumpet sat on a small table in front of him. "We'll try to contact Uncle Charlie," he said. Uncle Charlie was his uncle who had died a year or so earlier.

"His favorite hymn was 'Bringing in the Sheaves,' so we'll sing that."

We all sang "Bringing in the sheaves, bringing in the sheaves, we will come rejoicing, bringing in the sheaves."

Dad said, "Uncle Charlie, can you hear us? Come forward if you do." Nothing.

"I don't think he heard us. Let's sing again."

"Bringing in the sheaves ..." We sang a little more lustily this time.

"I can feel the trumpet vibrating. He's getting close. Let's sing."

"Bringing in the sheaves ..."

"There's a light over Eddie's head. If we can get two lights, we'll get a guide and the guide will bring Uncle Charlie in."

"Bringing in the sheaves ..."

"Arthur, thee's got a good imagination. I didn't see a bloody light," said Mrs. Taylor.

I was glad it was dark so he couldn't see us laugh silently. All except Mom. She laughed loud and long. I couldn't see his face, but I'm sure it was livid. I know he was saying to himself, "One of these days I'm going to throw that old woman out on her backside."

End of seance!

I think my dad began to realize that he had been duped, that his trumpet didn't have whatever magic power the other one had. The whole thing sort of faded away after that. No more meetings, no more trumpet.

When Mom Learned to Drive
October 21, 1995

I saw an old 1953 Chevy the other day and it reminded me of my mother. She used to have one just like it. It was a miserable old tank of a car and it suited her just fine. She never went over thirty-five miles per hour except once. She is the only one I know who ever got a ticket for driving too slow in morning rush hour. It seems that one of those caught in the mile-long traffic jam behind her was a state highway patrolman. He made her promise to never drive again in the car pool. When it was her turn, someone else drove her car.

After she finally got up enough nerve to divorce my dad, I built her a house next to mine. Since we lived in the country, she wanted a car so she could be independent. I helped her pick out the tank and tried as best I could to teach her to drive. She was absolutely petrified. It took months before she could manage to do twenty on the country roads and she never did master parallel parking. If she couldn't buy what she wanted in a shopping center, she did without.

She had nightmares about getting her driver's license. In fact, after she failed in Franklin County twice, she went to Madison County. She then went to Marysville in Union County because the Madison County guy "didn't like her." The Union County man was real nice, she said, so she went back to him twice and finally passed. I think the fellow was afraid to ride with her again and passed her in self defense.

Anyway, after she got her license, she was independent and happy even if the neighbors ran for their lives when they saw her coming.

One cold morning, Ol' Bessie wouldn't start and she wanted me to take her to work. Since she worked in downtown Columbus, it would have ruined my day because I'd have to go get her in the afternoon. I said, "This car starts easy. I'll give you a push and you'll be on your way."

"Oh, I can't do that," she said. "I wouldn't know how."

"There's nothing to it," I replied. "Just turn on the key, put it in drive, put your foot on the gas pedal, and it will start."

With much trepidation, she did as I instructed and we were off. Within 200 feet, her car started and she slowly pulled away from me. I watched her go gripping the wheel with both hands, hunched over like Barney Oldfield off to the races. I turned around at the first drive and went back home.

When she came home that night, she was fuming. It seemed to her that I was pushing her ever faster until she was going fifty miles per hour. She took off at the railroad crossing two miles away like a ski jump at fifty-five miles per hour. She said she'd never forgive me for pushing her so fast. She hadn't looked in her mirror and didn't realize I was no longer pushing until she went flying down Main Street in Hilliard and had to stop for the traffic light.

All this nervousness and fear started at an incident that happened when I was about five years old. My dad tried to teach Mom to drive back then. As usual, he yelled at her whenever she made a mistake, which made her so nervous that she made more mistakes, and so on. These sessions always ended in tears. My sister (who is two years younger) and I cowered in the back seat and prayed it would soon be over. Mom wasn't really mechanically minded, but I think she could have done all right eventually if he'd left her alone.

My dad drove a furniture delivery truck. One afternoon, he called to say he had a delivery near some friends who lived on a small farm near Westerville and for Mom to drive the car out there and meet him there for supper. Mom didn't want to go, but he was intimidating enough that she finally agreed. Packing some hot dishes in the back seat, she started up 3-C highway. She was doing pretty well, too, tooling along at twenty-five miles per hour. This was about 1932, and that was a reasonable speed for the time. She managed to stop for a couple of traffic lights and find the right gears to start up again. We were "yeahing" from the back seat and she was laughing and we had a grand old time.

After she got off the highway and onto the little country roads, she began to get a little apprehensive about getting lost, but we kids knew the way. Sure enough, we soon saw my dad's big furniture van in the driveway. At the sight of the truck, all of my mom's senses fled. As she turned in, she mashed hard on the gas instead of the brake and plowed into the tailgate, which was in a horizontal position, like a ton of bricks. We stopped very suddenly. My sister and I were thrown to the floor, followed by the food. She got smacked by the dinner rolls while I took a bath in the macaroni and cheese casserole, which luckily had cooled a bit by then.

The tailgate had sliced through the radiator of the car and a fountain of steam was billowing skyward like Old Faithful. The smell of alcohol antifreeze was sickening. My dad came storming out of the house and ranted and raved for about ten minutes. Mom flew out of the car because she thought it was going to blow up. Pretty soon, someone thought about us and rescued us from the macaroni.

After supper, we all crowded into the truck and had a long, quiet ride home. Mom never drove again until after the aforementioned divorce.

Johnny-One-Note
December 9, 1995

During the Great Depression in the 1930s, many people became entrepreneurs whether they wanted to or not.

Some men sold pencils or apples on downtown street corners. Some would buy a crate of strawberries or blackberries and carry it on their shoulders as they walked through the neighborhoods, crying out to sell their wares, "Strawberries! Strawberries! Two quarts for a quarter!" hoping to make a few pennies to support their families.

One old man came around about once a month, carrying a big foot-cranked grinder on his back. He rang a hand bell and shouted, "Knives and scissors sharpened!" When he got a customer, he would set the grinder down and peddle it with one foot and sharpen the instrument. He was a nice old man and did a good job, but my dad never would pay to have something done that he could do himself, so he never stopped at our house. I couldn't blame my dad, really, but it would have boosted my ego to have paid for something once.

There was a fellow who came around a couple of times a summer with a pony. You got to sit on the pony if you paid the man to take your picture. You even got to wear a cowboy hat and chaps. I would have died to ride that pony, but I never did.

There was a hurdy-gurdy man who came around occasionally with a street organ and a little monkey. After each tune, the monkey would go around and collect money from the crowd of kids that surrounded them. We could usually inveigle a penny or two out of Mom for him.

The champion entrepreneur of the neighborhood was Mrs. Tunny. She "wrote numbers." That was an illegal gambling scheme that was used extensively by poor folks because it was cheap and easy. You picked a three-digit number for three cents. For another penny, you could "box" it, which meant the digits could be rearranged in any sequence. Every day, a number would appear in the stock market page of the newspaper. If you picked that number, you won five dollars. After years of playing, my mother finally won. She figured it cost twenty-seven dollars to win five, so she quit.

Mrs. Tunny came every day to write numbers, and she was always selling something. It might be a chance on a punch board or candy or perfume. One day Mom called me in when Mrs. Tunny was there. She said, "Sit down. I want to show you something." I complied. Mrs. Tunny opened a funny-looking case and took out a guitar and placed it on my lap. She stroked the strings and said, "Ain't that purty?"

Mom said, "Would you like to learn to play that?"

I was taken aback. This was so sudden. I didn't know what to think. I didn't really want to play the thing, but I thought Mom wanted ed me to and I didn't want to disappoint her, so I said, "I guess so."

"Great!" shouted Mrs. Tunny. "Just go downtown to this address at three o'clock on Saturday and before you know it, you can play this thing." So the deal, and my fate, were sealed.

On Saturday, when everyone else was out playing, I had to wash and put on clean clothes. Mom gave me six cents for the streetcar — three cents each way — and fifty cents for the lesson, and directions. She said, "Take the streetcar downtown and get off at High Street. Turn right two blocks to this address." She gave me a slip of paper with a number on it. "It's upstairs, so look for this number on the door and this number on a door upstairs," she said.

I picked up the case and headed for the streetcar stop a block away. The case was huge. It was fully as tall as I was. (I was only eight at the time.) If I'd had only one leg, I could have gotten inside it myself. I struggled to get it up onto the streetcar. As I put my three cents into the fare box, the conductor said, "If that thing was wearin' a hat, I'd have to charge you three more cents."

I got off at High Street and after what seemed like a two-mile hike, I found the door with the correct numbers. When I looked up those stairs, I nearly died. They were the longest stairs I had ever seen. The building had a store on the first floor with fourteen-foot ceilings instead of the nine footers I was used to. After this trip, climbing

Mount McKinley would be a snap.

I found the door and knocked gently. A man opened the door and said, "Yes?"

"I'm supposed to take a guitar lesson," I said.

"Who are you?"

I told him, and he said, "I didn't know you were coming. You're fifteen minutes late. Take a seat."

There were about fifteen people of various ages all staring at me. I wanted to crawl in a hole. These people all knew how to play to some degree. I knew nothing.

"What can you play?" the man asked.

"Nothing," I replied.

"This is a Hawaiian guitar," he said. "You hold this steel bar on this mark and stroke it on this mark. Now we'll go on with the lesson. You follow along as best you can."

The next forty-five minutes were a blur. The other people took their instruction like they knew what they were doing, and I played that one note. I was never so relieved in my life as I was when that lesson was over. I gave the man the fifty cents and went home.

After supper, my dad said, "What did you learn on the guitar?"

"Nothin'," was my reply.

"Nothin'!" he shouted. "Git that guitar!"

I got the guitar. I knew what was coming.

"Now, let me hear you play that thing!"

I found the mark and put the steel there and played my one note.

"Go on," he growled.

I played the note again.

"That's it?" he asked.

"Yes," I mumbled.

"After me wasting fifty cents and sending you clear downtown, you can only play one lousy note? Well, I'll be damned if I'm wasting all my money on anybody that dumb!"

Inwardly, I rejoiced, but to make sure he didn't change his mind, I cried a little. And thus ended my short but brilliant career as a musician.

Remembering Lester
January 6, 1996

I had only lived in the Hilliard area a few weeks when I was introduced to Lester, or at least to his activities.

I was in the sixth grade at Hilliard Elementary School. It was 1939 and I was twelve years old. Several of my new-found friends and I were playing kickball out by the cesspool when an explosion rocked the sunny October afternoon. I happened to be looking toward the farm across the road. A small tree emerged from a cloud of dust, heading skyward.

"What the heck was that?" I asked of my nearest friend.

"Oh, that's just Lester. He's been clearing fence rows all fall. He loves to play with dynamite. He'd rather blow a tree to hell than cut it down."

"You mean he just dynamites trees here right across the road from the school and nobody cares?"

"Yep. He just spuds a hole under the tree, shoves in about a half stick of dynamite and touches her off."

"Where does he get the dynamite?" I asked.

"Hardware store."

"You mean anyone can go in a store and buy dynamite?"

"Well, not anyone. I think ya gotta be eighteen," he said.

"What a wonderful place," I thought. I couldn't wait to be eighteen.

The fence row clearing continued sporadically for another month or so, with only two or three blasts a week. I thought it was odd that he didn't just do it all at once and get it over with. I thought Lester owned the farm, but it turned out that he was the hired hand. The farm owner didn't really like him to blast that close to the school so he did it when the owner was gone. It was OK to blast on the back of the farm, but Lester was a little fuzzy on where the dividing line was, so he kept getting closer to the school. Actually, he never blasted closer than about 300 feet of the school, but it could be unnerving for the uninitiated.

I had seen Lester uptown but didn't know who he was. He was easy to notice. He dressed in typical farmer garb — bib overalls, a matching blue denim jacket buttoned to the neck, and a winter cap with ear flaps that you might expect to see on a Canadian trapper. His signature piece, though, was knee-high gum boots. He wore them every day, summer and winter. The only time he was without them was when he was dressed for church, and then he wore high-top tennis shoes. I often thought his feet must look like they had been parboiled. They couldn't smell too good, either!

You could spot him walking a block away and recognize him instantly. His back was bent so that he walked stooped over like he was carrying a heavy pack. He dragged his feet and the heels were worn off his boots. He was always walking uphill.

I didn't really get to know Lester until I was about eighteen. His face was absolutely expressionless and his complexion dark with undertones of red. I thought he must be an Indian. He looked like Injun Joe in the movie "Tom Sawyer," and I was afraid of him. I could visualize him cutting my throat some dark night or maybe blowing me high above the school with a couple of sticks of dynamite.

Several times my sister came home from town and told about some old man in gum boots buying her a candy bar. My mother was furious and told her to stay away from him lest he entice her away and do her bodily harm. Later after I got to know Lester, I saw him do this several times. In fact, any time he was in the grocery store and there were kids in there, he would buy some candy bars and come up to the checkout counter and just toss one down on the counter. When the kid would hesitate, he'd mumble, "Therz a canny fer ya," which when loosely translated meant, "There's a candy bar for you." Truth was, he just loved kids and they were afraid of him just as I was. It was a shame because a gentler man never drew breath.

Part of the problem was his method of speech. He talked so fast that all the words ran together and it really took concentration to understand him. Even then, you'd have to ask him to repeat about half of what he said. To the kids he loved he might as well have been speaking German, so they were understandably standoffish. With just a few changes, he would have been a pied piper.

Lester lived with his mother and took good care of her in the same house he was born in. It was a tiny place of about three rooms. The yard was neat but devoid of landscaping, save for a shade tree and a small flower bed. It was just two blocks from the farm where he worked. He never had a car or learned to drive. What a spartan life he must have lived. I don't think he ever made over twenty dollars a week.

Sometimes when the boss was away he would drive the old Ford tractor uptown in mid-afternoon and get a bottle of pop and a candy bar. He kept that tractor cleaner than most cars. He always wiped it off before his trip uptown. You could tell he was proud of it and thoroughly enjoyed the trip. He never looked back, so the line of cars behind him didn't bother him at all.

I don't know what happened to old Lester. I wish I had kept in better touch with the old timers I knew in my youth, but youth looks to the future and old age reveres the past and rarely do they meet.

The building boom hit in the 1950s and the farm was broken up and developed. Lester was sidelined, I'm sure. What a pity that he couldn't have lived out his life blowing up an occasional tree and putt-putting uptown for a pop and candy bar.

Saturday on the Farm
March 16, 1996

Farm work in the 1930s was about as hard a work as you could find. I spent the summer of 1937 on the farm of friends of my parents. I was ten at the time and had never done any actual labor beyond mowing the grass with an old push mower. I hated that as much because it was useless as it was hard work. When I was done there was nothing to show for my labor. To this day, I don't mow grass. The wildlife take what they want and the rest has to take care of itself.

On the farm, the work never ended. We toiled from before breakfast until almost dark. The corn was planted when I got there but it had to be cultivated at least twice, preferably three times if it didn't get too tall too soon. I was too young to be trusted with a team of horses alone, so I got the fun job of following after with a hoe and chopping the weeds that the corn plow missed. I hadn't had so much fun since I fell off the garage roof.

The hay had to be cut between plowing. Mr. Pepper would cut in the morning about what we could put in the barn in one afternoon. Then in the afternoon, he would rake what he had cut the day before. We would then load it on the wagon and unload it in the barn. I liked that part. I got to stay on the wagon and fork the hay around to build the load while he pitched it from the windrow onto the wagon. I got to drive the horses between two windrows across the field, turn them at the end and come back between the next two. Boy, I felt important.

After hay came cutting and shocking barley. As soon as it was done, it was time to do the same to wheat. Then came more hay. After that, the thrasher came to thrash the barley and wheat. More hay, then cut and shock oats. More hay, thrash the oats.

28

It was a neverending parade of events, all vital to the well-being of the farm and family. I soon became strong and more confident. I began to feel like a farmer and loved farming. I didn't mention that this labor was preceded by milking cows and feeding livestock, and followed by milking cows and feeding livestock in the evening. If I ever felt bad about having to work forty hours a week in later life, all I had to do was think of those days to put things into perspective.

There were days of more leisure, though, and I looked forward to them. Every Saturday, Mrs. Pepper and the girls went to town. She sold eggs at the Kroger store in Marysville. She then bought supplies with the proceeds. If we were caught up on work or the weather was bad, I got to go to town with them.

At home in Columbus, I played most of the time with my pals. Going to the drug store or the grocery was work. I never thought I would consider shopping as recreation, but after the back-breaking toil on the farm, it didn't take much to make me happy. I enjoyed carrying that big basket of eggs back to the produce manager. He never counted them. He trusted Mrs. Pepper implicitly. What tickled me was to watch him pour those eggs into a big wire basket without breaking them. I don't know how he did it. I would have broken them all if I had tried.

After Kroger, we would shop all the little stores on the main street of Marysville. There was a five and dime, and a dry goods store where Mrs. Pepper bought material, or "goods" as we called it, to make school dresses for the girls. There was a candy store that smelled so good we could hardly stand it. We didn't go in there but only drooled as we looked in the windows. I thought I would like to work in a candy store like that when I grew up.

The "piece de resistance" was the drug store. We walked up and down every aisle, looked in every case. This was all just ritual, of course. What we were aiming for was the soda fountain. The girls always asked their mother if they could get a "sody." She'd make a production of looking through her purse to see if she had enough egg money left. It seems she always did have just enough. We climbed up on the stools and studied the list of the kinds of "sodies" available. It was a tough decision, there were so many kinds. We liked to watch the "soda jerk" make the concoctions. They were usually high school boys and enjoyed putting on a show. We all got something different and tasted each others' and vowed to get "that" next time. Now I had lived one block from a drug store, and had gone there every day to get cigarettes for my mother, but I'd never had a "sody." This was a treat for me and I was glad to be in the company of "rich" farmers.

By the time we were finished, and we made them last as long as possible, it was time to go home.

While the women folk got supper ready, Mr. Pepper and I milked the cows. By this time, I could milk one to his two. It was a little early to milk, but there was a reason: It was movie night!

Every Saturday night that the weather was good, the firemen in the nearby town of Ostrander put on free movies. It was a great get-together for nearby farmers and their families. A big screen was stretched across the main street. I think it was two bed sheets sewed together. A rope was fastened to each corner and tied to the fronts of the buildings on each side of the street. The screen always seemed to have wrinkles in it, and if there was a breeze it moved about quite a bit so that the picture sometimes ran off the sides. The movies were several years old, and "B" quality to boot. Sometimes they were also silent. It was comical to watch their lips move and have no sound come out. They had the words printed on captions, but if you were on the wrong side of the screen it would be written backwards and we kids couldn't read backwards fast enough. All signs in the pictures would be backwards, too. They usually had a cartoon, a short subject and a feature. We took popcorn or cookies for a snack. There were intermissions often because they had to change reels three or four times a show. Then, too, the film broke occasionally.

The kids ran around and played while the adults sat engrossed in the movie.

When I look back at that unsophisticated time, I wish we could enjoy the high tech stuff as much. Them was the good old days.

The Mini-Farm
March 23, 1996

When I was very young, during the great depression, we lived in the east end of Columbus. It was an old neighborhood then. The houses were fairly large. Most had about seven rooms. All were two story. Some were doubles and some were duplexes. A double housed two families side by side, each with two floors. A duplex housed two families, too, but one lived downstairs and the other lived upstairs.

They all heated with coal. The air was so dirty in the winter that it always looked foggy. The soot from the coal furnaces fell lazily like black snow. In fact, the snow turned black after a few days and melted quickly. The soot blew around in little drifts on the sidewalks. My mother wouldn't hang her clothes on the clothesline outside even on warm, sunny days. She hung them in the dingy basement where they took longer to dry but stayed cleaner. No one dared put coal in the furnace until the clothes were dry and taken down from the lines.

We lived there five years, and I remember only one house being built in that time. There was one lot available on the far corner of our block. We kids made it a daily ritual to go down and watch the man dig the basement. It took almost a week. Today one man with a backhoe could do it in two or three hours.

This fellow had a team of horses and a single shovel, walking plow, and a slip scraper. He would plow the area and get the ground all loose, then hitch the scraper to the team and clean out the loose dirt. The scraper was like a big scoop shovel with two handles. He worked the handles as the horses pulled to fill the scraper. They pulled it up an earthen ramp, out into the yard. The man raised the handles at just the right time and the scraper dug in and flipped over, spilling the dirt out. This went on hour after hour, day after day. I marveled at the strength and patience of the man and his horses. I don't know where the man came from. At quitting time he just left the tools there and drove the horses off down the street.

Speaking of horses, we also had a milkman and a breadman who drove horses. They came every other day on alternate days. The horses knew the route so well that the men would just take a basket full of milk or bread and start down the street, dropping their products off at the houses as they went. The horses would walk along and stop at certain spots, the same every time, and the men would run out of things right there and they would go back and refill their baskets and proceed again. We couldn't figure out how the horses knew it would be at just that spot.

Of course the horses would leave piles of road apples along the street. That could have been a problem, but it wasn't. For one thing, the dogs would run out and eat some of it until their owners saw them and ran out in the street screaming and drove them home. The real clean-up came from Johnnie Hartig, our next door neighbor.

Johnnie was my age. He didn't clean up after the horses because he wanted to, but because his dad made him do it. It was needed as fertilizer for their garden. Mr. Hartig was from Austria. He didn't own a car, but rode to and from work on a bicycle. That seemed strange to me. He was the only adult I knew who rode a bike. I was only seven or eight and didn't know that bikes were common transportation in other countries. I don't know where Mr. Hartig worked, but he wore old work clothes to work, so I assume it was some sort of menial job. The Hartigs all spoke German among themselves. The kids — there were five — spoke English without an accent, but the parents' English was broken and hard to understand, so we rarely spoke. They kept to themselves.

Mr. Hartig was a hard worker. He was always busy. He scraped all the paint off his house with a blowtorch and putty knife and repainted it every two years. My dad said he was an ignorant hillbilly from the backwoods of Austria, so that's kind of how I saw him too. As I got older, my outlook began to change. His entire lot was productive. He had an immense garden, hence the horse manure. He had a big rhubarb patch and fruit trees. Every inch produced something. We had a small garden, but it was nothing like his.

I began to think that even if he was an ignorant hillbilly, he knew something my dad didn't. Any man who could raise five kids on guts and sweat through the depths of the Depression had to have something on the ball.

Out behind the garden was an area surrounded by a solid board fence about eight feet high. I could put my eye up to a crack and see a little bit of a garage or something in there but for about three years its contents remained a mystery to me. Then one day just as I passed the big wooden door, it flew open, nearly knocking me down. Mr. Hartig swept some water out onto the street. I stood still, almost in shock. Mr. Hartig motioned me in and said, "Come." I was afraid at first but my curiosity got the better of me and I cautiously went through the big door. What I saw was a surprise, a picture straight out of National Geographic. Here was a wire pen with about a dozen hens in the corner. Across the yard was a small house behind a board fence. It contained two pigs contentedly munching on weeds and vegetables tops and peelings from the garden. It was clean and neat as a pin with nearly no odor.

He said, "You like sausages?" I nodded in the affirmative. He opened what was once the garage door. Inside was a little building about the size of an outhouse. He opened the door and to my amazement it was full of smoked meat. It was a smoke house. There were hams and bacon hanging from nails. A string of sausages was draped between two pegs. He pulled two off and gave me one and bit into the other.

"Good, Ja?" he said. I replied, "Ja."

He showed me a big wooden barrel. "Sauerkraut," he said. Along one wall were bins with cabbage, potatoes, carrots and beets. This was the most amazing thing I had seen. The whole outdoor area was paved with brick and clean enough to eat off. Shovels, rakes and hoes were hung in their proper places.

He let me out with a smile. After that, I saw him in a different light and spoke whenever I saw him out. This ignorant Austrian hillbilly had managed to raise enough food on a small city lot to feed seven people and conceal a farmstead from prying neighbors and city inspectors and hold down a full-time job. Everybody should be so ignorant.

A Boy and his Dog
March 30, 1996

Like most people, I've had a fairly large number and variety of dogs in my time.

They've all been mongrel mutts but one. She was a purebred collie, and a sorrier bit of "canininivity" I've never seen. She was nervous, high-strung, neurotic and psychotic. She blessed my life for fourteen years. I thought she was destined to live forever. She raised my kids from babyhood to teenagers and managed to do something stupid almost every day.

All my other dogs were a delight. When I was a kid, people would give me dogs or they would "follow me home." This never sat well with my parents. After a few weeks, during which I would get thoroughly attached to them, they would mysteriously disappear. It wasn't until many years later that I discovered that my dad would load them in the car on the way to work and kick them out somewhere to fend for themselves.

This continued when we moved to the country. A friend at school gave me a real nice little black dog. I loved him. It turned out that he was epileptic. He had a seizure about once a week. My dad said he had worms and he would get rid of them. He made a concoction of a pinch of tobacco wrapped in a wad of Fels-Naptha soap and shoved it down the dog's throat. The dog had a wonderful case of diarrhea but continued to have "fits."

Dad was right, though; he got rid of the worms. The trouble was, they were still in the dog. He also went for a nice ride in the country early one morning. I was heartbroken that the dog would leave me. I assumed he left because of the soap-tobacco diet.

One day my dad brought home a little brindle pup that had been given to him by a lady to whom he had delivered some furniture. She was a rich lady so this was bound to be a wonderful dog. It was half registered German shepherd and half English bulldog. Since I also was half-German and half-English, I was hopeful that she would turn out as well as I did. I also hoped that the English would win out over the German. (My dad was the German half.)

Boots, as we named her, was the best dog we ever had. She was very smart and eager to please. She house-broke herself in a few days, as soon as she realized what she was supposed to do. She was happy to stay with us and was never cross. She never bit any of us, though she probably had reason when we played rough with her. She loved every minute of life.

When she was a couple of years old, we moved from our little sharecroppers shack to an honest-to-God farm. There she was in her glory. She was a natural-born ratter. She would spend hours by herself patrolling the old buildings, digging after rats or tearing boards off to get to them. She never eliminated them altogether — no one ever does — but she kept them under control.

By this time, I was in high school, taking agriculture. One of our Future Farmers of America activities was an annual pest hunt. This was a contest to see who could catch the most pests. Mice and sparrows were worth one point each, starlings two, rats five, owls and hawks twenty-five, and foxes were worth fifty points. Today, I shudder at the damage done, but we were all farmers then and we thought we were protecting ourselves.

All hawks were "chicken hawks" and we all had chickens. There was a bounty on foxes, too, because of their propensity to raid chicken coops. Probably 'coons did more damage to chickens than foxes, but foxes got the blame.

When fall came and corn husking was at hand, Boots was in her glory. She always was with me when I was outside. We went to the woods and fields, always together the way a boy and dog should be, but at corn husking we were a team. When I tore down a corn shock, mice scattered everywhere. We tore into them together, she grabbing them by the mouthful and I stomping the ones that ran. We would get about ten or twelve from each shock. I really had to hurry to take them away from her before she ate them so I could get the tails.

I always had a pocket full of mouse tails. My mother had a fit when she went to wash my jacket. She reached into the pockets to see if there was anything that shouldn't go into the washing and retrieving about fifty mouse tails from one and twenty-five sparrow heads from the other.

While I was husking the corn, Boots would dig out any strays that went into the burrows beneath the shock. That done, she would sniff and dig around the next shock, then come back and bed down in the fodder until I finished and we'd go on to the next.

The only problem was her fecundity. (I threw that word in for my neighbor, Nancy Buttrick, who said she had to get a dictionary to read my column. Since she has one, she might as well use it.) Boots had a habit of getting pregnant every year. She had eight litters of eight pups each. Sixty-four pups are a lot to palm off on friends and neighbors. In those days, it was almost unheard of to waste money on a dog by taking it to a vet. People just shut them up in a shed or barn until the season was over. They usually managed to get loose for a few minutes, and that's all it took.

I got the shock of my life when she had only one pup one time. At least that's what my dad said. Later that day, while looking after her and the pup, I saw a five-gallon bucket sitting nearby which shouldn't have been there. When I took the lid off there were seven tiny pups floating in the water. My dad had drowned them at birth. I can understand why he could have done it, but I never forgave him for leaving them where I could find them. It was deliberate, to let me know he was still in charge. I'm thankful that now dogs can be spayed or neutered to avoid that agony.

Boots and I spent several happy years together, roaming the woods and fields, hunting mice, rabbits and pheasants. That ended abruptly when I went into the Army. Mom said Boots moped around the house for a while, then took to roaming on her own. She ran the roads for miles around. She was hit by a car once and came home with an injured hip, dragging one leg. It eventually healed, but she limped after that.

When I was discharged, we resumed our fun on a limited basis. With work and college, I didn't have time for much mouse hunting. I married and moved away and saw her only occasionally.

One day when I came home, Boots wasn't there. I asked my mom where she was. She told me that she had slowed down on her ratting activities and the rats were making a comeback, so my dad had put out poison. Boots had eaten some and died. I was so angry with my dad for putting it where she could get it that I probably would have beaten him if he had been home. He knew better, I'm sure. Our relationship wasn't good anyhow and it went downhill from there.

I think back on Boots fondly. She was a wonderful dog and an even better friend. She gave me her full, unconditional love as only a dog can do. I hope she has plenty of mice where she is.

Pigs, Ya Gotta Love 'Em
April 13, 1996

It seems that, over the years, I've had recurring themes run through my life. One is pigs. Every now and then, I have something happen that involves pigs.

My first encounter was when I was ten. I spent the summer on a farm in Union County. My first day there, I helped Mr. Pepper put rings in the nose of an old sow. A little later, I became aware of the little pigs playing in the area fenced in just for them. They were cute little things. I would go in the lot and sit down (being careful as to where I sat), and they would come sniffing around cautiously. I couldn't touch them at first; they would stay just out of reach. By the end of the week, they would come up to have their ears scratched. Soon they would lie down beside me and sleep as if I were their mother. I guess by then, I smelled like her. It was nice to be accepted as an equal.

A couple of years later, when we moved to the country, we had pigs of our own. We started with two, brother and sister, named Polly and Ralph. After a few months, we ate Ralph. My dad put Polly in the back seat of the '29 Chevy and hauled her away somewhere. When he brought her back, she was smiling. He said she would have babies in three months, three weeks and three days. We marked that day on the calender. I didn't know how he knew that would happen, but he was wrong, anyway. She had them in three months, three weeks and two days.

When I went to feed her on that fateful morning, I was horrified. There were bits and pieces of baby pigs strewn all over the pen. Polly had killed and eaten parts of all of her litter. I went to tell my dad and he immediately had to fix blame. It was my fault for not watching more closely. It was the fault of the farmer he had bought Polly from.

It was the fault of the feed company for not selling him the right stuff. It was everyone's fault but his.

Truth be known, it was probably none of the above. Animals are born with instincts that guide their lives. Most know automatically what to do in certain situations. A spider knows instinctively how to make a web and trap prey, but he doesn't know where to put the web and it's up to chance if he chooses a good place and prospers or chooses a bad place and starves.

The higher we go in the order of life, the less we rely on instinct, and more on learning. Pigs are about halfway. Most can rely on instinct, but some must be taught some things. Polly had never seen another pig but Ralph and had no idea how to be a mother and there was no one to teach her. We ate Polly, too.

We then got an old sow from a neighbor. She was big and ugly and mean, but she knew how to mother a brood. She was already bred when we got her and soon had twelve tiny editions of herself. She was a spotted hog and all her offspring were spotted but one. He was black and very small. Since she had eleven active faucets and twelve active pigs, someone got short-changed in the chow line. It was the runt, of course. I named him Harry. He was my favorite. I'd slip into the pen when the sow was asleep and pull one of the pigs off a faucet and put Harry on. It didn't help much; he began to get weaker and showed signs of getting a cold.

Finally, my dad gave him to me to raise. I made him a nest out of an old carton and a feed bag and put him on the oven door of the old coal range. I fed him cow's milk from a baby bottle several times a day. I'd hear him in the night as he got up to go the bathroom. He could jump from the oven door, but couldn't get back up. I'd get up then and feed him again and clean up his mess. He'd always go in the same spot. I'd just put down a piece of paper and he'd go on that. Pigs are very clean if they have the choice and won't foul their nest area.

The cow's milk didn't have everything he needed, apparently, and he died in about a week. I was sad, but you learn to accept things like that when you live on a farm.

There was a fellow who lived about a mile away who had the contract to haul the garbage from Upper Arlington. In those days, Upper Arlington wasn't as big as it is now. He had a small dump truck and made two trips a day, five days a week. He hauled this stuff out to his farm and dumped it in a field. In this field, he had about a hundred hogs, and they eagerly awaited each load. They did a wonderful job as garbage disposals. They would run to the truck when they saw it coming, and dive in. They devoured the goodies quickly, then spent the rest of the day rooting through the wrappings, looking for more.

Everything was wrapped in newspaper, which blew all over on windy days. As a result, all the inedibles were eventually uncovered. Some of us boys discovered that there was treasure to be found there and went prospecting about once a week. We looked for silverware and butcher's knives mostly. We all had a stash of knives that we would practice throwing, thinking some day we'd get a job with a circus. There is something sort of humbling about getting down on your knees in a herd of hogs rooting for goodies. It puts things in proper perspective.

When we moved to a real farm, our hog operation expanded a bit. We had more room for them to roam and they grew better and faster on a diet of skim milk. We butchered about twice a year. One time I'll always remember. My dad had left one hog with all his facilities to serve as a boar to breed the sows. Several hogs were eating corn in front of my dad. They were all of the same litter and looked pretty much alike. He shot the boar. He was furious, mostly because he didn't have anyone to blame it on and I was a witness. We went ahead and butchered it. Mom cooked a pork roast for supper. It wasn't fit to eat. We had to throw the whole pig out and butcher another the next day that had been neutered.

I'm still dealing with pigs indirectly. All my shavings and sawdust go for bedding my neighbor's pigs. I'm happy about that. They deserve to sleep on something other than mud.

Pigs are now movie stars. There's no holding them back. Pigs, ya gotta love 'em.

Glimpse of the Inferno
May 18, 1996

When I started to work at the grain elevator in 1942, train wrecks were almost unheard of. In fact, I didn't hear of one for several years.

We were in the midst of World War II and the railroads were at their peak. Traffic was heavy and for the most part slow. Trains were sometimes backed up for miles waiting to get into or out of the rail yards. When they did move, it was slowly. The railroads were prosperous and maintained the tracks well. The chances of a wreck were slim.

After the war, trucks began to take freight business away from the railroads and airplanes took the passenger business. The railroads began to feel the pinch. They cut back on track maintenance and tracks became increasingly unsafe. By the early 1950s, they were dangerous. Since traffic was light, the trains could go faster. Wrecks became common.

The first wreck I became involved with happened two blocks from my home. Had it happened a half block farther west, it would have wiped out downtown Hilliard.

I heard a rumbling that sounded like a big truck in my driveway. I opened the back door just as the rumbling turned into a roar. The sky turned red and I felt heat on my face. I could feel the concussion from the blast and I saw the top hatch of a tank car soar to about two hundred feet into the air and fall back into the inferno below. I knew immediately that something blew up, but I couldn't guess what.

I jumped in the car and headed in the direction of the blast, fearing what I might find. I turned down Norwich Street and could see fire behind all the houses on the south side of the street. Ahead, I saw the red flashing light of a fire truck. I parked and ran toward it. The firemen were just pulling hoses from the truck. I grabbed some hose and followed. I wasn't on the fire department, but nobody ran me off. They seemed glad to have some help.

It was hard to believe the carnage that lay before me. At least thirty or forty cars were derailed, a twisted tangled mass, and they were all burning. This was the nearest thing to hell that I could imagine.

They turned on the water and a fireman near me was knocked down by the sudden pressure. I dived for the hose, and between the two of us we managed to get it pointed at the nearest burning car. The water had little effect at first. I couldn't see why they were burning because they were made of steel. Apparently whatever was in them was flammable.

In a few minutes, we began to hear small explosions coming from inside the cars. I surmised that canned goods, perhaps paint, had become superheated and were exploding. One of the cars was lying on its side and the door was knocked off. We began to see smoking streamers arching out of the door and flying in all directions like small fireworks or popcorn. They moved rather slowly and the whole scene was dreamlike.

We weren't particularly frightened because we could side-step them rather easily. It was dark and muddy and they disappeared as they hit the ground. Suddenly, something whacked me on the bridge of the nose, nearly knocking me down. Whatever it was lay sizzling at my feet. When it cooled, I picked it up for a closer look. To my amazement, it was the exploded brass of a twenty-millimeter anti-aircraft shell. I ran to the chief and showed him what it was.

"Oh, my God, let's get out of here!" he yelled. "Everybody back!"

We were standing within twenty feet of four or five cars of live ammunition! We tipped our hats and slowly rode away.

"Them cars ain't worth gittin' killed for!" the chief said. "Let 'em burn out!"

Meantime, the railroad people were trying to move the cars still on the track but weren't making much progress. The cars nearest the fire were burning, one after the other. They were out of reach of the hoses at the moment. Four or five cars burned before they were able to move the train. The chief was concentrating on saving some small buildings and protecting the houses nearby.

We worked well into the night without really doing anything significant. Most stayed all night. By the time a couple of hours had elapsed, there were several fire departments on the scene. Since I wasn't on the department and had no raincoat, boots, or helmet, I was nearly frozen. It was November, as I recall. I elected to go home about 2 a.m.

I was back early next morning. It wasn't until daylight that the full scope of the accident became apparent. We weren't dealing with one wreck, but two! The site was fully a city block long. I wasn't prepared for such a sight. As I walked up and down I was able to piece together the scenario. Two trains were passing each other at a pretty good speed. On the eastbound track, which is downhill, at about the middle of the train was a flat car loaded with huge rolls of steel cable. This cable was about an inch in diameter and capable of holding many, many tons without breaking. One of these reels fell off the car, between the two trains. It was probably battered back and forth until the reel broke, releasing the cable. The cable caught on the wheels of the cars of both trains, jerking the wheels right off the cars. Every car beyond that point derailed, piling into a jumbled heap.

Two of those cars contained gasoline. One of them landed on the grain dump of the Farm Bureau grain elevator and split open, spilling the gas into the basement. The other went end over end, spilling its contents all over the wreck, then blew up. That's what I had seen from my home. The other blew up then and that set off the gas in the basement. It exploded and blew all the floors and roof out the top like a cannon.

It was a fairly new, all concrete, fireproof building. Concrete and steel were scattered for half a block in every direction. The explosion ruptured a 2,000-gallon tank of molasses, which ended up in the basement about three feet deep. It was a terrible mess.

My boss farmed me out to the Farm Bureau to help salvage what we could. I worked there for about three weeks and was thoroughly sick of it by the time we finished.

I was involved in four or five more train wrecks which I might describe at a later date. But I'll probably never see such a wreck as that one again. At least I hope not.

'Deefie' Bit Off More than He Could Chew
May 25, 1996

A lot of farms in the 1930s and 1940s had a resident hired hand.

Some farms were just too big for the family to handle without help. If a farmer had several sons, they could farm a fairly large area, especially once tractors became readily available. A lot of farms were failing during the Depression, and if a farmer was doing well and had a little cash, he could buy another farm pretty cheaply. Thus, the rich got richer and the poor got poorer.

There were many men out of work in this era, and they would work cheap. Farm work was hard, but the hired hand didn't have the worries of the farmer. He did his work, ate his food, and slept well under someone else's roof. Usually, they were older men without much ambition.

Our neighbor, Jim Wright, had one such hired hand. Jim had a registered Guernsey dairy herd of about thirty cows and they had to be milked by hand. Cows are labor intensive and by the time they were fed and milked and the barn cleaned, the morning was pretty well shot. He hired an older man to do the feeding, cleaning, and help with the milking. It didn't take a great deal of strength or endurance to handle this job. It was a good thing; he didn't have either.

I worked for Jim when there was field work to be done. Another kid and I, with Jim, could put up most of the hay and plow the corn. This left the hand to do the barn work and help us when we needed it. Usually, we used him to help unload the hay wagons. He would lead the old mare as she pulled the rope that took the hay up into the mow, a job I did when I was twelve.

Most hired hands that I knew were happy, jolly fellows who were glad just to have a job. Not this guy! He was grumpy and morose. He felt as if he shouldn't have to work so hard and we kids should be under him, but Jim treated us as equals. He was such a miserable old reprobate that nobody liked him. To make matters worse, he was stone deaf, but he used it as an excuse to be rude. We wished he would go away. I don't recall his name. We just called him "Deefie." That's not very flattering, but we weren't trying to flatter him, anyway.

I had been driving the horses for a couple of years before Deefie came on the scene, but he tried to make me believe that everything I did was wrong and he would take over driving whenever Jim wasn't around. That really made me mad, because I thought I was a hot shot with horses. One time when Ray, the other kid, who was eighteen, and I were plowing corn on the back of the farm, we saw the dinner signal and came to the house for dinner. (Mrs. Wright would hang a white towel on a certain fence where we could see it and we would know it was lunch time.) Ray was from Kentucky and had a guitar and wanted to be a cowboy, so we rode the horses to and from the fields. We felt like Hopalong Cassidy as we plodded along on the gallant charges. As we approached the barn this particular day, ol' Deefie came out of the barn with a pitchfork in his hands. He stuck the handle under my ankles and flipped them in the air.

"You keep your feet outa them tugs," he said. "You'll ruin that harness that way. You ain't s'posta ride 'em, anyway."

Well, that really ticked me off. Jim didn't care if we rode them and we couldn't possibly have hurt the harness. We vowed to get him some way. We kept riding the horses and tried to show him he wasn't our boss. We never did get to him except in little ways that didn't seem to bother him. We put grease or cow manure on his pitchfork handle now and then, but we couldn't get him good.

I nearly got him for good one day. Late in the summer, it was time to get the silo ready to fill. Jim told Deefie to go down and clean out the pit at the bottom. He really grumbled under his breath. I didn't blame him. There was about a foot of silage that had been there all summer and it was really rotten. It stank to high heaven. I thought it was appropriate that such a rotten man should get such a rotten job.

I had never been to the top of the silo and I thought this would be a good time to do it. That way I could gloat without being close enough to smell it. A silo has a door about every two feet all the way to the top. All the doors are in place when it is filled. You take the doors out one at a time as you empty the contents. On each door is an iron bar that acts as a latch and also a ladder rung. As you step on the rung, it gets tighter. To take a door out, you lift on the rung and the door goes into the silo.

Now, a silo is about fifty feet high, and as you get near the top, it seems a lot higher. I was getting a little tense. Just as I got to where I could look into the top door and see what he was doing, my toe hooked on a rung below and the door fell in. I yelled as loud as I could but Deefie couldn't hear. That door must have weighed forty pounds and it landed beside him within inches. It made such a noise that it could be heard for miles. He heard that! He looked up as soon as he saw what it was and saw me looking down, frozen in place, eyes as big as saucers, mouth agape.

"You dirty little SOB," He yelled. "Get down out of there 'fore I break your head with a pitchfork handle!" I got.

When I got down, he was waiting for me and gave me a mighty chewing out. I couldn't do anything but stand there and take it because I knew he was right and I was wrong. It didn't make me like him any better though. Being wrong isn't any fun. It was obvious the man had no sense of humor.

Summer was about over and I had to go to school the next week and we still hadn't got our revenge. A couple of days later, as we were going in to lunch, Deefie was ahead of us. He put his cud of chewing tobacco on the gatepost, as he always did, so he could retrieve it after lunch and continue its dubious pleasure. Just then a light bulb went off in my head. I turned to Ray and he looked at me. I could tell he had the same thought.

"I'll be right back," he said, and headed for the stable.

Lunch was delicious, but I could hardly wait for it to be over. Finally, after the pie and ice cream, Jim said, "Well, we better get to the hay."

Ray went out quickly and I followed as soon as I could. We wanted to get a little distance between us and Deefie, but still close enough to hear and see the fun. It wasn't long in coming. Ray had chosen the perfect road apple. It was just the size and color of the tobacco. When ol' Deefie popped into his mouth and bit down on it, he lit out a roar that could be heard in Columbus. Never was a stream of obscenities spit out with more venom.

If words could kill, we would be a long time dead. I felt I had been vindicated.

It was obvious the man had no sense of humor.

Mom Goes Blackberryin'

June 15, 1996

When I was a kid, we relied quite heavily on wild fruit. We harvested raspberries, blackberries and strawberries, and occasionally dewberries. I say we, but it fell to me to do most of the picking.

Sometimes, I'd take one of my sisters, but I preferred going with the neighbor boys or alone. These guys had showed me where the good picking places were. I found some other good ones myself and could go any day and find something.

One day, when I was about fourteen, my mother said, "I'm getting tired of staying home and doing the canning while you have all the fun. I have an idea. We'll all go picking and we'll all clean and can them when we get back."

I had to agree. Mother makes the rules. We — me, my two sisters and Mom — got outfitted with pans and buckets and chigger repellent. In those days, the best way to keep chiggers off was to rub the bare skin with uncooked bacon rind. Not only was it messy, but it didn't work very well, either. I told everyone to wear long pants and long sleeves, but they said it was too hot. Mom wore a house dress as all women did then and my sisters wore shorts. I had an inkling as to how this expedition would turn out.

I decided we should go to Smith's Woods. It was a half mile away and had a lot of berries. I don't know how it got its name because there was no one near named Smith, but the name stuck. My neighbors rented pasture in the woods for two cows and someone else had three there, and they kept the brush down so it was easier to find the berries. The berries grew in large thickets that were almost impenetrable. To get to the berries, one had to pick around the edges, then try to tramp a path through the middle. There were lots in the middle if you could reach them. To get in there, you must use both feet and tramp down the bushes in front of you, picking the berries off them first. This involved a lot of scratches on legs and arms. Thus the long sleeves and pants. Mom tried to go in a path I'd made a few days before, and was having a tough time.

I heard her call my name in a very loud stage whisper. When I answered she whispered loudly, "There's a bear or something in there, I can hear him."

I knew it couldn't be a bear. She was insistent. I started to go around the briar patch when I heard the bushes breaking and a grunting noise. Now I was concerned. What was it? It surely wasn't a rabbit. I sneaked around quietly as I could, and peeked into the opening, and sure enough, there was a very large animal in there — Sam Cantrell's Jersey cow!

Mom was visibly shaken and sat down on a stump to regain her composure. The girls had a gay old time at her expense. She had about a handful of berries to show for her effort so far.

I went back to my task and in a few moments heard her scream. When I looked, she was pale as a ghost, staring open-mouthed at a small black snake spread out in the sun on a small branch a few feet away. I chased the snake away and tried to calm her shattered nerves, though I must confess, I was secretly enjoying the moment. The girls enjoyed it, too.

Finally she calmed down and decided she could pick some more, but it would be safer if we all stuck together. We picked quite a few berries in the next half hour, the only interruption being when we moved to another patch and came across all five cows lying down chewing their cuds. They stood up as we approached but didn't run away. I asked Mom and the girls to guess how many cows would have a bowel movement in the next minute. They guessed from one to three.

"Wrong," I said. "There will be five."

They all pooh-poohed that idea. Sure enough, within a minute or so, all five raised their tails and deposited a cow plop.

"How did you know that?" they asked.

"I can tell by their eyes," I replied smugly. I never did tell them that cud chewing is part of the digestive process and so is the plop. Almost every cow does that after resting and cud chewing. Every country kid should know that.

By then, clouds began to appear and we could hear faint rumblings in the distance. Mom said, "It's going to storm. We'd better go."

I said, "Oh, that's an hour away. Let's pick a few more." They grudgingly agreed to just a few minutes more. We found a nice patch and were happily gathering berries and kind of lost track of time. A very loud clap of thunder brought us back to reality. The sky was black and menacing.

"We'd better scoot," I hollered. It was too late. The rain began to pelt down before we reached the road. We decided to try to make it to the Wright farm, which was about a quarter mile away. We took off running. I grabbed my little sister under one arm and the berry bucket under the other and took off as fast as I could and didn't look back.

It rained so hard we were half drowned when we reached the Wright's front porch. I had expected the others were right behind me. My other sister was a few hundred feet behind, but Mom was still way down the road. By the time my sister made the porch, I decided to go back after Mom. I couldn't get any wetter.

When I got close enough to see through the rain, I began to laugh. Before me was the funniest sight I'd ever seen. It looked like the Tin Man from the Wizard of Oz! It had rained so hard Mom couldn't see, so she dumped out the berries and put the bucket on her head. She still couldn't see anything but her feet and was wandering all over the road.

I took her hand and led her to the porch. There was no need to hurry. She took off the bucket and we all doubled over with laughter. The juice from the berries had mixed with the rain on her hair and face and was running down in purple streaks. Her dress was plastered to her skin and her arms and legs were covered with scratches. She was a mess. At first she was furious but soon saw the humor of the situation and laughed with us.

I said, "Well, we'd better all go home and can these berries."

Mom handed me her buckets.

"Here, you go back and pick berries. I'll make the jelly. I've had all the fun I can stand for one day."

I don't know why, but she never did ask to go berrying again!

The Little House on the Prairie
June 22, 1996

I guess we all like to look back to our youth, regardless of our age, and reminisce. Some of those memories are golden and we wonder why we even remember others.

One in this category is the outhouse or necessary house or whatever pet name we had for it. I think you can guess what mine was, so there's no need to pursue it further here. I don't think I ever had a really joyful experience in one, so my memories are of a historical perspective. They were an absolute necessity and everyone had one.

Before the invention of the outhouse, it was common practice in the cities to fling the contents of the chamber pot, or slop jar as it was called in rural areas, out an upstairs window into the middle of the street. This got it out of the house but didn't do much for the sanitation of the streets. One had to keep one eye turned upward when taking a morning stroll. It was also an incentive to shorten ladies' skirts a bit.

I don't know just when the outhouse first made its appearance, but by mid-colonial times it was common. In colonial Williamsburg, Virginia, it was sort of a status symbol to see who could have the most elaborate one. In the more affluent neighborhoods four and even six holes were common, so that a group of ladies could retire to the restroom en masse and discuss ladies' topics away from the prying ears of the menfolk, as they still do today at dances and other social events. It's impossible for one woman to go to the restroom alone even today.

I like my privacy, so a one-holer is my outhouse of choice, though most of ours had two holes. It seems to make more sense, especially in the winter, to stand in line to get a warm seat than to warm two seats at once. The trick is to be more polite than your companion and insist that he or she go first. Perhaps this was the start of good manners.

I don't remember much about our first outhouse expect that it was in the backyard in east Columbus. There was a drainage ditch along the street with a wooden bridge at every house. Sort of a miniature Venice. This took the overflow to the safety of Alum Creek. I fell in once and came out covered with little worms that, looking back, I think were mosquito larvae. I didn't have to be told again to stay away from that stinking mess.

After living with indoor plumbing for five or six years, our next move was to the country again.

The outhouse there was less than an architectural marvel. My dad built it out of railroad car grain doors and tar paper. It was dark and unattractive and a two-holer. It would have been totally forgettable but for the location. In order to get it as far away from the house as possible, he built it down by the railroad tracks. Now these tracks were built up about fifteen feet higher than the surrounding terrain and on a fairly sharp curve. It didn't take too much imagination to figure out what would happen to you if a train jumped the tracks doing about sixty miles per hour, as they often did.

The ground trembled and the roar of the wheels and the scream of the whistle at the crossing created such a din that a stranger would swear the end of the Earth had come. It was not unusual to see visitors fling the door open and careen outside, clutching their pants with one hand and crossing themselves with the other. There was something about that place that created instant Catholics.

Alas, the property was confiscated by the Pennsy Railroad during World War II and a bulldozer put an end to that era of fun.

Our next move took us to a nineteenth century farm, formerly owned by a couple in their nineties. He had been born there and almost nothing had changed since his youth. They had a nice, roomy outhouse, but dark. Modesty prevented a window or opening of any kind. I soon made a startling discovery. There was no pit under it. Instead, there were two ten-gallon garbage cans. These had to be emptied periodically. The old man would hire someone to do this. My old man didn't. You can guess to whom this job fell.

I soon learned not to wait until they were full. They weighed close to one hundred pounds each when full. Lugging those things back to the orchard, contents spilling down my leg, was something less than a picnic. I had to dig a hole under a pear or apple tree and bury the mess. Come winter, it was even worse. The cans would freeze solid and the contents refused to leave their safe haven. This called for water to be heated and poured over the cans until finally everything came out in a lump. That required an even deeper hole be dug. Apparently the steam that flowed forth was good for something. I never had any sinus trouble. We had some delicious apples and pears, too.

Come spring, I wasted no time digging a pit under that little house on the prairie. I didn't actually dig it under the house — I dug it in front of it and with the aid of skid boards and pry bars, slid the house forward to its new home. That finished, I found a piece of glass in the barn and put a nice window in the side. My sister finished the inside with some leftover wallpaper, painted the seat, put an old rug on the floor, and it became a very nice bed and breakfast.

I do not look back fondly on that part of my life, but it was something that had to be done. As a feller once said, "I seen my duty, and I done it."

I'm not through with outhouses, though. A few years ago, my son and a friend and I built a cabin in the remote wilderness of Michigan's Upper Peninsula. An outhouse was the only option. I made the house here in my shop in sections and took it up there and put it together. It's small, a one-holer (I go there for privacy), and it has a large window in the door that overlooks a lake. It's the jewel in the crown. Thanks to modern materials, it's light enough that two men can pick it up and move it when necessary.

As the age of outhouses draws to a close, I can only doff my hat and say, "Flush toilets, I salute you."

When the Frost Is on the Punkin'
October 18, 1997

Well, it happened again. With all this gorgeous weather we've had this fall, I was caught with my pants down when the frost hit.

I have most of my firewood under roof. There are three or four trailer loads up in the woods yet, but it's been split and piled to dry. Three or four hours' work should get it. The wood shed is full at the house, so I'm pretty well assured I won't freeze. The rest is for the shop and the cabin and I think I'm covered there.

I still don't have anti-freeze in the motors yet. I have two tractors, a sawmill and three or four various trucks to be dealt with. Even that's a whole lot less work than we had to do when I was a kid.

The first priority was getting the crops in. All would have been harvested by now but for the corn. I read James Whitcomb Riley's poem the other day about "when the frost is on the punkin an' the fodder's in the shock." I wondered to myself how many young people of today know what fodder is, or even what a shock is.

This was before corn-pickers became plentiful. There were a few around, but only the rich farmers had them. We poor folks had to cut our corn by hand. The corn was cut when the leaves were partly or mostly dry. If you waited until they were all dry, you might not get done in time. We went into the field six rows and counted down six rows the other direction. In those days, corn was planted "checked," which meant the plants were evenly spaced in the row. We took four plants in a square and bent them over towards each other and twisted the tops together and sort of tied them in a knot. This made a foundation on which to stack the cornstalks.

Most people did the whole field before cutting. They would start early in the morning when the dew made the stalks wet and pliable. If they were too dry, they would break when they were bent.

We then took a corn knife, which is similar to a machete but lighter, and grabbed the stalks with one arm. We cut them off near the ground, and without straightening up went to the next "hill," as it was called, carrying the stalks we had just cut. This continued until we couldn't hold any more. We took that load back to the foundation hill we had tied and stood it up on one side. The process was continued with the next load put on the opposite side. When we had cut an area twelve rows square, that was considered a shock.

We carried a rope about fifteen feet long with a hook on one end. Lots of people made a wooden block instead of a hook. It had a slot cut in one side to receive the rope. Anything would do so long as it was heavy enough to swing it around the shock. A man would swing the rope almost like a lariat so that the hook went around the shock and back to where he could catch it. This was a little tricky. I was smacked aside the head many a time. (Maybe that accounts for me being silly enough to remember this job fondly.) The rope was hooked into the hook or block and pulled tight and tied, holding the shock all together and upright. We then tied some twine above the rope, tight as we could get it, and took the rope off.

It took a while to see if you did a good job. As the fodder (which was what the cornstalks were called after they were cut) dried and shrank, the shock settled. If you did it right, the shock stood straight. If you didn't get the stalks standing straight, the shock twisted and sometimes fell over. This led to razzing by neighbors and a butt-chewing by the old man.

The purpose of this was to dry the corn ears. If picked this time of the year, they were wet and would get moldy stored in a crib.

After a month or so in the shock, the corn could be husked. If we had a big barn, the shocks could be hauled by wagon or sled to the barn and husked there. Most was husked in the field. Usually, by then the weather had turned cold and sometimes snowy. The weather we're having now would be ideal. It was wonderful to work in the fields when the leaves were turning and the sun was just warm enough to keep your hands warm.

I loved to husk corn under the full October moon. I would come home from school and have a hearty snack of a half of loaf of warm bread and homemade butter. I'd then milk the cows and feed the hogs and chickens and gather the eggs. By then, it would be suppertime. Since I was a good kid and did my homework at school, I had my evenings free. I hadn't learned about girls yet.

I'd whistle up my dog, Boots, and head for the cornfield. Boots loved to catch mice as I tore down the shocks. I would tear down a part of a shock and kneel on it (or in it). I had a husking hook, which was a leather pad that strapped on the palm of my hand. Riveted to the pad was a steel plate with a hook on it. I would take an ear in my left hand and rake the hook across it near the small end. This would take off about a third of the husk and I grabbed the ear with my right hand and pulled the rest of the husk off with my left, at the same time snapping the ear off the stalk. I tossed it with my right while grabbing another ear with my left. With some practice, a well-coordinated person could keep two ears in the air at the same time. I could do it once in a while, but not all the time.

When the shock was all husked, I tied it in bundles as big as I could reach around and stacked three shocks together in a supersized shock and tied it with the rope as before. This could be hauled to the barn whenever it was convenient. We thought it was good cow feed. It wasn't until I took vo-ag in high school that I found out it wasn't worth hauling away.

Even though cutting corn was backbreaking work, I'm not sorry I did it. It's like going into the Army. I wouldn't take anything for the experience, but I wouldn't want to do it again. A modern farmer, with a four row picker-sheller, can harvest more grain in an hour than I did by hand in a whole winter. I don't think he enjoys it any more than I did, though. The corn leaves cut my neck and the corn-knife blistered my hand while my back was aching, but if I could look at a finished field of neat rows of corn shocks with punkins piled by each one, I couldn't help but feel proud of my accomplishment. Them was the good old days!

Remembering the Old Farm — Part I
March 14, 1998

I've read several books lately about the settling of Ohio in the late 1700s and early 1800s. At first blush, it sounds like a long time ago, but only 200 years ago there were almost no white men living in this state.

Two hundred years ago seems like a long time, but look at it this way. When I was born seventy-one years ago, it would have been only two more lifetimes ago. In other words, people who were about seventy when I was born knew people who were pioneers in Ohio.

I got to thinking about this after I read a book this week about the settling of Delaware County only a few miles from where I grew up. It mentions places I knew when I was a kid. I've seen the remnants of the old stone barns and mills standing forlornly near the Scioto and Olentangy rivers and wondered about them: Who built them and what happened to them that they were no longer used?

All this brought back memories of the old farm I grew up on. It was straight out of Currier and Ives. I loved that old place and marveled at its simplicity. It was a perfect eighteenth-century family farm. It was just the right size for a family to handle and be almost self-sufficient.

Before we moved there, we lived in what was nothing more than a sharecropper's shack. We had a farm of eight acres. All the buildings were hand built by my dad and me out of scrap lumber and old refrigerator crates. As long as we lived there I always felt inferior. In truth, we were "poor white trash" to the more affluent farmers. I never felt like trash, but I felt that other people thought so.

One day (this was during World War II), a man from the Pennsylvania Railroad, which ran through our back yard, knocked on our door. He said, "We are buying your place to put in a rail yard. You have two weeks to get out." Now, that gives you a jolt. We were devastated. We would be homeless in two weeks!

My dad negotiated with the company for a decent price and found the farm for sale the next day. It was owned by old "Uncle" Frank Nineger. I don't know if he was anyone's uncle, but everyone called him that anyway. He and his wife were a sweet old couple and they were sad about leaving but were getting too old to live on the farm alone and were moving to town. He was about ninety-five and was born on the farm in a log cabin which was out front of the "new" house. The "new" house was built when he was five years old. Since he was ninety-five in 1943 and the house was built when he was five, that meant it was built in 1853. To think that we knew a man who was born in 1848 boggles my mind. That was only forty-five years after the state was formed.

The farm consisted of fifty-two acres. It had six fields of seven acres each. They were divided by a lane about twelve feet wide that ran clear to the back of the farm and ended in a wood lot of about two or three acres. There was a gate in the corner of each field so that we could get to each field without going through any other field.

The house sat about a hundred yards from the road. Our front yard was about the size of a football field. We fenced it and used it for pasture. There was a row of huge osage orange (hedge apple) trees bounding each side of this field. The house was of brick. The bricks were made and burned right on the place. They were very soft and held water so that the house always was damp in the summer. The interior walls were also brick with plaster over them. There was no electricity when it was built, of course, so later when it was wired the wires ran exposed on the walls because there was no space in the walls to hide them.

Behind the house, connected by an enclosed porch, was another brick building. The first room was the laundry. There were a chimney and a laundry stove to heat the laundry tub and boiler to boil the clothes in. This building was built inside another building with about a foot between the walls. This space was filled with sawdust for insulation. It seemed odd to me that they insulated an outbuilding but apparently never thought of insulating the house.

There was a second room behind the laundry that was called an upground cellar. Here was kept the winter's food. There were shelves along the walls for jars of canned goods. Along one wall were bins for root crops such as potatoes, turnips, carrots, beets and such, plus cabbage. This room was insulated well enough — there was a foot of sawdust above the ceiling — so that we kept things from freezing when it got below zero by merely setting a coal oil lantern on the floor.

In one corner of the back porch was a small room about four feet square that was used to take care of the milk and store the cream. We had a cream separator in there. After I milked the cows twice a day, I would put the milk in the big bowl on top and turn a big crank. The separator had two spouts. The cream would come out one spout and the skim milk would come out the other into different buckets. After each use, the thing had to be taken apart and washed and disinfected. I never did know how this thing worked, but there were a bunch of funnel-like things called disks that spun when the crank was turned and somehow by centrifugal force the cream was separated from the milk. We fed the skim milk to the calves and pigs. My dad took the cream to the Blue Valley Creamery twice a week.

I hadn't intended to go into such detail and I thought I could tell about the old place in a regular column, but I see it will take another one. I hope I'm not boring you readers. I just feel that these details should be recorded before they are lost. The books I just read convinced me of this.

More next week.

Remembering the Old Farm — Part II
March 21, 1998

I hope you recall that last week I wrote about the old farm we lived on when I was in high school. I spoke of how the fields were laid out and described the milk house, laundry and upground cellar.

Just outside the back porch was a wooden building about sixteen feet square with a dinner bell on the roof, rung by a rope that ended just outside the porch door. We never knew what the building's purpose was. It might have been a workshop and harness room. We just used it for junk and occasionally, when the weather was bad, I would cut and split firewood in it.

Attached to this building, lean-to style, was the carriage house. It was just big enough for a buggy. There was no back door, so the buggy would have had to be backed in by hand. My dad used it for a garage, but it was just big enough to get his old '35 Buick in with room to get out on the driver's side. A passenger would have to get in or out of the car outside.

Behind the carriage house was the chicken house. It was L-shaped. One side of the L was open with chicken wire and a gate so that the chickens could get fresh air or be turned loose if we desired. The other side was closed up tight with only one window. The roosts were in here. It could be locked up at night to keep the foxes and 'coons out.

The nests were in the open side. It was pretty dark in there on cloudy days. I got the shock of my life one dark winter day when I was gathering the eggs. I had to just feel for the eggs because I couldn't see. I stuck my hand down in one nest and grabbed a sleeping possum! I don't know who was more surprised. We quickly went our separate ways.

Just beside the chicken house was a dug well, lined with limestone. There were three on the place, but this one wasn't used when we moved there. It had an old wooden pump which was broken. There was even a wooden pipe going down into the well. It was the first I had ever seen. This alone would give you an idea how old the well was. How I wish I had saved it. It would be a treasure today. In those days, it was just junk. My dad told me to get rid of it, so I just threw it on the junk pile. We put a more modern pump (which is now an antique) in its place and used it until the place was sold.

The lane started just beside this well. Right behind the chicken house and bounded by the lane on the south was the orchard. There were some forty apple, pear and plum trees there. Most of the apple trees were too old to bear well, but the pears always had good crops. The plums had dropped their fruit for years and I think all the seeds grew. The saplings were so thick you couldn't walk through them. What few plums we got weren't very good, so we never did clean that part of the orchard. We ran hogs in the orchard to eat the dropped fruit. While I was away my dad dug the trees out by the roots and plowed the orchard and that was the end of that.

Next to the old well by the lane was the corn crib. It was about twenty feet long and six feet wide. It was attached to the side of a machinery shed. You could pull a wagon inside the shed and shovel the corn into the crib. It only held about 200 bushels. That doesn't sound like much today, but that was about all the corn we could get off one of those seven-acre fields. Fifty bushels to the acre was about all we could expect in a good year. Any excess could be stored in the barn.

The barn was just to the south of the corn crib. The lane went between them. It was a nice old barn, hand-hewed beams mortised together, held by wooden pins or trunnels. (The word trunnel is a corruption of "tree nail." It was brought over here from England, I think, in the very early days of our country.) The barn had vertical tongue and groove (double V) siding of modern design, so I think it was probably built in this century. There was also the base of a silo outside, which was long gone when we moved there.

The floor of the barn was raised about three or four feet above ground and made of two-inch oak planks. The west end had stalls for horses and pens for pigs or sheep. The center was open for hay wagons. The east end had sheep pens on the ground floor and a hay mow above. There were doors on each end big enough to drive a team and a hay wagon through. There was a track attached to the rafters with a wheeled cart to which was fastened a huge rope and a big hay fork. We could unload a hay wagon by sticking the fork into the hay and pulling the rope with a horse.

Out back was an L-shaped loafing shed for cows and sheep. It had a tin roof. The side of the L that ran perpendicular to the barn also had a hay mow in it. It was about fifteen feet deep and thirty feet long.

Attached to the east end of the main barn was another building of some sort. I didn't know what it was for, only that it was filled to within three feet of the ceiling with sheep manure. Guess whose job it was to clean that out. Every afternoon after school and a 2,000-calorie snack. I worked on that. It was almost like an archaeological dig. The manure was five feet deep and dry as powder. I had to use a pick and shovel.

After a few days, I reached the floor in one end. To my amazement, it was concrete. Further excavation revealed a square trough running lengthwise of the room. As work progressed, I discovered another trough with a rounded bottom and a wall at the back about two feet high. The thing was a modern dairy milking parlor! Later I was rummaging around in a junk pile in the hay mow and found several cow stanchions intact. I put them back where they came from and used this room to do the milking for as long as we had cows. Apparently ol' Uncle Frank got tired of milking. He wasn't too hot on shoveling manure, either, I guess. At ninety-five, I couldn't blame him. It didn't take me that long to get tired of it.

The house had three rooms upstairs and four rooms down, the extra being the kitchen which was only one story. It had a big black cook stove which took up nearly half the room. A table and sink filled the rest. The sink had, at one time, a hand pump, but it had been replaced by an electric piston-type pump under the sink. It didn't work so we had to carry water from the cistern outside.

There was a stove in the "settin'" room and a fireplace in the living room, and that was it. It got so cold upstairs that the pot under the bed froze solid overnight. In spite of that, we slept well under a half dozen blankets. Nobody would get up until I got the fire going in the cook stove in the morning. Them was the good old days.

Even though it was a tough go, I thoroughly enjoyed life in the country. They were the happiest days of my young life, I guess, because even though my dad was a tough taskmaster and demanded I do things he couldn't or wouldn't, I found that I could do them and I became confident of my own ability. That was something new to me, having been told daily that I was stupid and useless. Since then I've been able to get by on my own. Something good comes of every situation if we look hard enough. Anyhow, I was sad to leave the old place. I drove past it early this week and nearly wept at what I saw. Everything is gone. I couldn't even find the boundaries. It is filled with businesses and houses. The back half, including my beloved woods, is a golf course. I suppose there's something good there. I haven't found it yet.

Ice Age
July 18, 1998

The spate of hot weather we've had recently has been uncomfortable for those who have to work outside. Ohio Department of Transportation is building a bridge in front of my place and I really feel for those guys who have to work out there in the sun. The blacktop gets hot enough to bake bread and the high humidity adds to the misery. They are as wet all day as if they were working in the rain.

There is no way to combat the heat except to try to get as much work done as possible before it gets too hot. You've never heard an alarm clock as effective as a big backhoe trying to bust up concrete at 5:30 in the morning. The first time I heard it, I thought the place had blown up. After I scraped myself off the ceiling, my first thought was to get the shotgun and make amends, but after a cup or two of coffee, I began to enjoy the early light. It must have awakened the birds, too, for they put on quite a concert, though at first it sounded like a protest. There are some advantages to rising early, but I like to do it at my own speed.

Though it seems very hot now, I've seen it a lot hotter. I heard the weatherman just the other evening talk about the old heat record for the date. It was 107 degrees in 1936. I was nine years old. We lived in Columbus at the time and I suppose it was almost unbearable on the city streets, but we had some large elm trees in our yard and we played under them quite comfortably. I really don't remember it being so hot, except one day that is imprinted on my brain indelibly.

We, like everyone else, had an icebox. This was before refrigerators were in common use. We had an ice man who delivered a fifty-pound block of ice twice a week in the summer. Because of the hot weather, we ran out of ice before his next visit. There was an ice house about six blocks away where we could buy ice when needed. I knew where it was but had only been there a couple of times and didn't realize how far it was. Mom sent me over there with my little red wagon to get a fifty-pounder.

Our street was shady and the sidewalks were fairly cool. When I came to Livingston Avenue, which was a street of commerce, there were no trees, the sidewalk was very hot and the asphalt street was twice as hot. I never thought to put shoes on. We went barefoot all summer. When I hit that street it was like walking on hot coals. I had to run like mad to get to shady spots, which were few and far between. I got to the place and couldn't remember what I'd come for. My memory was almost as bad then as it is now. (Mom said it was because I didn't listen.) I had to hot-foot it home (no exaggeration) and ask Mom. She said, "Fifty pounds of ice, you idiot. Go back and get it before the milk sours."

I recruited the kid next door to go back with me and help me remember. I had to promise to let him ride in the wagon to get him out of the shade. I told him to keep repeating over and over, "Fifty pounds of ice, fifty pounds of ice." He began to whine and say he didn't want to do it anymore when we were about halfway there. I said, "Cut the whining and keep saying 'fifty pounds of ice' or I'll dump ya out in the hot street."

That convinced him and I kept going as fast as I could. I didn't have sense enough to put shoes on before going back, so I was a'steppin' right out. When we got to the ice house he was still mumbling "fifty pounds of ice."

"What'll 'ya have, sonny?" the ice man asketh.

"Fifty pounds o' ice," I said boldly, as though I knew all along. He got his ice tongs and dropped the block in the wagon and I gave him my quarter and the deal was done.

Now, another problem arose. The ice took up about two-thirds of the space in the wagon and that didn't leave much room for Johnny. He tried straddling the block but he almost immediately began to complain that his private parts were freezing.

"Well, get out and walk, then," I said. I really didn't care to stand on that hot sidewalk and argue about trivialities. He didn't like that idea either and finally settled on facing the rear with his legs hanging over the back of the wagon and his back against the ice. It wasn't long until his teeth were chattering. I went as fast as I could go, stopping whenever a piece of lawn appeared and lying on my back to put my feet on the ice for a few seconds, then jumping up to run on before Johnny could get his teeth stopped enough to complain.

When we got home with our thirty-five-pounds of ice, I got out our ice tongs, and between Mom and me we managed to wrassle it up into the top of the icebox, and the day was saved.

It seems primitive, looking back, and I suppose it was, but we didn't know any better. That was just the way things were. There were more rewards, though. When the ice man came, he stopped his truck at almost every house. His truck had wooden sides about four feet high with a big heavy canvas draped over the top and down the back. The ice was in big blocks of about 200 or 300 pounds with seams in the sides at the fifty-pound mark. He would take his ice pick and jab it into one of those seams and the blocks would separate slick as a whistle. He'd grab one in his tongs and throw it on his shoulder and take off to the nearest house. He had a big leather pad strapped on his shoulder to protect it.

While he was gone, one of us would be a lookout like we were pulling a bank heist and the other would duck under the canvas and pick up all the chips of ice we could carry and take off up the street. We'd sit on someone's steps and chew those ice chips as though they were candy. I've always heard that forbidden fruit tastes best, and that holds true, even with something that has no taste. Them was the good old days.

Prom Night: The More Things Change ...
May 20, 2000

It's getting around prom time in high school again. It seems to happen every year about this time. It's a big deal — always was, I guess. The difference between now and my graduation is in the definition of big. Nowadays it's tuxedos and limousines. When I graduated, some 56 years ago, not everyone could scrape up a suit.

We were just coming out of the Great Depression and were well into World War II. I was lucky in that I had a summer job at a grain elevator and was able to save a few bucks for attending movies and school functions and even a date now and then.

Some weren't so lucky. The farm kids had to work at home and accept whatever they could talk their parents out of. Most had at least one pair of good shoes and a couple of pairs of pants, but suits were hard to come by. A school or FFA jacket had to suffice for dress-up occasions. I was on the low end of the scale, mostly because through the lower grades I didn't have girlfriends, and therefore didn't need any fancy duds even if I could afford them. By the time I could afford them, I was so used to scrimping that I didn't want to spend money on anything so frivolous.

When I was a junior, I began to notice that girls had bumps and curves, flashing eyes and flashing smiles. The first time I went to a dance and got up nerve enough to accept when a girl asked me to dance, I felt a warm body next to mine, and I knew I had been missing something. "Whoa," I said to myself, "I gotta get a suit."

The following Saturday, I talked my pal, Charlie, into taking me to downtown Columbus to look for one. Charlie was a sharp dresser (we were "sharp" before "cool" was in vogue) and knew more about clothes than I did. He had a tweedy type of a suit that I really liked, but after trying Robert Halls and the Boston Store, we couldn't find any that I liked. We ended up in Lazarus' basement, and there I settled for a blue one. "Ya can't go wrong with basic blue," Charlie said.

I sure hated to fork over fourteen bucks for that thing. After I'd gotten a white shirt, Charlie said I needed a red tie and black socks with a red stripe down the side. Man, I thought I had it all by then. I spent nearly twenty bucks that day and was torn between being happy because I'd be "sharp" and being sad because I'd be broke.

I wasn't as sharp as Charlie, but it didn't matter. He never dated girls in our school anyway. He said he wouldn't bother with "them hick girls." He preferred the more sophisticated chicks in Columbus. Charlie had a Model A Ford car and was as free as a bird to go wherever he wanted.

One night he talked me into going with him, and it turned out that his idea of a hot night with them sophisticated, uptown babes was to go to a skating rink and get girls to skate with him, holding hands. Around and around they'd go, never looking at each other or talking. The success of the evening was measured by how many girls he could skate with. I finally got up enough nerve to ask a good-looker to skate with me. I'd never skated this way before. Her hands were warm and her body felt wonderful as we rubbed together. I promptly got my feet tangled and we both fell. "Hick!" she shouted as she got up and skated away, leaving me there on my butt in the middle of the floor.

But I digress. Back to the prom. I dated a few girls during my junior and senior years, but nothing even semi-permanent developed. In about six weeks it would be over. It wasn't until halfway through my senior year that I found a girl (she wasn't lost, but it was just our turn I guess) who seemed to like me as much as I liked her. We hung around at school and dated whenever the chance for a double date arose. Only a few guys had cars and there was nothing much to do in town. We were fifteen miles from Columbus.

When prom time came, it was all new to me. I looked to my more knowledgeable friends for guidance. "Have you ordered the corsage yet?"

"What's a corsage?" I asked. "Flowers," was the answer. "Some of us are going to town to order ours after school, wanna go?"

"Sure, I have to do it sometime I guess. It's two weeks yet 'til the prom. What's the hurry?"

"If you don't order 'em now, ya won't get 'em," they said.

I thought to myself, "Why in hell would a girl want to carry around a vase of flowers at a dance?" I could visualize water spilled on my new blue suit. I looked in the dictionary and it said: "Corsage — a small bouquet of flowers usually worn at the shoulder." We had plenty of flowers in the garden. I didn't see why I had to buy some more, but not wanting to appear a hick, I went along. At the flower shop, I let the other guys go first to see what they got. They both ordered orchids. Orchids! The most expensive item on the menu. I was trapped. I had to order orchids, too.

"What color is her dress?" the clerk asked. "What?" was my sophisticated reply. "What color is the dress your date is wearing to the prom so I can match the flowers to the dress?" I had no idea, so I said white.

"Oh good. That's easy. Anything but white will do. That will be five dollars plus fifteen cents tax please."

Holy cow! This girl stuff was getting expensive. Put that on top of a fourteen-dollar suit and we're talking big bucks here. There was more to come. My date said that we should get some pictures taken to remember forever. I said I knew a part-time professional photographer and I would take care of it. In fact, I worked with him at the grain elevator. I talked to him at work and he agreed to do it for five bucks. "Just tell me when and I'll be ready. Come to my house before the prom."

My friend Marlin and his girl Elma Lou invited us to go with them, and they would get their picture taken, too. All was set. (They have been happily married for nearly fifty-five years.)

When I went in to pick up my date, my eyes nearly popped out. Her dress was actually a white, fluffy thing, and her hair was piled up on top of her head like I'd never seen before. To me she looked like an angel emerging from a white cloud. I handed her the box containing the corsage and she gushed over it, making me feel good.

"Will you pin it on for me?" she whispered. Oh, God, I thought. There wasn't much of a place to pin it except where I wasn't allowed to go, especially with her mother watching. My hands shook, but with a little help from her mother the mission was accomplished.

"We'd better hurry to get our picture taken or we'll be late," she said. So we did. We pulled into Reed Bidwell's farm right on time. Reed came to the door, still chewing on his supper. "Forgot you were coming," he said. "Come on in. Mary, push the supper aside and clean off one of the chairs, and we'll get these young people on to the prom."

And so it transpired. The dates sat on the old oak, straight-back chair (one at a time, of course), and the men stood stiffly behind. I'm sure glad we didn't look like hicks. He also lined us up together in front of a bare spot on the living room wall for a great shot. I'm sure glad we didn't look like hicks.

I don't remember much about the prom except that I was in heaven. Only the pin on the corsage kept me from enjoying it to the fullest. Her mother knew what she was doing when she helped me with that pin.

Chapter 2
Fun on the Funny Farm

A Fifteen-Minute Job
May 4, 1996

I've mentioned a few times my old Case tractor I've had so much trouble with. I thought my troubles were about over. With the help of my neighbor, Chuck, the world's greatest shade tree mechanic, I got it together and working pretty well (he did most of the work while I watched). It ran smoothly and quietly and we both got our driveways in pretty good shape by hauling gravel out of the crick and spreading it with my snow blade.

Last week, I parked it up on the hill by my house. I use one or the other (I have two) for transportation up and down my drive. I park crosswise on the hill and leave them in gear so they won't run away.

The next morning it wouldn't start. I had just put another battery in it and assumed that the battery cable wasn't making good contact.

My brain was still a little foggy that early and I wasn't thinking clearly. What I proposed to do was raise the hood and jiggle the cable with one hand and work the starter button with the other until the starter worked. This made perfect sense to me in my early morning fog. The only problem was I had to take it out of gear or it would move on the strength of the starter.

I gingerly took it out of gear and set the brake. It does have a brake on one wheel. I gave the back wheels a few tentative pushes and it stayed put. I started to go up front to raise the hood, and just as I got in front of it, it started to move. I tried to hold it back, but to no avail. All I could do was jump out of the way and let 'er go. And go she did. It went straight over the bank and into the woods, picking up speed quickly, and hit the first tree it came to dead center of the front wheels.

The tree top whipped down hill and back, showering dead branches all over. These tractors are tricycle-type, which means they have two small wheels close together. They are bolted into a large casting that makes up the front of the tractor just below the radiator and grill. The casting broke and the wheels were all but off. I knew they would fall off if the tractor was moved.

Now, a rich man would have called a tractor repair place to come and get it and fix it. Rich I ain't. This called for resourcefulness. I have another neighbor who has an old wrecker, and I mean old. I engaged his services.

He arrived early next morning, fenders flapping, exhaust roaring. We surveyed the situation and arrived at a plan. He would back down perpendicular to the tractor, lift the front end with the winch, drive back onto the driveway and haul it away. Simple. Shouldn't take more than fifteen minutes.

Phase one went well except the wrecker slid sideways a little and he missed his mark by about two feet. He was on the wrong side of the tree. He had shut off the motor when he stopped and when he tried to start it the starter wouldn't work. "It ain't never done that before," he said. "Just dirty cables I reckon."

With that, he pulled out a pocket knife big enough to skin a buffalo, scraped the cables and battery terminals and put the cables back on. When he tried the starter again, nothing happened. "Must be the solenoid," he said. He rooted around in a pile of debris on the floor and came up with a solenoid, which he installed. He tried the starter again — nothing.

"Must be the starter," he said. "If I could get it started I'd go home and put a starter on it."

"I've got another tractor," I said. "Maybe I could pull you and get you started."

"That'll work," he replied. I walked down the hill and came with the other tractor. I pulled his truck about five feet and it started. I unhooked the chain and went down the hill so he could go home for the starter. When I looked back up the hill, he had backed up to the tractor again. I went back up the hill and we hooked a chain around the tractor and hooked the wrecker cable to it. All this time the wrecker motor was running. He threw the winch into gear and started to lift when the motor died. "It ain't never done that before," he said.

Now we were in a pickle. We couldn't release the winch unless the motor was running and we couldn't get the motor running unless the winch was released.

"We got to figger out how to move the truck back about a foot," he said.

"I've got a hand winch," I said.

"That'll work," he replied.

Back down the hill. Back up the hill with the winch. We chained the winch to a tree and hooked the other end to the wrecker. We were able to move the wrecker about eight inches. It wasn't quite enough. The hook was loose but we couldn't unhook it.

"I believe I can drive the pin out of the hook and take the hook off," he said. He did exactly that. By using a screw driver and a hammer, he knocked the pin out into the woods where it has never been seen again. We got the hook off and I pulled the truck to get it started. He backed up again and we rigged the hook back on. He propped a stick against the gas pedal this time to speed up the motor and put the winch in gear again. He eased the tractor up a few inches and the wheels fell off, as I expected.

He started to pull the wrecker ahead and the tractor wouldn't turn. We were hooked too far back. We had to let it down and rehook farther forward. Of course, the wheels were off so we couldn't let it down. We were able to get some blocks under the front and get the chain in the right place. When he pulled forward, the tractor swung around behind the wrecker and followed it down the hill just as it was supposed to.

I knew it was only a fifteen-minute job. That's all it took once we were hooked up right. The other two hours were just practice.

Trip to the Tractor Retirement Village
May 11, 1996

Howdy, boys and girls. It's time for another excitin' adventure with TRACTOR MAN! You remember the last time Tractor Man and his trusted companion, WRECKER MAN, had just rescued the injured tractor from its place against a tree upon the hill. We join the hard-working pair as they get ready to unhook the tractor.

Wrecker Man speaks:

"That ain't very good, but it's about as good as I can get it."

Tractor Man replies: "I think ya done good. That's just about dead center of that mud puddle. I don't see how you could get it any better."

Wrecker Man departs and we listen to the continuing saga of Tractor Man in his own words:

My first job was to get the old casting off the tractor. I had to remove the grill and radiator before I could do that. It had only been a month or so since they had been removed, so the bolts hadn't rusted in place yet. They came off easily. Only big bolts held the casting on and they came loose without a struggle. I had the casting off in fifteen minutes. This was too easy. I knew I would have more trouble putting it back on. The casting weighed about seventy-five to eighty pounds.

I took the remaining tractor back up the hill to retrieve the wheels. This proved to be the hardest part yet. The tires were filled with water to make them heavier so the front of the tractor wouldn't rise off the ground on a hard pull. In addition, the spindle on which the tires were mounted was all iron and steel. Altogether, the assembly must have weighed 200 pounds. It proved most awkward because the wheels turned as I tried to lift them and spun out of my hands. I finally beat it, two falls out of three, and loaded it on the back of tractor number two.

After a cup of coffee and a short rest while my back and hernia healed, I rolled the wheel assembly off into a convenient puddle and proceeded to take the broken piece of casting off the wheel pedestal. Three of the four bolts came easily, but one held out for rough treatment. I tried leverage on the wrench and pounding on the wrench, all the while making acidic remarks about its ancestry, but it wouldn't budge. I finally got my propane torch and heated things up a bit, and with a little verbal persuasion, it broke loose. Now all I had to do was get another casting, and I was in business.

Dawn broke sunny and warm the next morning, so I jumped in my rolling rust pile and started north. I took along the old casting to be sure I got the right one. Before I was past Lancaster, it was raining. The farther north I went, the harder it rained. by the time I reached Morrow County, the fields were flooded and the streams were overflowing. Then it started to snow. A couple of places water was over the road.

When I approached the Tractor Retirement Village, I could see the tractors standing in ragged rows with water flowing between the rows. The place looked like a giant rice paddy.

I was greeted by Ed Axthelm, PARTS MAN, known around the world as "Reverend" or "Preacher." He's no more of a preacher than I am. He got that moniker by making a statement in front of witnesses along the lines of, "If that SOB is a farmer, I'm a preacher." It stuck.

It was warm and comfortable in the house and I was reluctant to go out in the blizzard. After a few minutes of chit-chat, he put on a pair of greasy coveralls over bib overalls, which were over more overalls. I think he'd done this before. God forbid he should get a sudden attack of diarrhea.

The Reverend mounted a large tractor hitched to an even larger truck bed loaded with tools and air tanks and an arc welder and acetylene welder. He indicated a small platform on which I could ride and away we went. He knew exactly which row to go down and soon found the unfortunate part donor. He attacked the bolts with an air wrench like they use to take car wheels off. Two came off; two didn't. Next he put a large wrench on and whacked it with a hammer. The wrench broke.

"It wasn't much of a wrench, anyway," he said.

Another heavier wrench got off number three, but four defied all efforts to extract it.

"Sometimes you have to speak in a language they understand."

He got out the acetylene torch and heated the bolt and casting thoroughly. The bolt came out easily.

"I think he understood," he mused.

I had only a light jacket and low boots and I was nearly frozen by the time we were ready to load up the parts. He let me wear a pair of his gloves, but they were so big I couldn't keep them on. He's a bear of a man.

Back to the house to warm up and exchange a few more pleasantries, including a hefty check, and I'm on my way. It was a pleasant visit and I hated to leave, but "miles to go before I sleep."

Next evening, I bolted the wheel spindle to the new casting. It took only a few minutes. Then I stood the whole thing up on the tires. It was an ungainly piece. (Imagine a 200-pound unicycle and you'll get the idea.) The tractor was six inches too low. I had wood blocks under the engine. I had to get another jack to raise the front high enough to get the blocks out and put the big jack under the transmission and raise it. Finally, I got it about right and tried the casting. Another inch or two and it would work. Blocking the wheels to keep it from rolling, I tried to work the jack left-handed and hold the casting with the other. (Where is CHUCKMAN when you need him?)

I finally got it so I could work the bolts in place. Only a few minutes to put on the radiator and grill and I was in business. I mounted the seat triumphantly and took off. It worked fine until I tried to go up the hill. It flat refused to climb that hill. Either it was afraid of heights after the trauma it had been through or the great tractor god in the sky was angry with me and needed to be appeased.

I might have to throw a virgin in Scott's Crick. I don't think that would please him, though — it's only six inches deep.

What this country needs is a good volcano — one big enough to throw a tractor into.

Caught Flat-Footed by Flood — Again
March 22, 1997

Well, it's happened again. We've been caught flat-footed by a flood. It seems, even though we know its bound to happen, we're never ready. Here in the hills, it can happen in minutes as the water rushes off the hills into the cricks.

The area where I live has been hit harder in recent years because of nearby strip mines. There are a couple hundred acres of stripped land. This was mostly forested before it was mined and the trees and the leaves and forest duff held water like a sponge. The water eventually got to the crick but the flow was slowed so that it was less likely to flood. Now it rushes into the streams as if the hills were concrete.

There have always been floods, of course, and there always will be. Floods didn't hurt anything a few centuries ago because there were no people here, or at most a few Indians who had the good sense to pick up their homes and move to higher ground when Ol' Man River threatened. It's only when man's homes and possessions are damaged that floods become a problem.

Floods are a natural part of Earth's plan. They tear down the hills and build valleys where the soil is deep and fertile, making places where man can raise his food. He just shouldn't live there. It seems we never learn. We love to be near water. We cuss and moan and groan and cry at our bad luck then move right back in as soon as the water recedes and wait for the next one. We say, "That was a fifty-year flood. It won't do that again for fifty years. By then I won't care." Here on Scott's Crick we've had three fifty-year floods in fifteen years.

I know that won't happen again for another fifty years. Last summer, my bridge was washed out five times. It was fun putting it back on the foundation, but I had other things to do and I felt guilty about playing when I should be working, so I decided to build a new one that would withstand whatever Mr. Scott could throw at it. Neighbor Chuck, the world's greatest shade-tree mechanic and all-around Jack of trades, and I constructed a beautiful bridge — longer, higher and stronger than necessary. All winter long Ol' Man Scott's Crick was docile and tame. He knew he was beaten this time so he didn't try to dislodge this masterpiece. I was lulled into complacency. I began to feel safe.

A couple of weeks ago we had a pretty good rain storm. I was staying with friends in Athens County. There were flood warnings on TV and radio. I was a little concerned but still fairly confident. The next day I came home to see what had happened. There she stood proud and strong. The water had almost entirely covered it. I could tell by the debris on the top. But the bridge hadn't moved an inch. "Well," I thought, "If it could stand that onslaught, it can stand anything the crick can throw at it." I went away feelin' good. It was starting to rain, but I wasn't worried.

I was listening to flood reports the next day. There was considerable damage. Hocking and Vinton counties were hard hit. It seemed it had rained another five or six inches overnight. I began to get a gnawing feeling in the pit of my stomach. That didn't last long, however. The phone rang and friend Chuck said, "Guess where your bridge is?" My first guess was Nelsonville. "Nope. It's still there, but it's pointing downstream."

"It might as well be in Nelsonville," I said. He said it didn't appear to be damaged. All we had to do was put it back on the foundation. That's all.

When I went to look at it, he was right. All we had to do was put it back. After chewing on several options and spitting them out, I decided that a crane could lift it back on with the least amount of damage or chance of anyone getting hurt. A few phone calls and I found someone who could do the job almost immediately. And he did. He and the crane and a rigger showed up at about 8:30 and had it in place by 9:30. There she sits, snugly chained to trees and bolted more securely to the foundation. It was simple and easy — but not cheap. I'm not complaining about the price. The man had a very expensive piece of equipment and help to pay besides other expenses that go with doing business. But it cost more to move it than it cost to build it.

My driveways, bridge approaches and a culvert had also been washed away, so I'm looking at six or seven hundred dollars of damage. I'd been hearing over and over that FEMA wanted to help flood victims and had a phone number to call. I've been under the weather lately and lost three month's income, so I thought I could use a little help. I called the number. I got ahold of a nice lady in the local emergency management office. She gave me an 800 number to call. This got me connected to a nice man in Texas. He asked all the right questions and I apparently gave the right answers and he said he could help — "however ..." I should have known there would be a however. However, I would have to talk to the Small Business Administration. I said that I didn't really want a loan, the radio said FEMA would help.

"Oh you don't have to take out a loan, but you have to fill out an application for a loan," he said.

Three days later two envelopes came from SBA. One for me, one for the business. A day or two later, on Sunday, the FEMA inspector called and said he would inspect the site that afternoon. I met him there and he said it looked favorable and he thought they could help me. "What about SBA?" I asked. "What do I do with those papers?"

"Fill 'em out and send 'em in."

"I really don't want an SBA loan," I said.

"Ya gotta fill 'em out and send 'em in."

I got out the papers to fill 'em out and send 'em it. I didn't fill 'em out or send 'em in.

There were some conditions to be met. First, I had to try to borrow money locally. Failing that, I could apply for an SBA loan. There were several pages to be filled out. It took a half hour just to read the instructions and forms.

I needed to file a complete financial statement, showing income for the last three years and a list of creditors. Then a list of everything lost (this would be a nightmare for a hardware store). Next, federal income tax forms for the last three years, a ninety-day balance sheet and IRS form 8821. An inspector from OSHA will inspect. SBA reserves the right to release this information to anyone who needs it.

To me, the price is too high. I don't like selling my soul to the government for a lousy 600 bucks. Whoever said "there's no such thing as a free lunch" was right. I should have known.

Hunting a Mastadon
July 5, 1997

When I built my present house, I hired a man to dig the basement with a bulldozer. It was dug into the hillside so that almost no dirt had to be taken from the front, but about six feet had to be excavated in the back.

The dirt was pushed to all four sides so that it could be graded easily. He went down to bedrock, which was fairly level. All went well until he reached the far left corner. There, he ran into a large lump of rock that was different from the rest of the brown sandstone.

It was white and sort of lumpy. It was fairly soft and broke into pieces as the dozer chipped away at it. He pushed it out with the rest of the dirt and it was scattered over the hillside.

After I had the block laid up and waterproofed, we had a big rain. I put plastic pipe around the foundation and gravel on top. I covered this area carefully with dirt and what was left was scattered over the hillside. As I was shoveling, I began to find pieces of the white stone that had been washed clean by the rain. It was funny-looking stuff. It appeared to be almost like fossilized meat, the muscles clearly defined. Some pieces were smooth with parts that looked as if they had been varnished. I was perplexed. I had never seen anything like it.

My friend, Marie, and her daughter, Jenny, came the next day to check on the progress I was making on the house. I showed them the rocks and we decided to gather a bunch of them together and try to make some sense of things. It became a treasure hunt, with, "Hey, come look at this one," being the call of the day, as we found more and more strange-looking pieces. It became "curiouser and curiouser!"

We began to speculate on what it could be. One piece looked for all the world like the inside of the mouth of a large animal. The palate looked real, though there weren't any teeth. Several pieces were tapered cylinders. The piece that gave me a real clue as to what it might be was found down below the driveway where it had rolled down the hill and fetched up against a tree. It was about eight inches in diameter and about two feet long. It looked for all the world like an elephant's leg from the knee down, even to the round of the foot. That got us really excited.

I got the tractor and wagon and loaded up the pieces (there were nearly a ton) and took them down to the crick and scrubbed them clean. We then laid them out on the ground and tried to piece them together. One huge piece, with the palate, seemed to be an elephant's head. Several of the tapered pieces formed a trunk and some of the smaller ones were the rudiments of tusks, and of course the leg was the crowning glory. There was no doubt in my mind that we had the remains of a mastodon here.

Mastodon bones are not uncommon in Ohio. Several have been found in the last few years. These were not bones, however; they looked like fossilized flesh. It is extremely rare that any soft tissue gets fossilized because it rots away quickly and it takes millions of years to make a fossil. I rationalized that these particular animals (there were some pieces left that didn't fit and I surmised that there were several animals together) had been trapped in a clay pit and had become sealed in clay and didn't rot because they didn't get oxygen. These pieces were smaller than the bones I had seen so I guessed that it had been a baby one.

That night I dreamed about how to make money off this thing. It surely would become a tourist attraction. There was still a lump of rock outside the foundation that could be more of the same. I thought of making a glass case over it so the tourists could see it. Then there would have to be a tram or some conveyance up the hill. I couldn't have people having heart attacks trying to walk up. Of course I'd have the obligatory gift shop. I'd have to hire someone to sell tickets while I lectured. I would probably have to pave the horse pasture to park all the cars that would come. This could turn into something big!

The next day Marie brought her video camera and we set about making a tape to get my find verified by some archaeology or geology types. We shot pictures of where it was found and shots of it put together. I explained how I came to my conclusions. I thought it came out well and surely someone would come and excavate the remainder.

I sent a copy of the tape to the Ohio Museum of Natural History and the head geologist for the State of Ohio. The museum never granted me the courtesy of a reply. I suppose they thought, "Here's another nut!"

Mr. Hanson, the geologist, wrote me a nice letter saying that he didn't know what it was, but he knew what it wasn't, and it wasn't a mastodon. Mastodons were here as late as 12,000 years ago and it takes millions of years to fossilize bones, but tissue doesn't fossilize. I knew that. I know that the last one was here 12,000 years ago, but when was the first one here? Isn't it possible that the first one arrived three million years ago?

Soon after, my nephew was visiting from Washington, D.C. He knew someone who worked for The National Geographic Society. He took the tape and the man viewed it in his presence. He said he didn't know what it was, but he knew what it wasn't, and it wasn't a mastodon. Sounded familiar. He said that their field crews had uncovered similar stuff, but they have never identified it. He did say it was a good tape, though.

Well, so much for dreams of grandeur. Two out of three can't be wrong. I still think it's something more than a pile of rocks, although that's what it is now. I piled the pieces next to my porch, threw a little dirt over them and planted flowers on them. People who come to my house have no idea that they are passing a three million year old rock garden.

I've told only a few people beyond my immediate family. Those who do know tend to make fun of me about it. I was sensitive for a while. Most people don't enjoy it when they make a fool of themselves, but I think I'm pretty well over it now, though not completely. The first guy that calls me a dumb rock saver — pow! Right in the kisser!

Do you suppose it could be a dinosaur? Too small for a T-Rex — maybe a masto-raptor.

Frightening, Fuzzy, Flying Things on Fassig's Funny Farm
August 2, 1997

It hasn't been a great week here on the hill.

We started off the week with a series of storms that were spectacular to watch from adequate cover, but had less than beautiful results. I never saw such lightning in all of my thirty-nine years. I sat on the porch and was fascinated by the display. The lightning was almost constant for nearly two hours on Saturday night. You could almost read a newspaper by the light.

The TV gave a running account of the progress of various storms and it was interesting to follow them, trying to guess if the ones approaching would hit here or not. The main storm hit just before dark and just wouldn't quit. For most of the evening, I was surrounded by lightning, which indicated that it was a big storm and I was right in the middle of it. I live in the woods and the trees are so dense that I have to lie on my back to see the sky, so I didn't see most of the actual bolts, just the glow.

Finally, it drifted off to the southeast and I was able to breathe a sigh of relief. I wondered how we managed to get through all that without losing power. Then the lights went out. They came back on in a few minutes and I thought, "That was quick work." Moments later, they went out again. They didn't come back on.

I have a twelve-volt lightning system in my house, so I had back-up lights but not enough power to run a TV set. Naturally, I didn't have any batteries for the radio. I read for a while, in the meantime enjoying another storm of slightly less intensity, then decided I might as well go to bed. That always seems to be a prudent way to solve problems.

Between showers, I scooted out to my screen house bedroom in the woods and crawled into the sack. I didn't stay long, however. As soon as my foot hit the blanket, I felt a searing pain. I thought I had put my foot on a wasp. Grabbing a flashlight, I started a site investigation (as they say in the cop shows). I didn't find a wasp. I found a caterpillar. He was a bristly devil. He looked like a tooth brush. I shook him off the blanket and he landed on the floor in front of the door. In anger, I opened the door and kicked him out. Big mistake. Instead of having a foot on fire, I now had two feet on fire. Boy, did they hurt. I'll bet not many of those babies get eaten!

After about ten minutes, the pain subsided and I was able to get to sleep. I must have slept pretty well, because when I went down the hill in the morning, a sizable tree limb was in the driveway and a large tree was beside the road on State Route 93. The evidence shows (more cop talk) that it had fallen across the highway and had been chain-sawed into pieces small enough to be moved off the road. We must have had another storm during the night, because there was no wind during the first two.

The only other damage I had was some erosion in the driveway. A half hour with tractor and blade fixed that. I didn't even break anything on the tractor.

One little thing I didn't mention, not storm-related, was that the deer had eaten almost all of my petunias during the night. They didn't eat much of the plants, just the flowers. I've babied those things all summer, mulching, watering, weeding and fertilizing, and they were beautiful. The blooms were large and colorful and so thick I could hardly see the leaves. Those and five tomatoes are the only things I cultivate anymore. Everything else is as nature intended. I gave up years ago trying to have a garden so I was particularly chagrined to find my only concession to civilization damaged.

I decided to try to prevent this from happening again. I had a box of mothballs that I purchased recently to try to discourage the flying squirrels from using my attic for a playground. Apparently, it's so hot up there that the resident black snake is on vacation.

I thought if I scattered the mothballs among the petunias, it might discourage the deer from picnicking just outside my door. I proceeded to do just that yesterday. As I started to go back into the house, a wasp took exception with my bothering his screen door and bounced off my leg a couple of times, then headed for my face. I swung the only weapon I had, the box of mothballs, scattering them in some places they weren't needed, and backed off. I saw then that there was a small nest under the crosspiece on the door. I had a can of wasp spray in the house, so I said, "I'll fix you, fella."

It was no good trying to get in that door, since he already had his dander up, so I decided to go in the rarely-used back door. As soon as I opened it, a wasp, without asking questions, flew in my face and stung me on the eyelid. Talk about something hurting! Holy cow, that did hurt. Now, going in that door was out of the question. I could see several more in there preparing to attack. I vacated immediately. I began to get a little perturbed at not being allowed in my own house. There was no choice but to make a frontal attack. Grabbing a piece of kindling from the woodshed (the shotgun was also in the house), I approached boldly and confidently. The wasps, seeing themselves outgunned, retreated, and I gained the fort without incident.

The first thing I did was give the back door bandits reason to regret their indiscretion. A shot of spray provided the front door bunch a little incentive to vacate. I looked in the mirror. My eyelid was already turning red and starting to swell. Ordinarily, I just shrug off bites and stings. They only hurt for a little while. But this was different. I didn't want to put any medicine or ointment in my eye, so I opted for an ice cube. That only made it cold. By nine o'clock, it looked like I had a slice of pickled beet plastered over my eye. When I got up this morning, it was swollen nearly shut.

It's a beautiful day in the neighborhood, and I'm looking for a better week. When you come right down to it, when you live in the woods, any week that you don't get stung or snakebit, catch poison ivy or "git et" by a bear is a purty good week.

Saga of the FEMA Memorial Bridge — Part I
November 30, 1996

You might remember last March, we had a rather disastrous flood here in Hocking County, as well as elsewhere. I wrote then about losing my new bridge and applying for flood relief funds from the federal government. They came through with adequate funds with a minimum of red tape. I was well pleased as well as embarrassed because I expected a paper work nightmare and said so.

The receipt of that check set in motion (slow motion, I might add), a chain of events that devoured the summer and most of the fall. FEMA, the Federal Emergency Management Agency, insisted that the bridge be done right this time, not the make-shift pile of junk that I've become famous for.

About the middle of May, I contacted Bill Shaw, our county engineer, who graciously consented to assist me in planning. He asked what size loads would use the bridge and how long it would be. I told him it must be forty feet long and should hold a fire truck. "Wow," he said, "Some of those babies weigh twenty tons when they're full of water. That'll take some iron. I'll have to check the load charts. Come in Friday and I'll have a drawing for you."

Friday, the drawing was ready. I think this was a great service. It was the type of thing public servants should do but seldom do for their constituents. I think we're lucky to have people like that in this county. It wasn't something he did for me as a friend, because I've never met him.

I can just imagine the response I would get if I had made the same request in Franklin County.

Anyway, the drawing called for five twelve-inch "I" beams forty feet long. In my mind, I pictured one of those cartoon balloons over my head with a flock of hundred dollar bills with wings flying away. I had thought two beams would do it, but the phrase "do it right this time" came to haunt me whenever I thought of cutting corners. Five beams it would be.

A perusal of the yellow pages revealed a local company that sold erected structure steel. I went to see them. They gave me a price that seemed reasonable, though it took just under half the allotted money. After all, that was the most expensive part, right? The owner said, "Why don't you let me figure what it would take to prefab the bridge? We can put it all together and weld it into one piece and haul it down to the site and with a crane set it right to the abutments and it will be done. You won't have to do anything. Of course, we don't do concrete work. You'll have to get someone else for that."

It was a couple of weeks before they had time to figure the price. When it came, it floored me. It would cost twice the money I had available. I opted for just buying the beams. By now it was mid-June.

That settled, I set about finding someone to do the concrete work. I had noticed a neighbor, whom I had never met since he had just recently moved in, building a bridge. I stopped in to see how he had done it. It was basically the same design as mine would be. He told me who built his. It was a local contractor. I gave him a call.

He said he would do the whole thing or just the concrete work if I wanted to set my own steel. I liked that. I always liked a challenge. I had neither the time or resources to do the concrete work, especially since I was still a little gimpy on my new knee. In a week or two he came up with a price which I thought was a little high but I accepted it. He said he was really busy right now but could get to it in a month or so. I told him I was in no great rush, I just didn't want to be working out in the cold or snow.

Having been a contractor myself, I should have known better. In the contracting business, the squeaky wheel gets the grease. Nice guys finish last.

Now that I had a cement man engaged, I ordered the beams so that they would be here when needed. I suspected it could take weeks to get them delivered. It took one week. The driver called to get specific directions. I was almost in shock. All those things I was going to do to get ready weren't done yet.

I put the snow blade on the tractor and plowed through wildflowers eight feet tall, not knowing what I would find. I found piles of dirt and tree limbs, logs and humongous rose bushes. These required a chain saw to eliminate. I'd just gotten a spot cleared to unload them when the truck came. As I went to the road to stop the man from coming in, he wheeled her around and, blocking State Route 93, backed in just like he knew what he was doing. He would have been a half an hour turning around in this place. I had him back in where I thought we could unload. "How are you going to get em off?" he questioned.

"I can pull 'em off with the tractor," I answered. "OK. Try it."

We got one off the forty-foot trailer, but then we were stymied. They had loaded the beams on either side and had a stack of other stuff in the middle, which made it impossible to unload them all on one side.

"Mind if I make a suggestion?" he said. "Nope." "Let me back right through these bushes," he indicated an old fence row, "and we'll chain 'em to that tree and I'll just pull out from under 'em."

Now here was my kinda man.

"Do'er," I said, "but there's still some fence in there. I don't want to hurt yer truck."

"Won't hurt a thing," was his reply.

He pulled up and over and backed into the fence row. Rose bushes flattened and fence wire popped. Back to the tree he went. He took a couple of chains and wrapped one around the beams and another around the tree and hooked them altogether. He pulled forward about forty-two feet, and with an eardrum shattering clang, they were on the ground.

To be continued ...

Saga of the FEMA Memorial Bridge — Part II

December 6, 1997

Last week I started the tale of replacing my washed-out bridge. I had just reached the point of unloading the new steel beams. By now it was early July.

I hadn't heard from the contractor, so I gave him a call.

"I'm not pushing you," I said, "but the water level in the crick is low and it seems like a good time to put in the footers."

"You're right," he said. "I should be there the end of this week or the first of next."

"OK. Just so I'm done before the first snow flies."

About the first week in September, I called him again.

"I'll be there the end of this week or the first of next," was his answer. It seemed I had heard that before somewhere. By now the wildflowers had reclaimed the space allotted for the steel beams and I could no longer find them. I had bought a welder and built a trailer just for practice so I could weld the beams when the time came.

The first of October I began calling around trying to find a contractor who could pour the concrete for the bridge abutments. I wasn't having much luck. Several were too busy trying to finish jobs before the snow flies. That had a familiar ring. Each gave me the name of someone who might do it. There were a couple who didn't answer. I would try them tomorrow. When I went down to work the next morning, there sat a backhoe. No people, just a backhoe. I took it as an omen.

An hour or so later, the original contractor showed up and started to work. I was torn between the urge to throw him in the crick or kiss him. Civility won out and I greeted him civilly, if not warmly.

By now we'd had some rains and the water level was higher than it had been in August. He was able to dig the eastern-most footer, but the water was too deep to dig on the western end. It would have to be pumped out.

Soon, two men from a concrete wall pouring company came in. They had been subcontracted to do the actual pouring. They ordered the concrete for shortly after noon. My old bridge wouldn't support a concrete truck, of course, so they came into the field down by the barn and hauled the concrete in the bucket on the front of the backhoe. It worked well, and in less than a half hour the footer was done.

The men tried to pump the crick dry, but couldn't get the pump started. They decided to try again on the morrow with a different pump. This one started and they got the water down enough to dig the footer. They poured the concrete under water because the water ran back as fast as they pumped it out. This doesn't hurt the concrete. In fact, it makes it stronger because it sets up more slowly.

The next day they returned and built the forms for the east end. They have standard-sized form panels that have steel frames around the outside edge with matching holes. They are placed side by side and metal clips are inserted in the holes to hold the pieces together. It goes surprisingly fast. In less than two hours the form is complete. Reinforcing bars are wired inside the forms to make the concrete stronger. Though this job goes rather swiftly, it's incredibly hard work. These guys earn their money.

They used the same procedure as before, hauling the concrete in with the front-end loader. It took only about a half hour.

They next day they stripped the forms off and built them on the west end. This was a little more difficult because there was about a foot of water over the footer, which was surrounded by sticky mud that wanted to pull their boots off. It was done eventually and the concrete ordered.

This time the truck was able to back right to the form and it took only a few minutes to fill it. I fully expected that no one would show up the next day, but they fooled me. They came about noon and removed the forms. All in all, they did a wonderful job, and I'm well pleased.

Now it's my baby. I can't blame anyone else if things don't move. They said to wait a day or two before setting the beams. They needn't have bothered. The October weather had been beautiful all week, and you know what happened. It turned cold and wet and miserable.

The formers left bolts sticking out of the top of the concrete abutments. The next job was to bolt a steel plate on top to which the beams could be welded.

My son took a couple of days off work to help with the steel. We worked all day getting one beam in place. They were a little awkward to handle. They weigh about 1,400 pounds apiece. We pulled them down on the old bridge with my trusty old tractor. Then, using chains and come-alongs and pry bars, we inched one end up on an inclined plank until that end was up on top of the wall.

We had some mishaps and had to change tacks several times, but we finally hit on a system that worked. On the second day we had the other four in place by mid-afternoon.

Before my son had to leave, he had welded them all to the steel plate that we had bolted to the top of the wall. Now it was beginning to look like a bridge.

While I was waiting for the concrete to cure, I had gone to a scrap yard and bought some pretty hefty channel irons. I rigged up a power saw with a metal cutting blade in high hopes of zipping the iron quickly into exact lengths. It didn't work.

I borrowed an acetylene torch from a neighbor. The acetylene tank was almost empty, so I had to have it filled before I could start. I was able to cut several pieces in pretty short order and then the torch quit working. I had to wait until the owner came home from work. He found that the torch itself was defective. He had a spare, so I was able to continue the next day. After an hour, the oxygen tank ran dry. Back to the supply company. Finally, I was able to finish.

These pieces were welded between the I-beams at intervals to give the bridge lateral stability.

Next, two-by-fours were bolted on top of the beams. I burned holes in the beams to take the bolts. It was much quicker than drilling. In order to bolt the two-by-fours I had to sit on the beams and slide along as I went. I was half done at dark.

The next day I awoke to an inch of snow and fifteen degrees. Since my posterior is sensitive to freezing to steel beams, I took the day off to meditate on the ancestry of the contractor to whom my only request was "get me finished before the snow flies."

One thing about this bridge that is different is its height. It stands head and shoulders above the old one. I tried to get it above the high water mark. This means that the approaches had to be raised. It needed five feet of fill on the east end. I put the scoop on the tractor and started hauling gravel out of the crick. It was a job that seemed endless. I worked a half a day on it. My son worked a whole day and then I hauled another whole day. We eventually got it filled.

The other end was at ground level, but there was a ditch three feet wide and five feet deep the width of the abutment. I was out of gravel that I could reach. It took four loads of limestone to fill that void, plus another to move the driveway over.

When the two-by-fours were bolted in place, I started taking the planks off the old bridge and tossing them up on the new one. (And I do mean up. The new bridge is six feet above the water.) I had gotten a flu shot the day before and my arm hurt, plus I had sprained my ankle a few days earlier, and the job wasn't fun for very long.

By noon, I was only a third done. I had to finish in one day because until the new bridge was finished I had no bridge at all. I had to resort to strong measures. At lunch time I went across the road and woke up my friend Chuck, the world's greatest shade-tree mechanic. (He's a night person.) When I returned from lunch, he was hard at it. It was about fifteen degrees and the planks were frozen down as well as nailed, and they didn't yield willingly. In about half an hour, two of Chuck's cousins showed up looking for him. After a few minutes of pleasantries, they were recruited and within an hour all the planks were on top. I thanked them profusely before they left. I thought they would be insulted if I offered to pay them. I'll certainly buy them a beer the next time I see them in the Waldorf-Astoria.

I spent the next couple of hours nailing the planks down. It was certainly a moment of triumph when I was able to drive my trusty rusty pickup truck across for the first time. It was also a little daunting, being that high with no guardrails on the side. I knew my flatland tourists would be afraid to cross it. The electric company had replaced a couple of poles during the summer and left the old ones. They were just as long as the bridge. I pulled them up on top and bolted one on each side. I don't know if they would keep anyone from driving off the edge, but they give one a feeling of security, anyhow.

At last, it's finished. My cabin people have driven across it for a couple of weeks now, and none have gone over the edge yet. If my luck holds, now that I've got a proper bridge, we'll never have another flood. It sort of boggles the mind, doesn't it?

I'm grateful to all those who helped, especially FEMA. It was a great experience, sorta like going into the Army. I wouldn't have missed it, but I wouldn't want to do it again.

All in a Day's Work
February 20, 1999

I've had quite a few people rent my cabin this winter. More than usual. As a result, I've been hard pressed to keep up with the demand for firewood. Them city folks do love to burn wood. This week we've had some really nice days, especially nice for February, so I decided to forgo shop work one day this week and get some wood in the shed.

I have a stack of red oak up on the hill that I cut last fall. It was from a blow-down and still fairly green. I stacked it outside where the wind could dry it. A foot of snow followed by ice and rain didn't do much to dry it, however, and it was still too wet to burn well. It was clear it would have to dry some more.

There was a dead elm down by the crick that should have been OK, so I decided to cut that instead. Elms dry pretty well if they are left standing. This tree had grown up into a couple of maples and the branches were intertwined. There was one branch about three inches in diameter that went twenty feet into one of the maples. It had been dead for some time and should have broken off as it fell. It should have, but it didn't. When I cut through the trunk, it just stood there and stared down at me.

No problem. I could pull it down with the tractor. The battery was nearly dead and the tractor wouldn't start. No problem. I put the battery charger on it. It was time for a cuppa coffee anyhow.

In half an hour, after two phone calls while I was trying to get coffee, it started right up. I backed it near the tree and got the cable. It was tangled almost beyond help. It's old and full of kinks and twists. After a few frustrating minutes, I was able to get the hook end untangled from the mess. There was a briar patch near the tree that had to be negotiated. I felt like a hog in a barb-wire fence by the time I reached the tree. These things can be positively infuriating, tearing at your clothes (and your hide). Eventually, I was in a position to toss the hook over a large branch. I didn't toss it over a branch — I was just in position to. There were numerous small branches from the maple trees that would reach out and grab the hook as it went by.

After ten or so tries, I finally got the thing over the branch. It didn't go over far enough that I could reach it, however. It took another ten minutes to flip the cable through the branches far enough that I could reach it. I seized the hook at last and engaged it around the cable.

Then it was back through the briar patch, all the while keeping the cable taut so that it wouldn't come unhooked. It was too short to reach the tractor! I had to let go of the cable and watch it contract its serpentine coils like a long, skinny boa constrictor and sneak back into that briar patch.

I moved the tractor back about six feet, fought my way back into the briars, retrieved the cable and hooked it to the tractor. I breathed a sigh of relief. I had it now. I eased ol' Bessie forward. The cable drew tight. The tree moved, and then zing! The cable went flying back toward the tree. The end had come loose from the tractor. I had no idea what had happened. Back through the briars. The end of the cable didn't have a hook — it just had a loop, held by a cable clamp. It had been on there twenty years and never came loose. This time it did. Of course, I had to go hunt up a wrench to put it back in place.

I hooked it back to the tractor and pulled forward confidently. The tree didn't move. The hook jumped over the limb and plopped into the briar patch. This was beginning to wear a little thin.

The whole process had to be repeated. It didn't go much better the second time around, but at last I was ready to pull again. The limb that was keeping it from falling broke off and the tree tipped over to about forty-five degrees and stopped. It resisted all efforts to dislodge it. A closer inspection revealed that I hadn't cut my notch at the right angle and the tree had gone as far as it would go. I cut off what branches I could reach before cutting the trunk farther. This I accomplished at arm's length, ready to run. The trunk shifted enough to start to pinch the saw, but I was able to jerk it loose before it was stuck permanently. Now, there I was. The tree was almost loose on the stump but hung on a couple of maple branches no bigger than my thumb. It was too dangerous to try to get the cable hooked up again, lest the tree fall on me. I had no choice but to tip my hat and slowly ride away.

So for a whole afternoon's work I had a wheelbarrow full of damp firewood, a butt full of thorns and high blood pressure. Actually, that's a pretty typical day's work here on the funny farm. I'm hoping for a good wind to come along and do what I couldn't do with a chain saw.

The Shiner
November 20, 1999

Do you ever have one of those days when everything goes wrong? I never do, but a couple of days ago I came close. I have a customer who wanted a few locust posts to repair a foot bridge. You used to be able to go to a nearby farm store or grain elevator and get them, but they're hard to find anymore. I have a friend who has some locust trees growing on her farm, and she agreed to let me have a few if I would cut them.

I arrived early Monday morning armed with chain saw and tape measure to cut a few trees. I thought about three would do it. She had to go to work so she said, "Take my tractor. It will be easier." So I did.

It was a lovely, bright, frosty morning for working. I had no trouble finding a patch of trees at the edge of the woods next to an open field. This would be easy. I selected one the right size, determined which way it would fall, and cut a notch in the correct place as any good logger would do, then cut it off. It fell ninety degrees from where I thought it would and hung up in an adjacent tree at about forty-five degrees from vertical. I'd failed to take into account a gob of grapevines near the top. The two trees were tied together. No problem. It happens all the time. I guestimated the length of the first post and, taking chain saw in hand, started to cut the trunk in two at that point. As I was about halfway through, the tree rolled about halfway over and pinched the saw. I'd again failed to take into account the gob of grapevines that tied the two trees together.

No problem. I'd come prepared with a chain for just such occurrences. I threw the end of the chain over the trunk as high as I could, secured the hook and gave a lusty pull. Nothing happened. "Oh, well, I guess I'll have to pull it down with the tractor," I said to myself. (I often do that, you know. I even answer myself sometimes.) I walked back to where I'd left the tractor and fired her up. I had the brush hog on, so I said to myself, "No use in being stupid; mow them briars as you go." "A good idea," sez I. So I did.

Only at the last second did I see that I was going to run over the chain. I stepped on the clutch to stop the mower, but I was going slightly downhill, and the momentum carried the mower right over the chain, and I heard it hit. Then the lights went out.

When I awakened some time later (and I don't know how much later), I was conscious of a lot of pain and the fact that I couldn't move. It took a few moments to realize that I was still on the tractor with the motor running. My foot was still on the clutch, and the tree was on my head and shoulder; my hand was pinned to the steering wheel, and my eye was full of steering wheel.

"Well, stupid," I sez to myself, "here's another fine mess you've gotten us into." I had to agree. I was able to hunch my right shoulder enough to get the tree to slide off my head and hand. In a minute or two I was able to raise my head. It's amazing how stiff you can get sitting in an uncomfortable position. My right hand was numb, so I took a swipe across my face with my left. It felt kinda lumpy, and there was a trace of blood, but no streams running anywhere, so I guessed I was in no immediate danger of bleeding to death. Tender words my dear old dad used to say to me came to mind. He'd say, "Come on. Get up. You ain't hurt. If ya ain't bleedin', ya ain't dyin'."

In a few minutes I was able to shut off the motor and get off the tractor. To my amazement, everything seemed to work. I was a little shaky on my feet, but nothing seemed broken. A little exploration of my skull showed that I had a lump on my eyebrow as big as a walnut. I picked up my hat and tried to put it on, but it was a couple sizes too small. Closer examination exposed a goose egg on the back of my head as big as, well, a goose egg. Neither hurt, but I decided to call it a day, just in case my skull split open and my brain fell out if I got too ambitious.

I retrieved the chain saw from where it fell, and luckily it started on the first pull. I cut the tree off the hood of the tractor and into appropriate lengths. One post was still chained to the blade of the brush hog. I started the tractor and raised the brush hog as high as I could. I shut off the motor (I thought it would be tempting fate to let it run) and wiggled under. The briars felt wonderful. Fortunately the chain wasn't badly wound around the blade, and in a few minutes it was free. I'm just lucky I guess.

By the time I reached the house, I felt pretty good, and I debated about going back and finishing the job. I went into the bathroom to clean up a bit and got the shock of my life. I looked like I'd just gone ten rounds with Mike Tyson. The knot on my eyebrow looked as big as my fist, and the skin was splitting. My eye was swelled at least halfway shut and growing. It was a lovely purple. My nose was skinned, too, though not badly. I reasoned that I'd better light out for home, post haste. It was probably the best decision I'd made all day.

The next day, my eye was swelled completely shut. My sister and her husband came calling in the afternoon and brought me some homemade jelly. She always wants the jars back, and I save them for her in a cabinet near the floor. I dug through the usual debris of bachelor living and found about a dozen. As I tried to stand up, I pulled myself up by lifting my bulk with the aid of the counter top, and an excruciating pain shot through my back and chest. It even hurt to breathe. (This was harder than trying to explain the shiner and then listening to advice about being careful.) I decided to take the rest of the day off.

The next morning it took a crowbar to get me out of bed. "Maybe I ought to get some help here," I thought. I called the doctor's office, and the nurse said she thought it wouldn't be a bad idea to get some X-rays. I could see the wisdom in that. Off to Hocking Valley Community Hospital I staggered. I won't go into that adventure. I got educated as I read magazines for three of the three and a half hours of my visit. Suffice to say that in the end the mission was accomplished in a friendly and competent manner. The X-rays showed that nothing was broken in head or back. That put my mind to ease, but I still hurt. To cough or sneeze is at least as painful as childbirth.

It's been a week now, and I still get stares from strangers and smart aleck remarks from friends. I'm thinking of getting a tattoo across my forehead that says, "Ya oughta see the other guy."

OHIO
HISTORICAL
MARKER

LOCK NO. 12
THE SHEEP PEN LOCK
(Continued from other side)

Stretching from Carroll to Athens, the Hocking Canal opened in 1843. The canal stimulated the growth of Lancaster, Logan, and Nelsonville, and opened the Hocking Valley to trade. Its major exports were salt, coal, and iron. Imports included goods from the East, such as cloth, shoes, and dishes. The advent of railroads in the 1850s meant the beginning of the end for canals. In 1894, the Hocking Canal was abandoned.

OHIO BICENTENNIAL COMMISSION, THE LONGABERGER COMPANY, SHEEP PEN LOCK COMMITTEE, HOCKING COUNTY TOURISM ASSOCIATION, HOCKING COUNTY HISTORICAL SOCIETY, THE OHIO HISTORICAL SOCIETY
1998
2-37

Chapter 3
History

Morgan's Raid
February 24, 1996

Most Hocking County residents have heard of Morgan's Raiders in the Civil War, but I wonder how many realize how close he came to ravaging and pillaging Logan. During the latter part of the war in 1863, as a diversionary tactic, Morgan and about 200 men on horseback crossed the Ohio border from Indiana, west of Cincinnati. From there, they traversed a meandering course across southern Ohio. Their purpose was to terrorize the residents and wreak havoc wherever they could, hoping that the North would pull troops out of the South to chase them, thus helping in the war effort against the North.

Morgan was a brave and wily leader. He traveled through Ohio for a couple of weeks without being caught. One morning, the driver of the Jackson stagecoach brought word to Logan that Morgan was encamped at Mount Pleasant. The first reaction was panic. There was no military attachment at Logan, and most able-bodied men were away at war. There was, however, a group of habitues of a certain watering hole which had earned the name "Squirrel Hunters." After a few rounds to discuss the situation, it was decided that an ambush was in order. There was a perfect place just south of town. The road, which is now State Route 93 South, was squeezed between Scott's Crick and a very steep hill. It was decided that they would lay in wait there. The whiskey seemed to obscure the fact that there were only about a dozen of them and about 200 raiders. I feel sure this would have been made clear to them in short order, but a later stage brought news that the wily Morgan had already departed, taking a back road toward Nelsonville.

Visibly disappointed, but I suspect secretly relieved, the Squirrel Hunters retired to the saloon to celebrate their victory. After a few rounds, someone said, "We oughta go down to Nelsonville and route them buggers outta there."

"Yeah, why don't we do that?" someone else replied. And so it was decided. A few more rounds stiffened their resolve and off they went. Since it was twelve or so miles to Nelsonville, they gathered up any means of travel at their disposal, some making the trip in wagons or buggies, some on horseback.

It was a hot afternoon and soon the sweat began to pour. The more they sweat, the more sober they got. The more sober they got, the more it seemed that this wasn't such a good idea. They began to drop out one by one. By the time they reached Nelsonville, there were only two or three left. As these brave souls got down into town, they found that Morgan had sacked and burned part of downtown and departed. The troopers had invaded the stores and taken what supplies they could carry and whatever else struck their fancy. Some came out of a women's clothing store wearing women's hats and shawls.

They set fire to some canal boats. They particularly liked the coal barges because of the dense smoke it created. That was more for effect than anything. Actually, little damage was done, but it had the desired effect of scaring the daylights out of the residents.

What they really wanted were horses. After two weeks on the run, their own horses were dead tired. Every horse in town was rounded up. It didn't matter if they were buggy horses or plow horses; all were saddled and mounted and the spent horses left in their places.

Remounted and reprovisioned, Morgan and his men proceeded on their mission. They had no particular destination in mind, so they proceeded on a whimsical course that took them east toward the Muskingum River. At the little town of Eagleport, they bivouacked.

Meanwhile, the Squirrel Hunters were on their trail. By this time, there were only two of them left. Apparently these two had a larger reserve of Old Stumpknocker and were able to maintain their bravado much longer. As they approached the rebel camp, the leader, one Henry Kelley, was promptly shot by Morgan's pickets. The other high-tailed it back to Logan as fast as he could. It was a good distance to Logan, so it was the next day before he arrived.

Upon hearing the news of Kelley's heroic demise, a small group left in a wagon to retrieve the body. It is supposed that Kelley's companion was among them to show the way.

When they returned, it was drinks all around while they pondered how to honor their fallen friend. It was decided that a proper funeral was in order. A coffin was procured from a local undertaker, and Kelley and a large quantity of ice were put in it. There was no use in wasting the ice, so the beer was also placed in the coffin to cool. A farewell party ensued until the wee hours of the morning when Kelley's wife got wind of it and arrived to claim the body. He was given a proper burial in Oak Grove Cemetery, where he remains today. The only man killed in Ohio during the Civil War from enemy gunfire. Henry Kelley — Hero.

More on Morgan and His Storied Raid
March 2, 1996

I've often wondered what route Morgan's raiders took from Mount Pleasant to Nelsonville. I've gotten a couple of clues since last week's column about Morgan. I was told about the episode by Jim Heinlein. The raiders encamped in his aunt's yard in Mount Pleasant. I always assumed that they went east on the county line road. There is no direct route. The roads wander all over the place at odd angles.

I got a call this week from Mrs. Harden Cremean, whose ancestors settled Ilesboro. She remembers hearing her great-grandmother tell of Morgan passing through Ilesboro. If he did that he would have had to go to Ewing and take Goat Run-Honey Fork Road or take Clay Lick between Ilesboro and Ewing. That's just a quarter mile from my home. If he went on to Ewing, he would have passed right by where my home is now, though it wasn't there then. That's rather exciting. It's almost like George Washington slept here.

Another clue comes from Mrs. Mary Combs of Athens County. Her great-grandfather lived on Cherry Ridge Road. Either course could have put Morgan on Cherry Ridge.

Here's her story as she related it to me:

"It was with great trepidation that the seven women watched my great-grandfather, George Souders, harness his best buggy horse that morning in 1863. All seven — his second wife, her daughters and his daughters — begged him not to go, but he would have none of it. After he left, they did as they were told, and hid the rest of their horses deep in the woods.

"Word had traveled from farm to farm that the notorious rebel general, Morgan, and about 200 troops were marauding in Vinton and Hocking counties and had eluded all efforts to catch them. They were reported to be stealing horses to replace their worn-out ones and getting food and supplies for themselves.

"Great-granddad lived near New Plymouth. He was deeply interested in the Civil War and tried to keep abreast of new developments. About once a week he went to town to get a newspaper. For reasons unknown to me, he went to Zaleski instead of New Plymouth. Perhaps there were no papers available in New Plymouth, or perhaps there was a saloon in Zaleski and none in New Plymouth. Anyway, off he went with his best trotting horse to get his paper. He wasn't worried about meeting Morgan and his raiders. That was just women folk foolishness. The trip was uneventful — a few stops along the way to chat with friends and neighbors and once or twice to water and rest the horse. All in all a right pleasant morning. It had rained heavily the day before and the fields were too wet to work. That eased his conscience a bit.

"He let the horse have his head on the way home as he glanced at the paper now and then and daydreamed. He liked to sit on the porch in his rocker and read it thoroughly. He was slouching lazily in his buggy as it topped a rise and ran smack-dab into Morgan and his raiders. He was stunned as much by the suddenness of if all as anything. The horsemen were a terrifying sight, though. They had been on the road for more than two weeks, having come from Kentucky through Indiana, entering Ohio west of Cincinnati. They were unwashed and unshaven and not in an altogether good mood after being chased all over the state by a company of inept troopers.

"Grandpa George had no choice but to stop. There was no place to go.

"'That's a right purty horse ya got there. The Capn' might like that'n,' a burly sergeant drawled. 'Git down.'

"'Ain't no Johnny Rebs takin' my horse,' Grandpa yelled.

"'You ain't got no choice. Git down!'

"'I'll be damned if I do,' was the reply.

"'Suit yerself,' said the trooper. He waved a couple of men forward. They unhitched the horse and left Grandpa holding the lines.

"'Gonna git down?' asked the trooper.

"'Hell no.'

"'Bye,' said the soldier as he gave the buggy a push an it went flying down the hill backwards. Great-grandpa had the ride of his life. Luckily, the hill was not too long or steep and the buggy sustained only a broken wheel. Granddad suffered a great indignity as he watched 200 jeering, laughing horsemen file by, one of them riding his horse. They left the worn out nag on the road. He caught it and led it the last two miles home.

"'Where's the horse and buggy and where'd you get that old bag o' bones?' his wife asked.

"'Been trading,' he said and sank into his rocker and buried himself in his newspaper."

I still don't know which roads Morgan took to Nelsonville, but there's a start.

There has been a lot of history come from this area and I wish I knew more. I guess I won't worry too much about it because I can't remember much any more. If I had learned it fifty years ago, it would be as clear as if it had happened yesterday. A lot of things are happening now. I hope someone is writing it all down.

Think You Had It Tough?

October 7, 1996

While searching my bookcase the other day for a particular book, which I still haven't found, I ran across a book I hadn't seen in several years.

It is a small, leather-bound notebook. At one time, it had a lock on it. One part of the cover is missing, so it now has only half a lock.

This book is a diary carried by a soldier in the Civil War. It was written by an uncle of my wife's grandmother, which, by my calculations, makes him no relation to me. My wife's grandmother gave it to me because she thought that I would appreciate it more than others in the family. She was right.

This soldier's name was John S. Ruhl of Findlay, Ohio. He was the son of German immigrants. His father was a minister in the German Reformed Church. John was a farmer in Hancock County. He was not drafted, but enlisted when he was paid a thousand dollars to take the place of a prominent doctor's son. This was legal in those days and quite common for the idle rich. John used the money to pay off his farm. Since he wasn't killed in the war, it made a good deal for both of them.

The thing that makes this diary so entertaining to read, other than its historical value, is his creative use of the English language and his spelling. Being a German, he spoke with a German accent. He spelled just as he spoke — with a German accent. For instance, he rode on a "boad" (boat). He also "road leters" (wrote letters). Among the pages of the diary are several letters from his father, who was apparently a well-educated man. The script is beautiful and flawless. Unfortunately, his letters are written in German, so I have no idea what they say. I'd like to find someone to interpret them.

One thing that amazed me about his odyssey was the amount of walking they did. They walked almost every day. From Findlay, they walked to Lima and "god on cars," which I take to mean railroad cars, and went to Cincinnati. There they "god on a boad" and went to "Loisville." From Louisville they walked to Savannah, Georgia. This was under General Sherman and his "march to the sea." Not for months does he mention any fighting or activity or enemy. His main concern was putting one foot in front of the other and finding something to eat. A typical entry might read: "Left camp 6 o'clock this morning and marched tell 1 o'clock and made diner. After diner marched tell 5 o'clock and com to camp in big woods. It was purty hot today. I'm purty tired tonight. We com 21 miles today."

About once a week they were given some food. They had to steal everything else they ate. One entry read: "Drawed rations today. They was a pound of coffee and two loaf of bread." Another read: "Drawed rations today. They was potatoes turnips and pickles." Can you imagine carrying several pounds of potatoes, turnips and pickles for several days? And wouldn't it be fun to build a fire and cook that stuff after marching fifteen or twenty miles in the rain?

Obtaining their other food was an adventure, too. One entry tells how they did it: "Went foraging today. Shot a pig. God all the pork I could carry." Or: "Caught some chickens today." Another entry tells of his chasing chickens at a farm. One chicken ran under the house and he followed. In addition to the chicken, he found the family treasure — a pile of silverware and a big gold watch. He kept the watch and still had it when he got discharged.

It wasn't until he was in Georgia that I had a hint of what they were up to. He tells of how tired he was one night after spending the entire day tearing up railroad tracks and then burning the town. He said they did that every place they went. That would coincide with what we know of Sherman's march. A couple of times, he tells of getting ready for battle and waiting all day for "the Rebs" and then getting back into formation and marching some more.

Only once does he mention any contact with the Rebs. The Rebs shelled the town they were working in, but "we had good 'brest works' and nobody got hirt."

Chattanooga was "cut up purty bad. There isn't much of the town left any more. The biggest part is burend and I seen the grade lookout maunden (Great Lookout Mountain)."

By the time they reached Raleigh, North Carolina, the war was pretty well over, but the Rebs wouldn't quit, so they started around again. They marched up to Washington, D.C. and camped on the outskirts. From there they marched to Parkersburg, West Virginia, "god on boads," and back down to Louisville.

Suddenly, it was over. They waited in camp to see when and how they would be discharged. While waiting, they were visited by General Hooker. He was much admired by the troops because he thought soldiers would be better soldiers if they had female companionship. He brought in some friendly girls that today are still called Hookers.

Though John was never wounded, he did come down with a sickness he called "ager," which is a corruption of ague. Ague was anything that gave you a fever and flu-like symptoms. He traveled in an ambulance for several days thereafter and later in a wagon until he was well enough to march again. During his tour of duty, he marched 1,155 miles, crossed twenty-one rivers, "payst" (passed) through eighteen towns "wich of them was 8 nice cyties." He was in the "staid" (state) of Ohio, Kentucky, Tennessee, Georgia, South Carolina, North Carolina, Pennsylvania, Indiana and Virginia. He received fifty-nine "leters" and "road" seventy-two "leters."

He stood "gard" sixteen times. On picket twenty times. "Worked on they ford 12 dayes and 6 knights." He was sworn in October 14, 1864 and discharged July 19, 1865 "and always don my duty as a good soldier."

I'm grateful to Grandma Eckhardt for entrusting me with these documents. They have given me an insight into the life of a foot soldier that was much different from my own.

Simpler Lifestyle of Ohio's Canal Era Is Appealing
May 9, 1998

I sometimes think about what it would be like to have lived at some other time in our history. Have you ever given that any thought? I probably would have gotten along a lot better in bygone days than now. I'm much better at dealing with natural situations than people situations. I would rather face an irate bear than an irate person.

I've often thought I would have liked to have lived on the early frontier in Ohio, but the thought of daily facing hostile Indians doesn't seem as glamorous when I place myself in the equation as when I read about some fearless pioneers such as Dan'l Boone, Jonathan Zane or Lewis Wetzel going blithely about the business of outwitting the Indians. I'll take the bears!

A time that really appeals to me, as I give it more thought, is the canal era in the Hocking Valley. The Indian problem had been taken care of by then. (I guess, when I think of it, if I had been here early enough, I would have lived peacefully with the Indians and not tried to take their land. There's something appealing about having an Indian wife to do all the work while I hunted and fished.) Life was slow and steady. The work was hard but how hard you worked depended on how much you wanted to acquire. It would have been nice and peaceful to sit on the bank of the canal and watch the boats go by. You could fish or swim whenever you took a notion.

The canal boats were slow by our standards today; but in those days, because they were pulled by horses or mules, they were as fast as wagons and a whole lot smoother since there weren't any bumps or potholes on the water. Everything you could think of traveled by boat. Some people lived on their boat and never had to worry about getting back home. I think I could have done that.

Logan would have been an interesting place to be. The canal went right through town. It came down along the river and sometimes in it. It came past the north end of the Falls Mill bridge and then behind the IGA supermarket and Hocking Valley Feed Mill. I'm sure the mill was served by it. There was an iron furnace near where Parsons' Laundromat now stands. Coal and ore would have been hauled in and then pig-iron hauled away. The canal boats also went in behind the Keynes flour mill and King Lumber. I've been told that the boats could come right inside the basement of the lumber yard and unload cargo. I don't know if the foundry was there at the time but it's located in just the right spot for it.

Just at the east edge of town, there is an aqueduct that carried the canal over Oldtown Creek. A little farther down on the left of Chieftain Drive is a crummy old swampy place, being filled in now, that was once a canal basin where boats could tie up for the night and/or turn around. The canal continued on through Haydenville and Nelsonville to Athens.

There were several locks along the way to keep the water level as the terrain went up or down hill. The one at Haydenville has recently been preserved and marked by local people and the Bicentennial Committee. Another one is in process west of town and will soon receive a historical marker from the Ohio State Bicentennial Committee. Gary and Sandy Starner have been active in the preservation of that one. Mrs. Starner, who taught school at Rockbridge Elementary School, had her school kids active in that project for years. It was used by the locals as a dump for generations. It has now been cleaned up and should be preserved forever and remain in that state. At least I certainly hope so.

There are surely tales of happenings on the canal, but I haven't heard many of them. Maybe I should learn to read. There must be some books about those days. The only story I can remember was about a fellow named Lutz, the inventor of the steam car now in the care of the Hocking County Historical Society. It seems that Mr. Lutz and his brother-in-law were driving around town and on the itinerary were several bars — one too many, I think. Anyhow, going home after dark, he geed when he should have hawed and drove right into the canal. They managed to wade ashore, soaking wet, and found their way home. He hired a team of horses the next morning and had the car pulled out, a little worse for wear but not seriously damaged.

Can't you imagine being able to walk around town and see all the activity going on? You could saunter over to the lumber yard and watch them maneuver a barge load of lumber into the basement. Then meander over next door and watch them unload a boatload of wheat at the flour mill. There were probably some restaurants along the main drag where you could get a cup of coffee and a big slab of pie while you listened to some travelers tell of a close call they had or a fight they saw between two teamsters over who would unhitch his team to let the other pass. There were laws governing such things, but sometimes the guy with the biggest fist enforced them. Just like today's road rage, I guess. There are some people who must be first.

Later you could hike, or hitch a ride on a boat if you knew the boatman, up to the iron furnace and maybe watch them dump a furnaceload of molten iron into the pig molds. What an exciting place to be. Logan was pretty much the center of things in the mid-Hocking Valley in those days. As an anticlimax, you could hoof it on out to the locks and watch the boats go through. There was somewhat of a bottleneck and there was usually a boat waiting its turn to go through.

The lock keeper lived in a house right at the lock and was always available, day or night. If there was no other boat there, you rang a bell and the keeper would appear. A lot of them were women. They did their cooking, cleaning and laundry between boats. Local historian Leland Conner told me that his grandmother was the lock keeper at Laurel Run Road for years.

The more I think of it, the better that era sounds. The canal brought peace and prosperity to the area, and though people were busy, the pace was unhurried. What more could one ask?

How We Extirpated Native Americans
May 16, 1998

Last week you might remember I wrote about how I would have liked to have lived on the frontier in Ohio, but what with the trouble with Indians it would not have been a very good time to live here.

I got a phone call from a lady soon after who wanted to know if I was for or against the Indians. She was part Indian and didn't know whether to take offense or not. I thought I had made it clear that I wasn't against the Indians, but when they were on the warpath they didn't make very good neighbors. I guess my obtuse sense of humor sometimes is misleading.

I am very much on the Indians' side. What we Americans did to them is one of the greatest travesties in world history. They would have been justified in shooting Christopher Columbus before he got off the boat. We eradicated a whole race of people in their own land. I think more people were killed then than on all sides during World War II, including all of the Jews in Hitler's death camps. We didn't really kill them; they were "extirpated."

To the shame of the human race, the same thing goes on today in many parts of the world. Several million Africans have been killed in Rwanda in recent years. And what about "ethnic cleansing" in Bosnia? What about the "trouble" in Ireland? It goes on endlessly. It must be part of human nature to kill neighbors.

I can't help but believe that the root of it is overpopulation in certain areas, if not the world in general. It seems that when people are crowded together, they are inclined to want to eliminate their rivals. This also happens in the natural world. Observations and experiments with animals have shown that overcrowding leads to wars over turf, whether it be a pride of lions or gangs of meerkats. Each wants to cut down on the competition for space and therefore food and shelter.

For some reason, certain animals have learned to live in large groups. These are mainly grass eating herds of cattle — animals which are prey for the most part, and pose little threat to others. These include buffaloes, wildebeests, caribou and such. They have learned that there is safety in numbers in their particular cases.

But man is different animal. He is selfish, greedy, aggressive and above all intelligent. That is a hard combination to beat. During the seventeenth and eighteenth centuries, Europe was getting crowded. People needed more space. The strong had kept the weak under their thumbs for centuries, and the discovery of the new world offered an opportunity for the oppressed to get out from under their oppressors and start new lives. There was plenty of land in the Americas and all they had to do was take it.

And take it they did. Since the people of the old world and the new developed at different rates and in different ways, the Europeans had technology far superior to that of the Native Americans. The Native American lifestyle was more primitive, as were their weapons. The Indians were no less intelligent that the whites and were fierce warriors, but bows and arrows were no match for guns and cannons.

Another great advantage the newcomers had was numbers. It didn't take long for word to get out that all this free land was here and the streets were paved with gold. They came by the thousands. It was an unstoppable tide.

When it came to greed, the Indians were no match for the Europeans. They didn't understand the concept of owning land. The land belonged to everyone. No Indian owned a square foot of land. When the white man came and claimed certain area as his own and put up fences to mark its boundaries, the Indians didn't understand and first gave way and moved over to make room. It didn't stop there, however. The next wave went just beyond the last and pushed farther. The next blow was the discovery of gold in the West. People pushed westward by the thousands, hoping to strike it rich, and viewed the Indians as just another obstacle to be overcome. Greed again!

Up to that point, the government dealt with the Indians by treaty. The treaties were broken by the government whenever it was more advantageous than keeping them. Finally, it became official policy to "extirpate" the Indians. Those who resisted were killed. Those who didn't were herded onto reservations on land that was useless to the whites. When it was discovered that some of the reservations were valuable, the Indians were moved again.

Nowadays, there are still Indians on reservations. The reservations are too small for them to live on in their former way of life, living off the land. For the most part, they live on government assistance in squalor. Alcoholism is rampant. They are free to leave the reservations but most are poorly educated and unable to adjust to the white man's ways. Some return to the reservations. Some inter-marry with the whites and are assimilated into the white society.

It's a sad thing, but in all fairness, the Indians were not immune to greed. Though they didn't care much about worldly possessions and owning land, they did have a passion for horses and would get them any way they could. Raids on other tribes were common in which they stole horses and women.

Their cruelty to captives was legendary. They were also very protective of their territory. They didn't own land as individuals, but each tribe had a territory it claimed as its own and guarded zealously. Several tribes were wiped out or run out of their territory in wars with their neighbors before the white men came. So I think greed is an innate trait in all races of people that we must constantly try to suppress in ourselves to avoid war between the countries and religious groups.

We might mourn the fate of our native people, but I'll bet that few of us would want to give the country back to them. I don't have a solution. What's done is done. The only thing we can try to do is help the original owners of this land as best we can. As a wise man once said, "You can't go back."

Looking at Some Historical Notes
October 16, 1999

We all are aware of the beauty of this wonderful county we live in, especially at this time of year when the fall leaf color makes the outdoors seem like an enchanted forest. When we visit the state parks, we usually wonder if Indians once lived in the caves so prominent there. We assume they did at one time or another, but that's as far as it goes for most of us.

Actually there is a tremendous amount of history here, both natural and man-made. I was talking to Jim Goslin a few months ago about this very subject. He is very knowledgeable about the history of this area. His father, the late Charles Goslin, devoted his life to studying the history of the Hocking Hills and was the author of numerous publications. He wrote a column for the Lancaster Eagle Gazette for many years. He studied the history and archaeology of the area with a passion.

As we were talking, Jim said, "I have a fifteen-page history of the area my dad wrote several years ago that I found among his papers. Would you like a copy?"

I jumped at the chance. In a few days he called to say he had left a copy at the Welcome Center for me. I didn't waste any time picking it up.

It's a masterpiece of condensation. In plain words, without wasting space, it covers the 200 years since the first white men came. He called it "Historical Ramblings, Hocking County, Ohio." It was written in 1971. I don't know just when he died, but I do remember reading about it in The Logan Daily News. In fact I read one or two of his columns in my early years here. I came in 1974, so our years overlapped a little. I wish I had met him. I wouldn't have had enough sense to understand at the time what a treasure he was, I suppose, but if I could go back in time, he would certainly be high on my list of things to see and do.

Here are a few tidbits gleaned from the pages:

The first residents here did indeed live in the caves in Good Hope, Laurel and Benton townships. The record is incomplete, however, because most of the excavations were done by amateurs, and there is little record of their findings. They were interested only in finding artifacts for sale or for their own collections. The true scientists were late in coming, and the pickings lean.

We do know that the Adena Indians roamed the area before the coming of Christ. There were some refuse pits that contained bits of bone and pottery, as well as crude tools and traces of clothes. A few remains of their dead gave small understanding of their size and state of health.

The rock shelters were not the only places where Indians lived. In the valleys of the various streams that drain the county were scattered villages, communities if you will, where people lived and made part of their living by farming. There are at least seventeen burial mounds in Hocking County. This is a small number compared to other nearby counties. Fairfield County has 112 and Athens sixty-three.

The first white man to record his findings in Hocking County was Christopher Gist, a surveyor from North Carolina who was hired by the Ohio Land Company. He and three helpers arrived in 1751. The French fur traders had dealt with the Indians for many years before that. They treated the Indians fairly and didn't cheat them as the English did and had freedom to travel the whole territory without fear of the Indians.

Lord Dunmore, in an effort to subdue the Indians, marched his army up the Hocking Valley in 1774. He reports an Indian village on the Hocking near what is now Logan. He called it "Oldtown" and named the creek emptying into the Hocking at that point "Oldtown Creek." It's located just at the edge of Logan near the Amanda Bent Bolt plant. There was another village between Logan and Rockbridge. It's assumed that these Indians were Wyandots.

The first settler in Hocking County was Christian Westenhaven, arriving in March of 1798. He staked his claim on the site of the Indian village of Oldtown. He was followed two months later by John Pence and Conrad Brian and their families. By the spring of 1799, the population of what is now Logan was twenty-two.

Look at us now. Most of the signs of the first inhabitants have been obliterated. We are quickly bulldozing up and paving over our history. That's progress I guess, but wouldn't it be nice if some trace of our heritage remained? There are some traces of later history still visible. I'm speaking of the Hocking Canal some 150 years ago. There are a few locks and small bits of the canal itself, but they will someday be gone. One unique lock near Rockbridge has been declared a historical site thanks to the efforts of Roger Shaw, who donated the site. An aqueduct which took the canal over Oldtown Creek remains near the site of the Oldtown village, but I'm sure it will go if someone decides to build on the site. Jobs, you know.

The old canal basin just east of Logan, where canal boats could be turned around or docked for the night, is being filled in and built upon by Canal Lumber Company. It will have to change its name someday to "Canaless Lumber."

We can't stop progress. One day there will be so many people here that every inch will be built upon. Just the other day, the United Nations reported that the population of the earth had reached six billion, having doubled since 1960. It's expected to double again in about thirty years. Do you suppose that in another thousand years some archaeologist will be digging through the rubble of our homes, trying to figure out who we were and how we lived? Maybe. Maybe there won't be anyone left to dig. Only time will tell.

Chapter 4
The Old Filosifer

An Epitaph for a Nobody
August 17, 1996

I don't think much about death — not my own, anyway. I'm reaching the age where some of my friends are beginning to slip away, but except for bad knees, a poor memory and a couple of other things I don't remember, I don't feel that old.

A year or so ago, I had a bad case of the flu or something that just went on and on. I finally got concerned about it and went to a doctor. I was having trouble breathing and was afraid it was some rare disease or the result of dust from my shop. X-rays showed nothing, so we decided to try some drugs, one at a time, and assess their effectiveness. None did much good, and I eventually fell into the trap. I was taking a drug to combat the side effects of another drug and another one to combat the side effects of that one and so on. Next, my blood pressure went up and I had to take blood pressure pills. Finally, I was taking five different prescriptions.

One night about a month ago, I had an experience that scared me half to death. I apparently had an allergic reaction between the prescriptions and a pain killer I had taken. I had a convulsive reaction which prevented me from getting my breath. I thought I was going to die! It was only by sheer will power that I was able to control it. This happened three times during the night. Each time, I thought "This is it! I'm going."

Between attacks, I thought of my mother and her wisdom. She

always told us before we went out to make sure we had clean underwear on. She'd say, "You could get hit by a car and have to go to the hospital and you don't want them to see dirty underwear, do you?"

It wasn't the underwear I was concerned about. It was the lack thereof. I like to be as uninhibited as possible when I sleep and was "in the buff," as they say. All I could say was, "Don't let me be found with my bare behind hangin' out."

I could see the headlines in that sensationalist rag, The Logan Daily News: "World Famous Columnist Found Dead in Shack in Woods — Body Nude — Sheriff Suspects Sexual Molestation Cause of Death." A little publicity wouldn't hurt, but that would be too much.

I didn't have a near-death experience, as such. There was no tunnel with bright lights and so on. There was, however, a black-billed cuckoo singing in the night, whatever that might mean.

All this got me to thinking about how I would like to be remembered when my time comes. The trouble is, I've never done anything memorable. I haven't found a cure for cancer. I haven't built any libraries. I haven't written any epics. I made a couple of kids. I made a little furniture. That's about it. Not much to warrant an epitaph. I hadn't thought of an epitaph before. Most grave stones say "Born ____, Died ____." I guess that would about cover it.

There are a few epitaphs that I got a kick out of. I have a book of famous ones somewhere, but I can't find it. The one that comes to mind first is that famous one up in New England somewhere. It says, "I told them I was sick." That's simple eloquence that says it all. There's a cemetery in New Albany that has a grave stone I think is funny, though it's not supposed to be. There is an immense pair of hands coming out of the ground, holding a huge round stone. It's not perfectly round and smooth, but irregularly shaped.

My first thought when I saw it was the deceased wasn't dead yet when he was buried and was crying out for help. "Get this damned rock off my chest." A closer inspection reveals the inscription — rather small so you have to look close to see it: "And in the beginning, God made Heaven and the Earth." I think that's quite pretentious, unless of course God was buried there. If so, I haven't heard about it.

For my part, I don't even want to be buried. Some day, at the present rate, the Earth will be one big cemetery. We are overpopulating the

Earth while we're alive, no use overwhelming it when we're dead.

There is a series of lakes in Quetico Provincial Park in Ontario, Canada, that cascade from one to the other over granite parapets. This is the nearest thing to Heaven I've ever seen. There is one waterfall in particular that some friends and I named "Dancing Falls" because the huge, smooth boulder, a quarter acre in size, over which the water runs, makes you feel like dancing. It's a most happy place.

If someone could take my ashes there and pour them slowly in that waterfall, so they didn't pollute anything, then scratch on a board "Here passed Ed Fassig. Just a man, but he did the best he could," then stick that board between a couple of rocks in a place where it would go out in the spring flood, no man could ask for more.

Under Cover People Watcher
January 18, 1997

Every once in a while, I get the urge to study people. I study nature from my home in the woods almost every day, but when I want to study people, I have to go where they are.

I racked my brain, trying to figure out a good place to conduct my studies. I could have gone to Florida and laid around on the beach, but that didn't appeal to me because the people who do that would be categorized and pretty much alike. The study would be biased. The same would be true if I went north. Snowmobilers and snow-shoers hang out there.

I needed a place that would be warm and comfortable. It had to be far enough from home that I wouldn't know anyone but close enough that I wouldn't have to travel far.

Then it hit me. A hospital would be a perfect place. People from all walks of life enter hospitals. It would be a representative sample. I packed a few things and arrived at a nearby town in short order.

A nice lady at the admissions desk said, "We'd be happy to have you visit us for a few days, but you just can't 'stay' at a hospital. We have to cut on you or something. Do you have any life-threatening maladies?"

"No," I replied. "I have some moles that could be removed."

"That's not much," she answered. "How about some brain surgery?"

"No, I don't want to ruin my haircut. Maybe some new knees. The old ones are about worn out."

"That sounds wonderful," she said. "We'll run some tests right away. Pick a surgeon from this list and then we'll assign you a room."

Then came a parade of people to study. All the technicians and nurses that I met were extremely friendly — or so it seemed at first glance. I began to see a pattern emerging. These people were trained to be friendly.

After I lay around awhile, I became invisible. The interaction between them wasn't always friendly. Some didn't get along at all, but when forced to interact with me and each other, they became friendly again. It reminded me of Pavlov's dogs: a conditioned response. When someone rang a bell, they smiled.

The patients benefit from this policy immensely. I never had better care. The whole experience was a positive one. The nurses assigned to my own room were superb. They all seemed to have my comfort in mind. It was funny to me to hear them whisper behind each others' backs. In short, people are people, wherever they might be.

As of this writing, I'll have another week to continue my studies. It seems that I have developed blood clots in my leg that has the new knee. I'll have to stay a while before starting rehab at square one. I have a week to ten days to continue. This morning, I learned how to put on my pants and socks. This was taught by a young man who seems genuinely interested in my welfare.

I've had a chance, also, to observe friends and relatives who visit. Since I'm not one to do much visiting, I'm surprised to have so many friends drop in and call on the phone. Truly, I'm being showed up as a rather casual person. I must try to do better. I'm sure these friends really do have my welfare in mind. I guess I'm luckier than I thought.

I got to thinking that if these people can be taught to be nice to other people, why can't we all? If we could be taught to be nice, wouldn't we all be better off? I kinda think we would. Let's give it a try.

Cabin Fever
February 1, 1997

When I was about twelve years old, I read a book about two young brothers who were left alone to winter in a cabin in the north woods. They trapped for game and hunted for food and were snowbound.

I have always thought that would be a wonderful way to spend a winter. When my son and I built our cabin in the wilderness of Michigan's Upper Peninsula, this thought was in the back of my mind.

I have made lists of what I would take. First and foremost, of course, would be food. It would have to be dry for the most part. Beans, flour, sugar, spaghetti, et cetera. Hunting would be out of the question after deer season. When the snow gets deep (three to four feet or more), the deer "yard" up in a swamp somewhere and stay there until spring. They would crucify me if I shot a moose.

The more you think about this, the tougher it gets and the less it seems like a good idea. Did you ever calculate how much toilet paper one would use in five or six months? Number two and three would be books and music. How many books? How many batteries and tapes? This gets complicated. Those old-timers knew something about primitive living.

I think I'll put the trip off till next year. I'll just have a dry run this year. Since I'm stuck with a bum leg for several more weeks, I'll just pretend I'm snowbound. I've laid in a supply of unread magazines — maybe twenty-five or so. I've got around twenty tapes and eight or ten CDs. I have friends taking care of the food part, so I'm OK there. It looks like a lovely vacation.

I woke up the other day and the ground was white. There was at least a half inch of snow. I'm snowbound. So much for atmosphere.

A week has passed and I've spent many happy hours reading and listening. I can't believe I've read twenty-five magazines already. I'm on the third round of the tapes. We had a January thaw and the snow has melted and the earth has returned to its drab (earthy) color. More snow is predicted for tonight.

This morning I decided to take a nice long hike, to take advantage of the nice weather. I made it from the bed to the front door twelve times — on my walker — a total distance of sixty-four feet. A new record. It's a good thing I had my global positioning unit or I might have gotten lost.

I ran the trap line early this morning. I caught two mice and a woods cricket. I expected the mice, but the cricket was a surprise. Usually, they have been eaten by the mice by now. I guess this one was smarter than most. My stack of fur is growing. I'll have enough for a fur coat by spring.

The deer have been yarding up of late. They are yarding in the door yard. Between twelve and fifteen show up at daylight for breakfast. They reappear in twos and threes all day, expecting the corn goddess has returned just for them. At about four in the afternoon, they begin to drift in and stand and stare at the house until the corn goddess feeds them. They are fat and beautiful. The goddess treats them well.

When I'm not watching deer, I can watch birds. At least 300 to 400 are constantly feeding at any one of the dozen feeders and porch railings. They are beginning to look more and more appetizing as the spaghetti wears thin. I'm visualizing them as tiny turkeys on tiny platters with their tiny drumsticks sticking up at their sides. They don't look like they'd hold much dressing. I think the cardinals would be more meaty than the chickadees. Actually, the crows would make a bigger meal, but I bet they would be tougher'n whang leather.

I'm into the third week now and I've read everything I can lay my hands on. I've listened to all my tapes a dozen times. There is very little on the radio that I enjoy. I'm going mad, I tell you, MAD, MAD, MAD! If this inch of snow doesn't melt soon, I'm going to break out of here. It's only a few miles to town. I can make it to the doughnut shop in a couple of days if my walker doesn't break down. Modern man wasn't built to take this hardship. My ancestors could do it, but I've been acclimated to malls and movies and hardware stores and doughnuts. I can't stand this isolation anymore. I'm at the breaking point. I'm leaving now. I'll see you at —

Sign Language Lessons on the Open Road
August 9, 1997

When I was young, I liked nothing better than to drive all day — forever.

If I could have driven after the sun until I chased it into the Pacific, I would have been happy. To sit behind the wheel of a car or truck was the ultimate high. Most of my cars were severely used before I got them, so it wasn't the cars that thrilled me, but the freedom to just go anywhere I pleased that made it so exhilarating. I still like to drive the back roads, especially here in Hocking County. There's a peace that falls over me when I'm on a tiny road with no traffic.

All that goes by the boards when I have to go on the highway. I had to go north of Lancaster the other day and it was like a trip to hell. For one thing, I was driving a borrowed car. It was a Suzuki Samurai, which is nothing more than a baby buggy with a motor, a very small one at that. I don't know how fast it will go and I hope never to find out. At fifty-five, it rides so rough that my head shakes like I was riding a trotting horse. My eyes kept lighting up and saying, "TILT!"

The speed limit on U.S. 33 is sixty-five as far as State Route 180, but my body couldn't take it over fifty-five, so I was the slowest one on the road. Everyone else was going seventy. It seems everyone has to go at least five miles an hour faster than the speed limit, whatever that might be. At first, I thought everyone was friendly but tired and could only hold up one finger as they passed. It dawned on me after awhile that they weren't smiling. In fact, some looked downright hostile.

The trip to Lancaster wasn't too bad, though longer than I remembered. It was when I hit the first traffic light that all the fun ended. I had to go from fifty miles an hour to stopped in a very short span. From there, traffic crawled at a snail's pace. It was a hot day and the heat from the road compelled me to open the window. The heat from the glass factory and fumes from the cars compelled me to close it again. Finally, I couldn't stand it and had to open the window again. As we began to move, an errant breeze came in and messed up my hair. Both of them were standing straight up. I hoped no one saw me.

It was stop and go the entire way to my destination. The addition of all those stupid traffic lights by the mall and beyond make that strip a nightmare. Everybody was jockeying for position so they could get away from the lights in a hurry. When I was first in line in my baby buggy, I got off the line just a little bit slower than Bobby Rahal and people showed their pity for me by waving a finger at me again. It's so nice to have a special signal just for us poor folks who can't afford a Cadillac.

As I returned to Lancaster, things were getting hectic. I pulled into McDonald's to get rested and refreshed. The parking lot was almost filled with cars and a huge line was at the drive through. I found a parking spot and stepped into the cool of the blacktopped area. It was about 110 degrees Fahrenheit. I zipped inside where it was air-conditioned and stood in line for about ten minutes to get cooled off. I ordered my usual — soggy cheeseburger, over-salted fries and almost chocolate shake.

Feeling cooled and bloated, I emerged into the inferno and climbed into my oven on wheels. I had to go clear out to the east end of Lancaster to find a bike shop to get parts for my exercise bike. That street changes from four lanes to two in a couple of places, squeezing the traffic into one lane. Horn blaring and more finger waving. This driving wasn't near as much fun as it was awhile ago. Going back was more of the same. I was certainly glad to get back on Interstate 33 and headed home.

I always welcome that first Hocking Hill at Horn's Mill Road. It feels like I'm coming home. There was even a welcoming committee there. I saw brake lights come on ahead for no apparent reason. There, just off the highway, was a patrolman looking through a telescope at me. I smiled and waved like a friendly fella should. He didn't wave back. It seems people aren't very friendly on this road. I had smoothed my hairs down by now so I wouldn't look so bad if he wanted to talk awhile, but he didn't.

Finally, I came to home ground, Logan, where things moved at a slower pace. There was a wreck at State Route 664 and Hunter Street and traffic was piled up. That was the second one there in a week that I had seen. It's a lot more fun there now that they've fixed that bottleneck. I don't recall ever seeing a wreck there before.

The people there weren't any more friendly than in Lancaster. It must be contagious. At last we are getting just like the big city folks. Who said we hillbillies ain't got no culture?

When I finally got home, I heaved a big sigh of relief and vowed to venture away from home only out of dire necessity. I drew a big glass of well water and sat down on the porch swing to contemplate. What has happened to us as a people? Where once we were helpful and friendly, we are now aggressive and mean-tempered. I even found myself getting aggressive and mean by the time I got home. This thing, whatever it is, is getting to all of us. Surely it can't be that everyone is in a hurry to get where they're going. That could be cured by leaving home a few minutes earlier.

The cars are faster now than they ever were and are easier to drive and more comfortable. When I was a kid during WWII, the speed limit was thirty-five miles an hour and we always left home in time to get to our destination. So it can't be the time element.

I guess there is no one answer. Perhaps we see this kind of behavior on TV and movies so much that we accept it as the norm. Could it be that there are just too damned many people and we are getting in each other's way? I think that both of these things are contributing factors. If we all lived by the Golden Rule instead of trying to do unto others before they can do unto us, life would be so much easier and simpler.

In the meantime, I hope that pretty little blonde in that pretty little red car that tries to run over me in the mornings as I head to the hardware store leaves home ten minutes earlier from now on.

Neighbors — Quality, not Quantity
January 24, 1998

Neighboring, at least here in the country, doesn't seem to be as prevalent as it once was.

I suppose that in the city, where you can hit your neighbors with a spitball, people are more closely associated. In fact, in that last two-year period when I lived in town, we had so many nice neighbors that we actually got sick of them. All day long people were in and out of each other's houses. We had parties and dinners at least once a week.

What I mean by neighboring is helping each other with our work. A couple of generations ago, most rural people were farmers and needed to be home working most of the time. When we needed help, a neighbor always was willing. When he needed help, there were no questions asked — we went. There are very few farmers left, especially here in the hills where most farms are too small to make a living in today's economy. Most people are working at a job somewhere and by the time they drive home in the heavy traffic they're in no mood to go visiting.

Something brought this thought to mind the other day and I got to pondering about it. I suddenly realized that neighbors play a greater part in my life than I thought. I have some wonderful neighbors. Not all of them, of course — some who live less than a mile away I have never met. That's my fault as much as theirs. I'm just not a social animal. I'd rather have a few good friends that I can count on than hundreds that I can't keep up with. That's especially true in my later years since my memory isn't what it once was. I have trouble remembering someone I met just last week. When I see them again, I could swear I never laid eyes on them. It's no disgrace to get old, but it's mighty inconvenient! On the other hand, a fellow came into my shop about a year ago that I hadn't seen in more than forty years and I recognized him immediately.

Anyhow, look to what I'm trying to say. I have neighbors that I don't socialize with, that I couldn't do without. For example, one fellow who modestly admits to being the world's greatest shade tree mechanic (and I grudgingly admit that he might be right) will come help me at the drop of a hat. Any problem I'm having with one of my vehicles is promptly taken care of. I don't have to ask him to fix it, just casually mention that I'm having a problem and he will at least come and diagnose it even if he doesn't have time to fix it at the time. He will, at the first opportunity. It doesn't have to be a mechanical problem, either. He lives close enough that he can hear my sawmill start up. As soon as he hears it, he's right there. He'll work all day for lunch and a couple cups of coffee. I feel slightly uncomfortable because he won't take money and I seldom get a chance to reciprocate.

When my cabin burned, he was right there helping to put out the fire. He helped me tear down the remains and worked tirelessly to build the new one.

A couple of weeks ago, I bought a used engine for one of my pickups and he volunteered to help put it in the truck. When I say "helped," I mean he did it. All I could do was be a gopher, since I don't know anything about cars. It took us a week to get it in. He never wavered or thought of quitting. To him, it was fun; to me, it was a nightmare.

One of the problems I have working on vehicles is that I don't have a warm garage to work in. When I do shade-tree mechanical work, it's under a shade tree. Another neighbor volunteered to let us use his heated garage and tools. That was a godsend. All he wanted in return was for me to plane a few boards for him so he could pursue his hobby of making clocks. I am glad to help him in this regard. Actually, we've had this relationship for several years. He sharpens my planer blades and I plane and glue his clock boards. He has good tools, where mine are mostly El Cheapos, and when I really need a particular tool, it's nice to know where to find it. We don't run back and forth and get in each other's way, but we consider each other friends as well as neighbors. That's how it should be.

I also have for neighbors three brothers who are, for the most part, loggers. They deal mostly in firewood nowadays. They are always more than willing to help.

One has a truck to haul logs. He hauls logs for me and I also buy logs from him from time to time. He will never take money for hauling. He occasionally needs a few boards for a doghouse or a gate in the barn. I just give him what he needs and we call it square. He uses sawdust to bed his pigs. I'm glad to get rid of it, so it works for our mutual benefit.

One of his brothers has a team of huge horses that they use for logging. If I have a tree go down that I can't reach with the tractor, he will walk one or both of his horses a mile to my place and pull it out for me and act like I'm doing him a favor. I can't go to their place without being loaded down with garden produce or eggs. That's neighboring.

The third brother has left the farm for a city job, but he still lives there. He helps his brothers when he can. He works a rotating shift job, so sometimes he has to sleep during the day. He will gladly help me if the timing is right. I made a wooden stove handle for their mother last week. It took fifteen minutes. Today they brought me a pumpkin pie she'd baked. It brought tears to my eyes.

Another neighbor is located right next to my place. He helps me sometimes and I help him if he needs help, though my ability to do much work has diminished in the last year or two. He graciously allows my cabin guests to hike in his woods and sometimes fish in his pond. He's a good friend and a fine fellow. We've known each other for nearly thirty years, from another galaxy far, far away.

Last weekend, my son came to help me repair some flood damage. I rented a jackhammer to break up some concrete so we could tear out the remains of my old bridge. While my son manned the hammer, I hauled crick gravel with the tractor. It was slow going. While we worked away, a large backhoe pulled in the drive. The driver said, "It sounded like you could use a little help. What needs to be done?"

I was dumbfounded. It was a neighbor whom I'd only met once. He had similar damage and had rented the hoe to repair it. He jumped right in and pulled the old bridge out and put several large buckets full of gravel in the appropriate places. He was done in less than a half hour. When I offered to pay him, he refused.

"That's what neighbors are for," he said.

He was so right. As I consider what the neighbors have done for me, I realize how lucky I am to be living here. I get so much more than I can give. I feel somehow inadequate. There are many others, of course, that I don't have space to mention now. I think of them, though, and regarded them as friends as well as neighbors. Hurray for all those people who give of themselves. There will be a reward some day.

Old Friends
June 5, 1999

I've been racking my brain for days now, trying to think of a subject for a column, but nothing came to mind. I chanced to run into an old friend in the grocery store today. It seems that I almost always run into someone I know in the grocery or hardware store. That's one of the things I love about living near a small town. I've made so many friends here and see them often.

Anyway, as I was saying, I met Jimmy Stewart. He told me how much he enjoys reading the column. I told him that I'd drawn a blank for this week and he said, "I've got just the subject for ya. Why don't you write about old friends?"

He then went on to tell me about a reunion he'd attended in the small town where he was born in West Virginia. It was for anyone who came from there, regardless of age. They had the Armory rented for a sit-down dinner. It could accommodate about 450. It sold out a month early and they told late-callers to come anyway, even though they couldn't feed them. Several hundred did.

He said that he met more people than he thought he ever knew. They had name tags of course, or most would have been strangers without them, but once their names were known, they remembered old times.

Jimmy is a long-time resident of Logan, having served on the town council for several years. He's an all-around nice guy. He is approaching his seventy-eighth birthday and doesn't look a whole lot different than he did when I first met him some twenty-five years ago. He told me something that warmed the cockles of my heart, whatever they are. He said that in recent years, he has made it a point to tell his friends how much he likes them and that he loves them in a Christian way. Because of his age, he has looked in many a casket and smiled because he had told the friend therein how much he or she meant to him. That is a wonderful idea.

Personally, I am rather reticent when it comes to expressing such feelings. I figure they know I like 'em, or I wouldn't hang around with 'em. But do they really? I think I will try to do as Jimmy is doing. I have dear friends that I've known since high school and some even from grade school. I love them dearly, but I guess I've never really told them so. I'll have to be careful and break it to 'em gently. The shock might kill 'em.

We had our fiftieth high school reunion in 1995 and there were some people there I hadn't seen since 1945. Some I knew immediately, some I didn't recognize at all, but once I knew who they were, the good times came flooding back. If we have another reunion as we are hoping in 2005, I hereby resolve to make my feelings known.

My best friend through high school and ever since is a guy named Marlin Hurd. He's retired now and lives the good life with his wife, Elmie, who was also a good friend in high school. In fact, the three of us were nearly always together. We'd double date a lot — the two of them and whatever girl was tolerating me at the time. Marlin's dad sold his farm and moved to Delaware County during our senior year, and Marlin lived with our family for several months until graduation. We were like brothers. Later when I married, he was my best man and Elmie played the organ. She also played for my wife's funeral. People like that are priceless.

There was a sort of "rat-pack" of us that ran around together. We still do when we can get together. We do a couple of times a year, and they are joyous occasions.

I thought of one fellow yesterday. It just popped into my mind as

I was eating an apple. I know that sounds strange, but you have to follow my train of thought. Dick had a cider press and we had an orchard. Several of my pals and I belonged to the FFA (Future Farmers of America). He was the only one who farmed most of his life. Anyhow, we were on the committee to provide the refreshments for the October meeting. Dick and some of the guys loaded up his press and came to my house and we picked up all the dropped apples we could find and made cider, and it was good. We didn't think that was enough for thirty guys, so we started on the pears. We were running out of them and started throwing in rhubarb and anything else that had juice. It was awful. We marked the jugs of the good stuff, so we wouldn't get the junk at the meeting.

It was a grand time on a glorious early October afternoon. What's better than good friends having a good time at a wholesome job? It was work, but many hands make the work light.

It must have made a lasting impression on Dick because he always brings it up whenever we meet. As I said, you have to follow my train of thought. I was eating this apple and I wondered just what percentage of it was water. Then I thought it must be pretty high because when you make cider there isn't much solid stuff left. When I thought of making cider, I thought of Dick. See?

This goes to show that good times and good friends are inseparable. I think I'll call Dick and see if he's had any good pear-rhubarb cider lately.

Happiness Is ...
July 10, 1999

During a recent trip to our cabin in Michigan's upper peninsula, my son and I had many happy experiences, but one stands head and shoulders above the rest. We had found a lake in a state park system that virtually nobody used. We had to make a path to the water's edge. It was through dense forest and not easy to do. My son carried the canoe while I trailed along with the paddles and fishing gear.

The lake was about 400 acres in area and absolutely gorgeous. It reminded me of some of the lakes in Ontario's Quetico Provincial Park that I love so much. The water was black as ink and deep. The breeze rippled the surface and moved the canoe along at a slow even pace so that we could cast the banks and only now and then have to paddle. The only fly in the ointment was that the fish refused to bite. We really didn't care.

As the evening wore on, the breeze quit and the lake became as calm as glass. We noticed some ripples as fish rose to take insects as they hatched from the depths below. We switched to fly-rods with tiny poppers and began to catch small fish that were new to us. I don't know what they were yet, but they were fun to catch and release. Finally dusk was upon us and we headed for the put-in place. The lake was like a mirror and we felt as though the canoe were floating in mid-air; the forested hillside was reflected perfectly, upside down. We stopped the canoe and just sat. The sight brought a feeling of complete happiness over me. The emotion was so compelling that I couldn't speak, and tears came into my eyes. Finally darkness and the buzz of mosquitoes broke the spell and the moment was over.

That one moment — and I don't know how long a moment is — was worth all the expense and discomfort of an 800-mile drive. If I live to be a hundred, and I intend to, I'll never forget that one short moment. I'll file it away with hundreds of others forever. I can take it out and remember and enjoy it whenever I want to.

I got to thinking afterwards how lucky I am and how precious happiness is. So many people are looking for happiness and don't even recognize it when it comes. They are looking to be made completely happy all the time. I have that. I can take my happiness in small doses and savor it over and over.

I remember, years ago, when I participated in a craft show at Old Man's Cave. A fellow in his forties approached me and asked a lot of questions about where and how I lived, if I could make a living doing what I do and if I were happy doing it. "I guess I'm just searching for happiness," he said. I noticed that his wife hung back and listened but didn't participate. She looked rather glum.

I don't know why I said what I said. I'm certainly not a philosopher, but I made what was a rather profound statement for me.

I said, "My friend, I'm afraid you're in for a disappointment. It's not those searching for happiness who find it. It's those who give happiness that are truly happy. If you make someone else happy, you will be happy, too." He looked sorta confused because that wasn't what he wanted to hear. His wife broke into a lovely smile and her head nodded in affirmation. It was exactly what she wanted to hear. I never saw them again so I don't know how things turned out, but I hope he took the hint and learned to appreciate what he had.

I certainly did. I decided to remove my main source of unhappiness. I divorced my wife and went on with my life. Maybe that thought was meant for me and just needed the right moment to come into being. Since then, I've learned to be happy unless there is something to be unhappy about. There are a lot of people who are unhappy unless there is something to be happy about. I take my happiness in small doses and am glad for them.

At this moment I'm sitting on a mountaintop in West Virginia, taking advantage of bad weather and good company. It has rained at least ten times today and twice yesterday. In spite of that, we've had some wonderful times. It was lovely sleeping in, hearing the rain on the tent and the wind howling through the pines. I took advantage of a lull in the rain and brewed coffee and retreated to the tent with it as it started to rain again. It never tasted better. Complete happiness!

Since I've had a rental cabin, I hardly ever have a weekend off, so I can't have a full-fledged vacation anymore. I have to steal a few days at a time, whenever I can. These mini-vacations are filled with happiness. A few days in a beautiful place with the best of friends are worth a world cruise to me.

As you might know, I make furniture for a living. It gives me pleasure to take logs and saw them on my sawmill, dry them and shape them into something usable and, if possible, beautiful at the same time. The real pleasure comes if the customer appreciates them for what they are — pieces of art that are also utilitarian. I have a small stack of letters from satisfied customers who do appreciate the beauty of hand-formed wood. I'm extremely happy when I receive one of those. Of course, not everyone feels that way. I have just finished the third top for a cherry table that I finished a year ago. The gentleman loved it when he picked it up, but after he had it home for a week, he called to say he didn't like the top. I made a new one and he loved it. A week later he called and said he found a place on the top that looked like I had filled a defect in the wood, and he wanted a new top. I can't wait for him to see this one. I know that he will never be satisfied and will find something wrong with the new one.

The poor fellow must be unhappy. If he would enjoy the beauty of a handmade article and accept that almost anything handmade will have defects, he would be happier than he is. So would I.

The old-time Japanese artisans deliberately put defects in their work because they believe no one is perfect but God. If I could just introduce this fellow to eastern culture, maybe he could be happier.

Anyway, happiness is a matter of attitude, a frame of mind. We can train ourselves to accept happiness. Our lives are peaks and valleys. When we realize that after every valley there is a mountaintop from which we can see the big picture, we can know happiness. When we help someone out of his own valley to his mountaintop, we are happier for the effort.

As I finish this, I'm home again, sitting on my screened-in porch. It's twilight. The stillness in the creeping darkness is broken only by the twittering of birds as they settle down for the night in the woods and the buzzing and bickering of six or eight hummingbirds at the feeders as they fill up to make it through the night. I think to myself, "What complete peace and happiness I have in my little piece of the world." If I were any happier, I couldn't stand it.

Reflecting on Armistice Day
November 13, 1999

When I was in grade school, about fourth or fifth grade, we learned a little bit about World War I. It was twenty-five years earlier, and it seemed to me that it was ancient history. I heard my dad talk about things that happened way back in 1917 or 1918, but it didn't relate to anything that I had experienced, so it didn't have much impact on me or my friends. We were mainly concerned with just getting by during the "great" depression.

We had heard that President Woodrow Wilson had declared it to be the "war to end all wars." Of course, we believed it. Since there were to be no more wars, we didn't worry about war. I never knew anyone who had been in the war. When we went downtown in Columbus, there would be a few people sitting on the sidewalks selling pencils or apples for a few pennies. One or two were blind, and some were missing an arm or a leg. There was one fellow who had no legs and would travel up and down Livingston Avenue on a little wooden platform on small metal wheels. He propelled himself by pushing and lifting on the ground with some homemade things that looked something like horseshoes covered with pieces of car tires. The streetcar line ended near our house, but he couldn't climb the steps to get on. I'd seen him on High Street way downtown. My heart went out to these people. When I asked Mom about them, she'd just say, "They were in the war."

We heard about men who were sick because they were caught in mustard gas. I never did understand that, because once in a while we could afford mustard for our hot dogs, and it never hurt us. That's about all we knew about "the war." It seemed so distant and remote that it had no bearing on our lives, or so we thought.

I can see the same thing happening now. World War II was over fifty years ago, and today's kids probably have no more idea of what happened then than I did when I was ten or eleven. We hear daily about wars and bombing all around the world, but we still think it can't happen here. To kids today, that is ancient history. I hope it never happens again, but I'm sure it will someday. When it does, it could truly be the war to end all wars. Well, maybe not. If there are two groups of people left, they will fight over something using sticks and stones.

Reality came to me on Dec. 7, 1941. The Japanese bombed Pearl Harbor, and the war was on. We flocked to theaters to see pictures of the carnage. There was no instant television coverage in those days, so we went to see Pathe news on the big screen, and we were shocked!

I was fourteen at the time and pretty scrawny, so I gave no thought to enlisting. We lived the war at home, glued to the radio every night. The news was usually bad. We had only a vestige of an army and navy. We didn't even have guns to train with. Valiant men and women flocked to enlist. Thousands were drafted. They had to use props for training. The newsreels showed soldiers carrying broomsticks instead of guns and using stove pipe for mortars and artillery. It was heartbreaking to think that our leaders didn't see it coming and prepare for it.

It took a year or two for the suppliers of arms, ships and planes to get geared up and running. When they did, we began to make some progress. It took four years to do it, but we finally gained victory in

Europe and the Pacific Theater. The most important ingredient though was the people.

Those gallant men and women went into battle, knowing that the chances of living through it weren't all that good. Yet they gave it all they had and prevailed. We owe them so much. I'll bet we don't even know who most of them are today. Most don't brag about it. They know, and that's what counts, I guess.

That's why I was so happy to see Kristy Wadsworth's piece in this past Wednesday's Logan Daily News about the Jurgensmier brothers and their service in what we now call "the big one." Not only was the piece well done, but she managed to make them look like real people and not made-up heroes. There are no doubt hundreds more in Hocking County that we don't know about. "Bless 'em all, the long and the short and the tall," as the old war song goes.

It wasn't just servicemen who were heroes in "the big one." All citizens helped, and they deserve some credit, too. They bought War Bonds to help finance the effort. They had scrap drives to salvage metal to be melted down for guns and vehicles. They went without new cars for several years and without tires for the old cars. They had food, gas and many other commodities of everyday life rationed. It took a total effort to win against overwhelming odds, but we did it.

It is Armistice Day as I write, and I hope we all honored and revered our veterans of all the wars on this day. They are a priceless treasure, and we're losing them all too soon.

Confidence
February 5, 2000

My neighbor, John Brennaman, told me a story the other day that tickled me and also made me think. John's had a couple of geese for several years that served no purpose but to make noise and poop on the porch and driveway. A month or so ago, the gander disappeared, probably the victim of a fox or coyote, since no corpus delicti was found in the road. This was of no consequence to John, but another neighbor, who raises geese, thought that the remaining goose would be lonesome and so gave John a big old blue gander. The pair seemed to bond all right and everything was rosy.

A few days later, John noticed some white blobs moving around in the horse pasture. It puzzled John because from a distance they appeared to be a couple of feed sacks blowing in the wind. On closer inspection, they proved to be a hen and a very large rooster. He found a cardboard box on the porch of the barn that contained some feathers and chicken droppings. Some kind soul had donated him a very small egg factory. John didn't really mind because he kinda liked to hear the rooster crow, and it gave the place a country atmosphere.

In a few days, the birds wandered up near the barn and seemed to be fitting in. Then the rooster discovered the geese sitting peacefully in the sun. (Maybe squatting would be more appropriate.) The rooster had probably never seen a goose before and looked them over carefully. Then he jumped up on the back of the gander and tried to attain what is sometimes called "the marital impulse." Of course the gears didn't mesh correctly, and he gave up. He walked all around that gander and stared at him from every angle. He jumped back up and tried again. He finally climbed down and walked away with a puzzled expression on his beak, like he was thinking "That thing's gotta be good for something." He'll be back!

This is the part that got me to thinking. That old boy's got confidence. People are always telling us we have to have confidence in ourselves, but sometimes too much confidence can get us in trouble. One day that ol' goose will get tired of being walked on and give that rooster the whoopin' of his life.

I can feel for him because I've always had confidence that I could get out of any predicament that I got into, in a physical sense, anyway. A couple of months ago, I confidently dropped a tree on my head. I did manage to get out of the predicament, but at a cost. That episode brought a smile to the faces of a couple of neighbors, but they are suffering from the same malady.

One neighbor, who shall remain nameless, is a logger, and a pretty good one, too. A harder worker you'll never find. Last summer, he cut some trees near home and for some reason, one log was left in the woods. It had rolled partly down an incline and stopped against a couple of small saplings. He left it there until a couple of weeks ago, when he went to haul it out. Since it had lain there for three months, he knew it was firmly embedded in the ground and wouldn't roll farther. With the confidence of a man who knows his business, he cut the saplings out of the way. The second he cut the last one, that log rolled right on him before he knew what happened. It was too heavy to move, and he lay there with his legs pinned, yelling his lungs out until, by chance, his brother came to visit and found him. That seemed to me another case of over-confidence.

I have another neighbor, who also will remain nameless, who modestly admits to being the world's best shade-tree mechanic. He is supremely confident that he can fix anything that can befall a machine — and most of the time, he can. He's good. He takes long trips in some of the junkiest old vehicles without the slightest trepidation. He carries a few wrenches, a pair of pliers and a screwdriver. That's confidence.

Last year, he went to a New Year's Eve party where he got into a holiday mood. There he met a guy who had a heavy-duty pickup for sale, and the price was right, so he agreed to buy it. The only problem was it was in South Carolina. They climbed in his old truck and took off for Dixie. He saw the truck, paid the man, got a temporary license and lit out for home, thinking to come back later for his old truck. Now, you would think that a mechanic would give a used vehicle a pretty good going over before he plunked down the green, but here's where confidence got in the way. He knew he could fix anything that was wrong with the thing.

He started down the country road toward the highway. The road followed a river part of the way. Without warning, a tie rod end came loose just as he was on a curve right beside the river. The truck made a sharp right turn, and he found himself sitting in cold water up to his shoulders, watching fish swim by his windshield.

After some difficulty, he removed himself from the river and pondered the future. He was only a mile from where he bought the truck, so he walked back, perhaps with humility or perhaps with anger. (He didn't say, but mentally kicking his own butt, I'd wager.)

He managed to engage a guy with a wrecker to retrieve the truck. This meant that he had to get back in the river and hook up the chain while completely submerged. Not too much fun I would imagine, since it was in January. Even though it was in South Carolina, that water came from snow melting in the mountains.

To make a long story short, it took two days to get it out of the river. He took the motor apart and dried and cleaned it. The same with the transmission and differential. They had to be drained, rinsed and refilled. After all this, the motor wouldn't start. Two more days were spent changing and cleaning parts, and it still wouldn't start.

The wrecker man came after his money (he owed him $900 by then) and said in his colloquial way, "It ain't never gonna start. You done ruined the computer, and it'll cost more than the truck's worth to get a new one." That just about fried it. He talked the wrecker man into taking the truck to settle the bill. He had just enough money to get home on, and he made it in the "old" one, somewhat chastened but unbowed. He still has confidence, but tempered by wisdom, I hope.

Chapter 5
Pure Fantasy

Holiday Shopping Tips
December 23, 1995

Since the season of giving is upon us, I thought I would pass along some tips on how to shop and keep one's sanity. My vast experience of being a tightwad fully qualifies me as an expert on the subject.

Number one: Be timely.

Never start any later than December 24. Any later than that puts you in a position of having to rush. Most stores don't open until noon on Christmas Day. If you can delay your gift exchange until Christmas evening, you can take advantage of the after-Christmas sales that start at about 1 p.m. By 2 p.m., people are returning gifts, so you might find something that the store was out of the day before. Of course, this puts you in a rush situation as far as wrapping goes, but the paper is cheaper so you can afford to use more.

Number two: Whenever possible, give something you can borrow.

Don't waste time trying to find something they like; find something you like. You must use discretion here. You would be a little suspect if you gave old Aunt Mary a power saw. You could say that it would be to help when you build that wheelchair ramp to her back porch, but then you'd have to do it. Better to be a little more subtle. Maybe a few cans of fruit and some ready-made pie shells would be more appropriate, but you get the idea.

Number three: Keep track of how much each person spent on you last year.

Good records are in order here. Don't rely on memory. You must be careful not to escalate the pricing. If you can keep it to about a dollar less than he gave you last year, it won't get out of hand. If you spend more, he'll spend more, then you will have to spend more and the first thing you know it's up to ten dollars.

Number four: Shop locally whenever possible.

This is especially important in a small town. To be caught in a store in another city can be embarrassing. A few years ago I spotted a local shop owner in a Columbus department store buying jewelry for a pretty young girl. Don't think he wasn't embarrassed.

Number five: Save useless gifts and give them next year.

This is pretty well self explanatory. Keep the tag with the gift so you know who gave it to you. You certainly don't want to give it back to the same person who gave it to you, although it might be interesting to see what the hell he would do with it.

Number six: Be of good cheer.

Hunting a place to park, fighting crowds and seeing your money disappear can put you in a bad mood if you let it. You can change the mood all around you if you know how.

I discovered this by accident a couple of years ago. I was shopping for something nice for a young lady of my acquaintance. I was shopping in the lingerie department of a local store. (Why is lingerie pronounced "lawngeray?" I know it's French, but we've Americanized everything else. Why can't they just call it underwear?) Anyway, I had already found a tasteful see-through negligee (another one of them French words) with hearts and bows on it, and a lovely teensy-weensy pair of panties with hearts in appropriate places, and I was looking for a bra to match. At last I came upon the perfect one. It had little gold tassels on it. The problem was to find the right size. I knew it had a thirty-six in there somewhere, but I didn't know the size of the pockets.

I had come from the grocery store before coming in the department store and had with me a bag of grapefruit. I felt around until I found one about the right size and proceeded to put it in a pocket of each bra. It took several tries, of course, and every time I tried one a little old lady beside me would yell "that ain't it." When I would lay the grapefruit down, she would grab it and try to take a bite out of it. I'm glad she didn't have any teeth. She dang nigh gummed it to death as it was. I had to wipe the saliva off each time. I don't mind telling you that was wearing thin, and my mood was beginning to slide down toward mean.

I took a dollar bill out of my pocket and threw it on the floor, then said to her, "Is that your money down there?" She said "yes" and bent over to pick it up. I did what any red-blooded young man would do. When she reached for it, I stood on her hand.

That solved one problem, but caused another. Though she couldn't reach my grapefruit, her screams of agony and pleas for mercy were beginning to attract attention and soon a crowd gathered. To cover up the noise, I began to sing Christmas carols as loud as I could while I kept trying the grapefruit. By the third verse of "Joy to the World," everyone was singing. After I'd gone through "Hark the Herald Angels Sing" and "O Come All Ye Faithful," the woman was down to a whimper, so I slowed down the tempo with "O Little Town of Bethlehem" and closed with "Silent Night." By then, I'd found the perfect bra size and everyone was in a good mood. Even the old lady thanked me for getting off her hand.

So you see, anyone can make the best of a bad situation and make a chore seem like fun, just by being a good fellow.

That's the last time I'm taking little old Aunt Jennie shopping, though!

Resolution Conflict
December 30, 1995

I've never made a New Year's resolution in my life. I'm not making any this year. They are, for the most part, unachievable. When you fail, you feel bad. I feel bad enough having all these shortcomings without piling failure on top.

I've come up with a system that allows me to try to improve my lot without making promises I can't keep. I merely make some suggestions as if they came from someone else — maybe someone I don't like. If I succeed, I can say, "I guess I showed him." If I fail, I can say, "I wouldn't do anything he wanted anyway." That way, I can have the best of both sides.

This past year has been particularly rough. I rebuilt a cabin that burned last year while at the same time trying to keep up with orders in my shop. There just wasn't time to do everything that needed to be done. What suffered was my housekeeping. Now I'm not the world's best housekeeper, but I at least try to keep the place so that I don't get typhoid fever or something just by association. I'm pushing the limit now.

When someone suggested that this might be a good year to clean the refrigerator, I really couldn't argue. I'm going to make that high on my list of things to do that are not New Year's resolutions. I've been meaning to do it for some time now, but I've been afraid. There are things in there that scare me. Some are black and slimy. Others are shapeless, pulsating masses of matter that glow in the dark. What if they should escape and wreak havoc on the helpless citizenry of Hocking County? I open the door only sparingly, and slam it shut immediately to guard against that eventuality. I think I will contact the haz-mat team before I try. Space suits and oxygen masks might be in order here.

If I survive that ordeal, there has been a suggestion made that I clear some floor and table space by eliminating some printed material. This consists mainly of unread magazines and mail telling me that I would be a millionaire if I would buy only one more magazine. It appears that by eliminating one or the other, I could break the cycle. T'ain't so! Once you've bought a magazine, you're on a mailing list that reaches the world around. There is no escape. My plan is to put an incinerator behind the mailbox. I'll have two slots on the mailbox — one marked "bills" and one marked "other." The "other" would feed directly into the incinerator. That would stop the growth of the piles in the house and give me a chance to wade through them. It would take until October, so there would be no connection with New Year's.

I have a passive solar house that uses a concrete floor as a heat sink. It is painted, with scatter rugs to accent the color scheme. By now, the color scheme is dust. I can't make up my mind whether to paint it or just plow it and plant potatoes. Given my record in gardening, I'm sure the deer, groundhogs and 'coons would break in and devour everything.

I think the best thing for me to do is sneak up on this easy. Test the waters, so to speak. I could start with the cobwebs. I think I could get them in just a few days. Then I could brag to myself that I had achieved one of my goals and, after a week's rest, could tackle the window washing. Outside wouldn't be bad; the rain keeps the film from getting too thick. But the inside could be more of a challenge. I would have to be careful not to spill water on the floor and make clean spots. Then I would have to do the whole thing, and I'm not mentally prepared for that just yet. Getting the windows clean would let in more light and give the whole place a rosier appearance. It might look so good that I wouldn't have to do any more. Maybe not.

I'm hoping I can get the ring off the bath tub with just a hammer and chisel. Renting and air hammer would be just too expensive. Maybe if I just take most of the light bulbs out ... Nah! Hammer and chisel.

This is getting too involved. Perhaps I should just move.

To get back to my original premise, I haven't made any commitment, so I don't feel guilty about not doing anything I didn't want to do. I think I'll take a sabbatical year off while I think about it. Maybe next year I'll feel like really getting into it. In the meantime, I can relax and not feel guilty. It's all in how you look at it.

Baring of the Soul
December 31, 1999

Dear Friends,

I've received some sad news from my doctor that I feel I must share with you. He seems to think that because of my lavish lifestyle, I have only about thirty years to live. That would date my expected demise at about 103 years of age. That comes as a shock to me because the average age of my ancestors' passing was about 120. My parents both lived to their mid-120s.

This revelation demands that I confess that I have lived a double life. My parents both were of noble birth. My father was a Prussian prince, second in line to be the emperor of Austria. After having several torrid affairs with ladies of low station, he married my mother who was a cousin to the king of England.

There issued from this pairing eight children, and the oldest five, who were in line for succession to the throne, mysteriously died within a three-year span. Our parents decided to send us to America to pose as commoners to protect us from harm that might come to us from political foes. Three common children who died of the plague were stolen, dressed in royal finery and buried in our stead.

We were shipped off to Columbus to live with and be raised by dirt poor, depression-era, shirt-tail relatives of our gardener. There was a small stipend that provided for our wants. We learned to speak the language of the commoners and know their habits.

I managed to get through grade school and high school without too much trouble. My parents both had IQs of about 240. Mine was only about 190, but it gave me an edge over my classmates, who averaged about ninety-five. I had to pretend that the subjects were difficult, while in reality I never studied. I was rated number seven in my graduating class, though I could have easily been first, had I chosen to. It never pays to show all your cards, you know.

I spent a couple of years in the Army, and although it was difficult to conceal my intelligence, I was discharged as a colonel. I could have easily made three-star general had I chosen to.

When my parents died, their fortune had been eroded by the ravages of war, and our inheritance was only about thirty million dollars each. My sisters married well and were able to have comfortable lives. I, on the other hand, married unwisely, and after seven or eight wives, found my nest egg somewhat diminished. I invested my share wisely and after a while was able to parlay it into a modest fortune.

When I decided to live in Hocking County, it seemed best not to reveal my true situation, so I took on the dress and mannerisms of a country bumpkin. I hid my assets, literally. I converted half of my cash to gold, which I buried in a nearby cave. In the dark of night, I would trundle wheelbarrow load after wheelbarrow load through the woods, choosing a different route each time so as not to wear a path, and then dig a large hole and bury the gold bullion. I took several nights to accomplish this task. When I was finished, I carefully spread the sand and erased all traces of the digging. I then sprinkled bits of vegetation and rocks over the disturbed area and threw a few 'coons and 'possums in there to make some tracks, so that nobody would suspect that a fortune lies buried there.

Now, you might wonder why I'm divulging these secrets that I've kept hidden for more than seventy years. I don't blame you. Herein lies the predicament. I'm ashamed to say that even with my superior intellect, I've made a fatal mistake. I had planned to dig up a small amount of gold whenever I needed it and have money to finance my villa in Spain and my mansion in Las Vegas. I had my broker invest the balance, some forty million, in U.S. government bonds, just to show support for my adopted country. It was a grand gesture, I thought.

I just found out he bought thirty-year treasury bonds, and I can't get them redeemed for twenty-nine years, the year before I'm scheduled to die, according to my doctor. To make matters worse, the roof of the cave fell in last week, burying my gold under hundreds of tons of rocks, some weighing tons apiece. Since I don't own that cave, and I don't have any money and won't have any for twenty-nine years, I can't even buy it. I can't dig the gold up without heavy machinery, so I'm up against it. Thank goodness I have this writing job to fall back on. I guess I can eat on the three dollars a week. I need to lose a little weight anyhow.

To show that I'm not at all stuck up because of my station in life, I'm not requesting that you kneel when you meet me in town. It wouldn't hurt if you slipped me a Little Debbie once in a while, though.

Country Politics
February 19, 2000

Ever since David Knight's letter to the editor urging me to run for public office appeared in The Logan Daily News, hundreds of people (at least three) have taken up the cry. I've spent several sleepless nights trying to sort out the whys and wherefores. After careful consideration, I've decided to run for county commissioner.

It won't be soon, however. I don't feel that I'm fully qualified for such an important office. The natural thing to do would be to run for a lower office and gain experience there. Age is against me, however, being already over thirty-nine. I think the thing to do is start at the top and work my way down. I'm going to run for president of the United States first.

It's an ideal place to start, since the president doesn't really have to do much. He hires someone to do every job there is to do. I can do that. The salary is good and the perks are great. The retirement plan is adequate. Once elected, all there is to do is not offend anybody and not get shot.

I don't think I'll have any trouble getting elected. Everyone is so sick of all the television commercials and hype that all I'll have to do is show up on election day. The only problem will be convincing them I'm not a Washington insider. People will love a fresh face with no past. The most scandalous thing I've ever done (mainly because I haven't done much of anything) is kick my brother-in-law's dog for pooping on my porch.

After I'm elected president, I'll take some local people with me to fill the important jobs. As vice president, I'll run my neighbor Chuck, the world's best shade-tree mechanic. Since the only duties of the vice president are to attend state funerals and vote in the Senate in case of a tie, which happens only once in a blue moon, he can sleep 'til noon, as is his habit, and still keep the presidential limousines running. Being also an accomplished carpenter, he can keep the White House in good repair. He is also young and virile and could easily entertain the young interns who like to hang around the president.

I'll take another neighbor, John Brenneman, as secretary of state. He's had years of experience with horses and gets things straight from the horse's mouth. He also knows how to handle the other end of the horses, of which I understand there is an over-abundance in Washington.

Another neighbor, Roger Cordle, I'll take along and make the secretary of agriculture. We'll haul his team of work horses along and keep them in that pavilion in the rose garden. He's a great gardener. He can plow up all that lawn and plant a garden. I plan to save the taxpayers some money and pay down the national debt. I'll do that by selling vegetables through that big iron fence around the White House grounds. There are millions of tourists hanging around, waiting in line to get in the White House. I'll bet they'd pay a pretty penny just to get something to eat that grew on White House grounds. We'll sell them tomatoes for a buck a piece and clean up. We could even buy some stuff wholesale and scatter a little horse manure over 'em, and they'd never know the difference. We could sell ten times what we raised. I'll have Roger shut off the drinking fountains and get my granddaughter to sell lemonade through the fence. The possibilities are endless.

When Roger isn't hoeing or selling, he could walk down to the agriculture building and make things happen. Whooee, that's a big building. It must be two blocks square and eight or ten stories high. They've got thousands of people sittin' around there in itty-bitty rooms, staring at computers and writing checks to farmers for not planting things. I'd have Roger fire all them that ain't wantin' to work and put the rest to shovelin' that place full of corn, beans and wheat. We could put millions of bushels in there and sell 'em at good prices to them countries that are starvin' instead of giving it away.

Then I'd take Mike and Donna McKnight along. Donna, being an accomplished innkeeper, would be in charge of the bed and breakfast business in the Lincoln Bedroom. I hear they get about $25,000 a night for that place. I think she could clean that and a couple or three more rooms and make the place pay. I can see we'd pay off the debt in my first term and maybe accumulate a little for myself the second.

I don't know what Mike's good for other than to entertain Donna. I guess he could attend to the plumbing in his spare time.

The biggest leak we've got in our national budget is the United Nations. I've got the perfect solution for that. I'm going to appoint Mike Nihiser Ambassador to the UN. He would fit right into an organization that takes two years to decide on the shape of the table before they start to negotiate. By the time he picked his way through the charter one line at a time, the term would be over and that would be wonderful. I think I'll give him a bonus.

After my two terms are over, I guess I'll get elected to the U.S. Senate. Most presidents don't do that, but they don't have the work ethic that we Hocking County boys do. I'd thought of being governor next, but since most governors run for the Senate, I guess I'll hit governor on the way down. While I'm in the Senate, I pledge to do absolutely nothing. The Senate spends all its time thinking up new ways to tax us and make us think we're being helped, and I don't want any part of that. They've been doing better lately, though. Since this is an election year and their main thrust is getting re-elected, they haven't passed a bill in months. That's great! The less they do, the better off we are.

I'll have to do a little figuring here. I'll be president for eight years, plus one before I take office. Then I'll probably stick around the Senate for eight or so, and eight as governor; that makes about twenty-five. (I don't think I'll bother with state senator or representative.) By that time, I'll be about 104. I'll have plenty of law-making experience by then, and I'll sleep a lot and won't pay too much attention to what's going on. Then, and only then, will I feel that I'm fully qualified to be a county commissioner.

Don't forget to vote for me in the primary election. You'll have to write me in as an Independent, since I started a little late. I'd appreciate it if you could put up a few hundred signs along the road with my campaign slogan on 'em: FASSIG FER PRES — HE AIN'T NO CROOK.

It wouldn't hurt if you could slip me a dime or a quarter. I'll have to save up for a bus ticket next January.

The Signs of Fall
October 21, 2000

About every ten years we have a fall in which the colors are way above average, and this is it. The political signs are really colorful this year, and the leaves ain't bad either.

I don't remember seeing these little signs all over the place like they are this year. I particularly like the color combinations on some of them. I don't know how, or why, those candidates pick the colors they do. Do you suppose they consciously or unconsciously pick the colors or leave that up to the printer? As I think more about it, I think that there is a conscious effort to project an image here.

Some of these people I know, but most of them I know only from seeing their names or pictures in the paper.

I know Charlie Morehead, who is running for county commissioner, and he is trying to project an image of someone who is interested in preserving the natural look of the county. His signs are a light green on a white background. I think that works.

Roger Hinerman and Gary Starner are both incumbent commissioners and are a little bolder, I guess. Hinerman's are red, white and blue to give the impression he's all-American; and Starner's are purple and white, the school colors, meaning he's local all the way, I would suppose.

Larry Householder's signs are red and white, which isn't all that exciting, but they are bigger. He has three sizes: big, large and humongous. Since he's the incumbent state representative, they deserve to be bigger; and since he's running for Speaker of the House of Representatives, they should be large and extra large.

Lanny North, who is running for sheriff, has the least attractive signs, to my notion. They are a garish yellow and black which gives an "in your face" impression, and I guess that's the kind of impression a sheriff would want to project.

Tom Wheeler, the opposing sheriff candidate, sticks with the tried and true red, white and blue, saying "you can trust me."

Mike DeWine, the incumbent U.S. Senator, has a plain blue and white sign that cries out, "I'm true blue," while the candidates for coroner have wildly differing colors. David Cummin's is the old trusty school color purple, exuding home-town trust, while Doug Carr's are a neon green lettering on black, which says nothing about his character or ability but it sure gets your attention. I can't get that excited about whether or not a coroner is loyal and trustworthy. What's he gonna steal, some old used body parts?

Renee Tschudy makes her signs clearly visible. They are neon orange and dark blue. You can see them a mile away.

These signs seem to gather together like wild geese. Where you see one, the next day there is one of his opponent's beside it. I gave permission for a friend put a sign for his friend in front of my place a few weeks ago, and a day or two later there was one from someone else nearby. Every few days thereafter, another would appear, until now there are ten and growing. I don't really mind because they each have a nice piece of heavy wire inside that I can use after the election to repair things around the place. They make a dandy hinge for a gate or to keep the muffler on my pickup from dragging on the road. In a pinch I could even make a hook for the outhouse door. The cardboard signs make good fire-starters for the old wood stove, too.

I was thinking the other day there are so many signs that with a little organization, we wouldn't even need an election. We could just count signs. Whoever has the most wins. It would be a heck of a job to count 'em, I know. We could just make each candidate show an invoice from a printer showing the number of signs purchased. In case of a tie, an independent committee would decide whose sign was the purtiest, and that candidate would win.

There's one more sign that I need to see out there. That's my own. I've been a little lax in my campaigning lately. I didn't get invited to share in the presidential debates because I'm just a write-in candidate for president. I can't afford to buy a gang of them store-bought signs. I thought about sneaking out one night and borrowing one of Householder's great big signs, but that wouldn't be right. Honesty is the best policy.

Besides, my campaign motto is "Vote fer Fassig for Prez. He ain't no crook." It wouldn't look right to get arrested for stealing just a couple of weeks before the election. I guess I'll just make one. I've got a bunch of sawmill slabs down at the mill. They'll do. I've also got several cans of old paint in the shop and some twenty penny spikes. I could make a right purdy one with Caterpiller yeller and John Deere green.

I'm asking you all to give me your write-in vote come election day. I don't have any party backing, so I'm running as an Independent.

I hope you remember my platform. Remember, I'm going to appoint Roger Cordle secretary of agriculture so he can take his team of work horses over there to Warshton and plow up the rose garden and plant corn and taters and maters to sell to the tourists through the fence, so we can save Social Security. I'm taking Donna and Mike McKnight. Donna's going to run the bed and breakfast in the Lincoln Bedroom. Mike will fix up a couple of other bedrooms so we can expand the business, and he'll keep the White House plumbing in good repair in his spare time.

Mike Nihiser will be the Ambassador to the U.N. His job, which he is very good at, is to keep things at a stand-still so that nothing gets done, thus saving us millions of dollars.

I'll still need secretaries of labor, energy and a few others, plus the FBI and DOE. I can make up a lot of other agencies and departments and take about all of the unemployed in Hocking County. This begins to sound better and better. The only thing we have to be careful of is that we don't get mistaken for Warshton insiders.

Well, I better get busy makin' that sign. Don't forget — "Vote for Fassig — he ain't no crook."

Election Time
November 4, 2000

I hope you're enjoying the presidential election campaign as much as I am. In fact, you're probably enjoying it more than I am because I'm sick of it. It seems as though this has been going on for years. When you stop and think about it, it has. It really never ends. When a man gets elected president, his every word and action is slanted toward getting re-elected.

We don't get bombarded every minute of the day or night with local candidates and issues like we do for national elections (though we do have some pretty signs to beautify our yards and roadsides). I don't mind local politics because they affect us directly. We know most of the candidates, or at least who they are, and the issues are more directly connected to our everyday lives.

The presidential candidates rail on about whose "plan" for Social Security or prescription drugs is the best when they know and we know that they as individuals can't do a damned thing about them. It's up to Congress, and they can't agree on anything or it would have been done years ago. President Clinton has had eight years to do something and he hasn't. The decisions aren't made on the basis of what is best for the country or its people. They are made by wheeling and dealing between members of Congress who are trying to get something for their voters, and to hell with the rest of the country. If they succeed, they get re-elected. It's as simple as that.

I know this sounds cynical, and it is, but how did I get that way? Just by observing the passing scene, that's how. It is they who have made me the way I am. It's the same story every year. They never seem to learn. A very wise man, and I can't remember who it was, once said, "Those who don't learn from history are doomed to repeat it." Truer words were never spoken.

I tend to lean toward the espoused philosophy of the Republican ideology — that is smaller, less intrusive government. That doesn't mean that I vote a straight Republican ticket. There are just as many charlatans in the Republican party as there are in the Democratic party. I tend to be more of an Independent voter than a party one. If I were a straight-laced, tried and true Republican, I'd vote for Bush, no questions asked, even if Gore were a better choice. As it is, I can't in good conscience vote for either one.

I think Gore has laid out a better platform. His approach to the environmental issues is better than Bush's. The Social Security issue is rather clouded. I don't think either one is good. The funding is an issue, but I guess Gore's would be acceptable. The main problem is, I don't believe a word he says. He has turned me against him by talking out of both sides of his mouth. The more I hear him the more obnoxious he seems to be. He probably would fit right in with the rest of the Washington insiders.

I like Bush personally better than Gore. He seems more down to earth. He exhibits good leadership qualities. After all, though he is governor of Texas, he hasn't been in the capitol building in six or eight months and Texas hasn't floated away or burned down. Somebody must be doing something right. (To be fair, Gore hasn't been to a state funeral lately either, so his office is still intact.)

The thing that bothers me about Bush is his attitude toward the environment. I think, or at least he gives me the impression, that he would sacrifice wilderness areas to drill for oil. He said that he would encourage drilling in Alaska. Wherever exploitation of the earth's minerals takes place, the earth suffers, and there is no more being made. When this is gone, where do we go?

We know that someday the last drop of oil, the last lump of coal, the last cubic foot of gas will be gone. I don't hear either candidate saying a word about finding or inventing a substitute for any of them. Neither do I hear anything about the most pressing issue of our time — population control. We are using our resources at an ever-increasing rate. The population of the earth is doubling about every hundred years. The attitude seems to be "OK, we'll do something about that in a hundred years. In the meantime, look at all those voters out there."

I don't think the politicians realize that the voters are so disgusted with the political process and the politicians that they aren't voting. We have the lowest percentage of voter turn-out in the industrialized world. Somebody had better wake up.

There are several more candidates for president that I haven't mentioned. One is Pat Buchanan, who has taken over Ross Perot's Independent Party. He runs on a platform of the radical Christian right. He has about as much chance as a snowball in hell. The others are so obscure that they're hardly worth mentioning. In fact, I've forgotten who they are.

The only other viable candidate is Ralph Nader, and he is expected to get only about eight percent of the votes. He has some very good ideas, but has gained such a reputation as a radical over the years that he scares people. The Green Party that he heads is a radical environmental group that has the same reputation.

After going over the points in my mind countless times, I still don't know what to do. I've voted every election since about 1950 and I will vote this year, but it's a sad thing to vote not for the best man but for the least bad.

Perhaps there is a ray of hope. I'm running for president myself. Since I don't have any party backing, I only made one sign and it's environmentally friendly. It's made of an old sawmill slab. I did, however, have to spend six bucks for paint, so your campaign contributions would be welcome. Remember, "Rite in vote fer Fassig. He ain't no crook."

How About a Recount?
November 22, 2000

The days leading up to the election were hectic. There were signs to put up, speeches to make and dinners to attend. The dinners were the most fun. It took only a week to put the eight pounds back on that I had spent two months losing.

Now that the election is over, I still don't know if I won. When the results were printed in the newspaper, they somehow forgot to say how many votes I got. When I checked with the editor, he said that the election board didn't report any votes for me. That is surely a mistake, because I've spoken to eight or ten people who said they voted for me. Maybe they lied. I know I got at least one because I voted for myself.

I think there's a conspiracy afoot. I'll bet Gore and Bush have gotten together and had their lawyers file an action in the courts to have my votes thrown out. That has to be it! After two machine recounts and one by hand, there is still no sign of them. It just dawned on me that it couldn't be the "chads." It was a write-in vote and had to be handwritten on the envelope. Someone connected with the opposition must have sneaked into the township house and swiped the envelopes. You just can't trust these guys.

I'm really in trouble here. The secretary of state, who is a Republican, has declared that all ballots must be certified by Friday, which was yesterday. I tried to get a lawyer to go to the Supreme Court and get this travesty stopped. He said he didn't have any use for possums; he wanted cash money. That put me on the spot.

After spending six bucks on my sign, I was pretty well strapped. I pleaded for campaign contributions, but I only got one. A secret admirer sent me a penny taped on the back of a coupon for a Big Mac at half price. The lawyer said that wasn't quite enough, though he would consider writing a letter to Janet Reno if I'd throw in the Big

Mac, some fries and a coke. I've already eaten that.

So it seems that all my hopes and dreams are splattered like a cow plop on a flat rock. I've lain awake nights trying to figure out a plan for plowing up the White House lawn and raising vegetables to sell through the fence to the White House tourists. That, along with running a bed and breakfast in the Lincoln Bedroom, would save Social Security without raising taxes. I think that's a better plan than either of them yahoos had.

I admit that sounds a little far fetched, but we free-thinkers have always had to endure criticism from the masses. The problem is that I'm just ahead of my time. Within the next century, it will come to pass, mark my words.

I had another grand idea this past week that would have helped me repay my campaign debts. Wednesday morning I gathered up all of the campaign signs I could get on my pickup. It didn't take long. I had it full by the time I got to Ewing (about a mile and a half). There's about six feet of number nine wire in each one of them. I took them all apart and salvaged the wire. There was a good bit of weight there, so I took it over to the scrap yard at Union Furnace. The man said, "Unload it in that bin there." So I did. Then I asked him how he was going to weigh it.

"Don't need to," he replied. "It ain't worth nuthin'. Them Japanese is shippin' the stuff over here so cheap I can't sell it. It'll cost ya a buck to leave it here."

I gave him a buck rather than crawl down in that dumpster. He's a smart man. I think I'll make him the Secretary of Commerce in 2004.

Well, that left me seven bucks in the hole. I'd better quit before I'm any worse off. I still have the signs, though. I'll bet everybody will run again next time. I could sell them cheaper than they could print new ones. All I'll have to do is buy about $20 worth of wire.

Well, it looks like I've had it for this time. I'm just about fifty-six million votes shy. I'm not going to phone my rivals and concede just yet. Gore made that mistake and had to take it back. I'll wait until the votes have been recounted and certified in Rhode Island.

I want to thank all my supporters out there. I love you both. Now as I ride away into the sunset I'll have the satisfaction of knowing that the big networks won't have Fassig to kick around anymore.

Election Day 31
December 9, 2000

A few weeks ago I sorta halfway conceded the election to Al Gore and George W. Bush. Today, the result seems in doubt, so I'll sorta halfway take back my concession. If Gore can do it, I guess I can too. Since there are forty-one lawsuits filed in the case, it might be a while before the final count is final.

In addition to a whole raft of local state courts, circuit courts, appeals courts, tennis courts and so on, the Florida State Supreme Court and the United States Supreme Court also are involved. By the time they all get through rasselling, Clinton will be halfway through his third term.

The big argument centers around chads. I can honestly say that I have never impregnated a chad, though I must admit that I lusted in my heart for a chad's dimple once. I couldn't afford to rent a Ryder truck to take my ballots to the state capitol to be counted, so, since there were only twelve of them, I put them in a cardboard box and sent them by UPS. I gave a neighbor kid three bucks to ride along and guard them with his slingshot. He wanted me to go up to Columbus to bring him home, but his mom gave me ten bucks not to. I knew there was money in this politicin'.

We think that this is a most unusual election, and I suppose it is, but it happened before 100 years ago or so. I can't remember just when or who was involved. We've been fed every detail of this process from day one. I never heard of the word "minutia" until the O.J. trial, but we've certainly come to know the meaning of it in the last month. Every minute detail of this debacle has been spoon-fed to us by the national TV networks, local TV, radio stations and newspapers.

Almost every program through the day is interrupted with "breaking" news about the election minutae, and they're getting more and more minute. I wonder what else is going on in the world.

I don't have time to petition the Ohio Supreme Court to act on my behalf, but maybe the county commissioners could send a letter. Probably not, since my reason for running for president was to get experience in politics so I could replace one of them. I don't think they have much to fear from me. If my plan works out, it will be nearly forty years before I work my way back down again. Most of them would be ready to retire by then anyhow. C'mon fellers, help me out here.

I'm sorta getting desperate now. Clutching at straws as it were. I tried to get Charlie Gibson and George Stephanopaulas to come down and do their show from here so I could get some free publicity. They said they tried, but couldn't get a hotel room because of the rush of tourists here to watch Wal-Mart destroy the hilltop.

I guess I'll have to withdraw my concession withdrawal. It's tough, I tell ya. I just don't get no respect.

Just wait til '04. I'll run again. Next time I'll be better prepared. I've learned a lot this year. Politics is a dirty business. You have to get down and dirty in the trenches. I think I'll start out by getting a truck load of chads. I'll bet I can get 'em purty cheap next week.

I do thank all my supporters out there in never-never land. I wish you both a Merry Christmas and a chad-free New Year.

Chapter 6
Travelin' On

Serendipity
February 10, 1996

I've been poor all my life and never considered it a handicap. I'll admit it's inconvenient at times, but it never was a handicap. In fact, it's led me down some interesting paths. I never could afford a deluxe vacation, so I had to go the hard way. Instead of staying in a posh hotel, I had only a tent on some hidden lake or shore. The solitude I gained in tune with nature more than made up for the shortage of cash. I've been poor so long that I'm not comfortable in glitzy situations.

The most inconvenient part is having to drive junky old cars and trucks. Some of my trips have been adventures in themselves. This continues today. My present transportation is a thirteen-year-old pickup that is melting away before my very eyes. It runs good, but I'm afraid to turn a corner too fast for fear the body will fall off and leave me upside down in the middle of the road. There is a similar situation with my tractor, as well. I have two. One is a 1945 Case. In spite of using a quart of oil a day, it provides yeoman service. It also leads to some exciting adventures because it doesn't have brakes. My "new" tractor, a 1958 Case, has been out of service more than in. There is something radically wrong in the engine so that it keeps breaking the distributor.

Last week, I was determined to get to the bottom of the problem. The ground was frozen too hard to bury it, so I decided to tear into the engine. The problem is I don't know a damned thing about engines. They are a complete mystery to me and I have no idea what makes them run. I do, however, have a repair manual. I drained the oil and took off the oil pan. One look up into the engine convinced me that I was beyond my depth. I fetched my neighbor, Chuck Randolph, who modestly admits to being the world's greatest shade-tree mechanic.

With me slowly cranking the engine, he stuck his head up inside and soon determined that there were teeth missing from two gears on the cam shaft, whatever that is. Chuck made me stick my head in while he turned the crank. Now I know what a crankshaft is. It's that knobby thing that throws oil in your face when you put it where it ain't supposed to be.

Then came the task of finding parts for a nearly forty-year-old machine. I let my fingers do the walking and after a few calls found a dealer in Circleville that could order the parts. All but the cam gear, that is. Now what? The parts manager suggested I try to find a used one. Where? "You might try the Tractor Retirement Village," he said. "It will be cheaper, too. You're looking at at least $300 here." I knew he had to be pulling my leg, but he produced a phone number, so I decided I had nothing to lose.

A gruff voice answered my call. He asked me a number of questions about the tractor that I was able to answer with the aid of my book, and he was able to determine that he had what I wanted. The only question unanswered was about the governor. Did it have sliding weights or balls? I couldn't answer that without taking the cam shaft out. It seems they changed the system mid-year and the later models have sliding weights on the cam gear. He said he had both, so I asked directions to get to his place. We'd decide later.

He thought that taking State Route 664 to Bremen then State Route 37 to Sunbury would be the best way. From Sunbury, there were five or six turns involving churches and bridges and such landmarks, which I jotted down in my own shorthand. "Ya think you got that?" he asked. "I think so," I replied.

"Read it back to me," he said. I did, I think to his amazement.

"You'll know it when you git here," he said.

I immediately marked it on my map so I wouldn't forget it. I probably couldn't have read it an hour later.

I started shortly after noon the next day on what was to prove an adventure of sorts. If you've ever driven State Route 37, you know that's an adventure in itself. It meanders all over the state. It took hours to get to Sunbury. It was a pleasant drive, however, through rolling countryside and quaint little villages. I would have enjoyed it more if it were not for a full bladder and a bumpy road. I finally found relief in Granville and enjoyed the rest of the trip. I even navigated by the churches and bridges. By this time, the country had turned flat, and he was right, I could tell when I got there. In fact, I could see it a mile before I got there. I always feel naked in flat country. I can see houses miles away and I know people can see me. Here in the hills, I can't see anything but woods from home.

Anyway, when the place came into view, it was comprised of an old farmstead with acres of tractors in rows — row after row. As I approached the house, a nice lady came to the door. "He's out there somewhere," she said. "Maybe in one of them house trailers."

I turned and started the hunt. I was fascinated by the sight of hundreds of tractors — a lot of them in better shape than mine, all in "retirement." I walked down one row and back the next. There were several house trailers, all with radios blaring, and some barns and sheds, also with radios. Finally, I spotted the proprietor of the establishment. He had just removed a radiator from some poor unfortunate retiree. I introduced myself and he said, "It's over there in that red van. I'll get my tools."

I looked in the van. There were several partly dismantled engines in there. He came with a large tractor pulling the body of a utility truck such as those used by telephone or electric companies. There was an electric welder mounted on the tractor, an acetylene cutting torch and an air compressor on the front of the trailer, and hoses and various large tools hanging all over the sides. There were several tool boxes filled with wrenches. I said, "It looks like you're prepared for any eventuality."

"When I go after sumpin, I genly get it," he grinned.

This was Ed Axthelm, a bear of a man with a grizzled beard, huge farmer hands that seemed to defy the cold wind that whistled through the tractors, and the bearing of a man who knew what he was about — the mayor of Tractor Retirement Village.

"I still have to get the cam gear," he said. "That one has the ball governor. This motor has the right one."

It took only ten minutes and three or four trips to the tool trailer to remove the gear. He knows his stuff. He knows those tractors like the back of his hand. If he wants a certain part, he knows just where to look. He has piles of generators and wheels and whatever in all those sheds.

He climbed on the tractor and I rode the tongue back to the house. His office is on the back porch. On the way, I asked how many tractors he had.

"I got no idea," he said.

"Where do you get 'em?" I asked.

"Most come here," he said. "Some I go out and buy."

At the office, he looked up the prices in greasy old books, then charged me half price. I thought that was fair enough, but at the same time he made pretty good money, too. After I paid him, we chatted for almost a half hour. He is well-read and intelligent and well-versed in local geography and history. It turned out that he had a nephew in Rockbridge for whom I had made some furniture. Small world! I enjoyed my visit with him and I'd like to go back. Given the tractor's propensity to break down, I probably will. He's a fellow I'd like to get to know better.

All in all, it was a fine little adventure, one I would have missed if I were a rich man.

Fun in the Woods
July 27, 1996

This year, I opted to spend my vacation a little closer to home than the Canadian trip that I love so much.

A friend, my son and I built a cabin in the Upper Peninsula wilderness of Michigan. It's only 800 miles from Logan. It's a beautiful spot. There is a small lake about an eighth of a mile away. Its drainage has been dammed by beavers in a series of ponds that cover about ten acres, coming to within sixty feet of the cabin.

As I write, I'm on the screened-in porch overlooking the largest pond. I'm being serenaded by dozens of frogs of various lineages. The sky is blue and a light breeze keeps us comfortable at seventy degrees.

The only problem is, I'm being held captive and leave the safety of the porch at my peril. Outside lurks the enemy, the state bird of Michigan — the mosquito. Here, they've had a spring and summer much like ours: lots of rain.

Luckily, the black flies are gone. They usually expire by the early part of July. I have never seen the mosquitoes as bad as they are this year. They are thicker, meaner, trickier and hungrier than I've ever seen them. Special measures must be taken if one is to survive.

First, of course, is repellent. We never go outside without dousing liberally with at least two kinds. The ads all say that this or that kind is the best, but no one brand is perfect. I always carry a spare squeeze bottle in my pocket. A good sweat will wash it off and woe to the one without a replacement.

I found that even with the repellent I was losing a good bit of blood. As I was browsing a mall in Marquette, looking for more repellent, I found myself in the sporting goods department. Golf tees caught my attention and I bought a package on a whim. They work beautifully.

Now, after a particularly brutal attack, I just stick a tee in the larger holes in my skin to stop the bleeding until I can make it to the safety of the cabin and staunch the flow surgically. My companions laugh at the odd patterns achieved by the many-colored tees, but I remain strong and they grow weaker daily.

One of my friends weighs only eighty-five pounds and I no doubt saved her life by throwing her a large rock as she was being carried away by a blood-thirsty horde. Had the rock been a few pounds lighter, she would have been lost forever. We managed to fend them off with clubs and stones. By fighting a delaying action, we were able to make the safety of the cabin.

She developed a mean streak after that and now spends her time with a hammer, bending the ends of their stingers over when they stick them through the screen so they can't pull them out. The whole north side of the porch is covered with captive mosquitoes. She likes to hit the screen with a broom to make them all fly at once. They do make some nice harmony, though.

There is at least one body function that we must go outside to perform. The forty or so yards to the necessary house can be traversed in a few seconds. I usually wait until I can wait no longer to make the trip even quicker. The first few minutes are spent killing the dozen or so mosquitoes that come in with you. After that you can enjoy the view, for it does have a picture window from which the lake can be seen.

It doesn't take long to realize, however, that a few of the tricky devils were either smart enough (or dumb enough) to hide down the hole and are enjoying a meal at your expense. I have several dozen bites, arranged in an elliptical pattern, on a part of my anatomy that I don't usually show in public. It's hard to scratch there and be inconspicuous about it. I'm designing underwear with velcro lining so I can walk and scratch at the same time.

Of course, I'm exaggerating a little bit (not much). We've enjoyed this magnificent country. The black flies and mosquitoes have actually saved this area from overdevelopment. If it weren't for them (and the four feet of snow in the winter) this area would be fully as well-developed as Hocking County. The invention of the snowmobile has helped the people survive here in the winter because people come by the thousands just to ride snowmobiles and spend money. If we had more snow at home it would happen in Hocking County. I don't know if I'd like that. Peace and quiet would be worth more than the money, I think.

There is very little private land in the Upper Peninsula. Most of it is state or national forest or is owned by lumber or paper companies. Mead owns thousands of acres hereabouts. Most is available as public recreation area as long as certain rules are followed.

We have ridden miles of forest trails on our mountain bikes. Most are rugged but ridable. The biggest problem we faced was the abundance of puddles. The heavy rain this year has left quagmires on most trails. In some places, beavers have flooded the roads to impossible levels. Last time, we even encountered beavers on county roads. A good four-wheel-drive pickup is a necessity for those who live here year round.

Wildlife abounds here. There are deer, moose, bears and even occasional wolves. One seldom encounters them in the daylight, but their tracks show evidence of their passing. A local reported seeing a mountain lion a couple of times last year. All these apparently pose little threat to humans. It's nice to know there is a place east of the Rockies where things like this can survive. I know I'll keep coming back as long as I'm able.

"Sods" Revisited: Still a Great Place to Unwind
Sept. 20, 1997

Having lost nearly three months this year to a knee operation, I had given up any thought of a vacation this fall. However, a glance at my calendar showed that I had a vacancy in my rental cabin one weekend. That would give me about ten days uncommitted to someone else, and the urge proved too strong to resist.

Not that I had time to waste. I certainly had work to do, but it doesn't HAVE to be done this week.

I would have liked to go to our cabin in Michigan's Upper Peninsula, but the thought of a fifteen-hour drive palled on me. Having only a ten-year-old pickup that's getting a little tired helped sway my opinion. It just wasn't worth it. Marie, my best friend for sixteen or seventeen years, and I decided to revisit West Virginia, my second favorite place.

A drive of only five hours over an absolutely fabulous road (once we got out of Ohio — U.S. 50 from Athens to Parkersburg is a nightmare and Parkersburg is the pits to drive through) took us to Dolly Sods in eastern West Virginia. We arrived after dark because of our usual late start and set up camp by starlight.

The sods are on a mountain top of about 4,000 feet and the air is pure and sweet. The stars were about as bright as I've ever seen them. Each stood out as an individual and shone down with a visible light that made it possible to see to walk without a flashlight. After the tent was up, we just sat and stared at the sky. We don't often see air this clear in Hocking County because of the humidity we have in summer. Anyhow, we should take advantage of it whenever it occurs.

We were awakened about 4 a.m. by the violent shaking of the tent and the roaring of the wind. It was a little unsettling for a while, but soon we slept again. I was just getting up to make coffee when it started to rain. I slumped back down into my sleeping bag to wait it out. It proved to be only a few sprinkles and in an hour the sun was shining.

Within the sods, there's a wilderness area where you may camp anywhere as long as you are no closer than one hundred yards to a road. We moved from the U.S. Forest Service campground to a spot where we were completely alone. We could neither see nor hear another person. We could well have been in another time, centuries ago. What a delightful feeling! The forest service campground is nice, but there are other people around and driving in and out. There are only eleven spaces and we were lucky to get the last one, but we were also happy to leave. We still go there for our water and to get rid of the trash, but only every other day or so.

I wrote about Dolly Sods a couple of years ago, but I'll recap briefly for those who might not remember. The word "sods" refers to a grassy area that was used for livestock grazing. The people who originally owned this one were German immigrants whose last name was Dahle. It was pronounced "Dolly" and through time began to be spelled that way. There are several hundred acres here on this mountain top that belonged to Dahle plus more than 10,000 belonging to the forest service. When we first came here, there were still cattle free-ranging here. One had to be alert while driving because the cows liked to stand in the road.

The atmosphere is Alpine in nature. It's a harsh environment, especially in the winter. The plants are those that you would find in Canada. The snow lies deep and the winds blow strong and hard — so hard, in fact, that the trees only have limbs on the east side. The Dahles didn't live here, although I think they had a small cabin here that they used when checking on their cattle. They lived down the mountain aways where the weather is more amenable.

The sods has been badly used over the years. During World War II, it was used as a practice range for artillery by the Army. There are signs around telling people not to pick up mortar shells if they find them. I've never seen one in the last fifteen years.

The Dahles set fire to the area periodically to discourage trees from growing so they would have grass for their cattle. What didn't burn was cut for timber. Since the government has taken control of it, there haven't been any fires and trees are coming back over most of it. Soon it will no longer be a "sods." That might or might not be good. I think, at least, part of it should be burned. That's what makes it unique.

We had planned to make this area a central stopping point and go sight-seeing from here, but Marie is a photographer by trade and has a new camera. Our sightseeing has been confined to places we can walk to. She finds it impossible to walk more than ten feet without seeing something that cries out to be photographed. I don't mind, because it's nice to be with someone who appreciates her surroundings. I've been guilty of taking pictures myself. I have hundreds that I rarely look at. I prefer to catalog memories. I fear that her pictures will outlast my memories, however, because my memories fade much sooner.

You must always be aware of weather in a high place like this. The wind was from the west when we arrived. It blew incessantly at about twenty-five miles per hour for forty-eight hours straight. We had to put rocks in the tent to keep it from blowing away. As we were retiring last night, there was distant lightning and I was afraid we were in for a storm. Not good on a mountaintop! During the night the wind stopped and today it's still and muggy. The wind is from the east, bringing moisture and pollution with it. Occasionally, a low cloud comes by, engulfing me in fog. It's rather eerie to see a cloud come at you, then pass by.

I'm sitting on one of the highest parts of the mountain. This place is called Bear Rocks. It was so called because of the many crevices in this big jumble of rocks that bears would use as hibernation places. Maybe they still do. The valley below me, some thousand feet, is filled with haze. I can't see the bottom. The ridges of mountains beyond are visible only as subtle changes in color as they fade into a blue oblivion. This magic place has me in its spell. I find it hard to leave. If there is no column next week, send the forest service looking for me. They'll find me sitting on a cliff, staring into space. I think they'll also find Marie, camera grown into her forehead, looking for just the right angle to photograph me.

On West Virginia Highways, Danger Happens in Threes
September 27, 1997

I recently had a week's vacation in West Virginia. It's a beautiful place and the people are friendly, at least when they're not driving. I had three near-death experiences that made me question whether any long drive is worth the risk anymore.

Now I consider myself a good driver. (I suppose everybody does.) I drive conservatively and defensively. I don't take chances. I drive the speed limits on major roads and try not to impede other drivers.

Last week, I was driving in West Virginia on a road that compares in size and configuration to State Route 93 South in Hocking County. It was a good road, well-maintained, but hilly and curvy. There were few places where one car could pass another. It was raining and the road appeared slippery. I was driving the speed limit, which was fifty-five miles per hour. I noticed a semi-truck coming up behind me at a pretty good clip. He kept getting closer. He was very close behind me. Realizing that most people drive a little over the speed limit, I stepped it up to sixty miles per hour. The truck got closer. Soon he was only about twenty feet from my back bumper. That can be a little unsettling. To be followed at twenty feet, at sixty miles per hour, on a rain-slickened, unfamiliar, hilly, curvy road didn't add up to a great vacation to me.

I spied a wide place in the berm and a driveway about a quarter mile ahead and I decided to get out of his way and let him kill himself without involving me. I put on my right turn signal and hit the brakes. The truck got closer. I whipped into the wide spot and barely got stopped before going into the ditch. The truck was so close behind that the driver couldn't see my signal, I guess. He came so close to hitting my pickup that I couldn't believe he missed. The truck went left of center and forced an oncoming car to the berm.

As he passed, I saw that the trailer was loaded with wood chips. Now, what is so important about a load of wood chips that a man would risk killing several other people as well as himself, not to mention wrecking a $50,000 rig? I'll never know. Marie, my traveling companion, and I agreed we needed a change of underwear after that episode.

We decided from there on to take the road less traveled. We would take only little back roads wherever possible. We did just that and saw some absolutely beautiful country. The only problem was that the major roads follow the valleys and are therefore less steep and curvy. The little roads go over the top of the mountains and are extremely steep and crooked as a snake. They are well-paved and maintained, however, and not hard to drive, except that you can't go as fast. That suited us just fine. We came to look and see. Most of eastern West Virginia is in the Monongahela National Forest and there are few houses along the roads, just scenery. The people are congregated in pockets of private land.

We were traveling one road that went northwest, over mountain after mountain. It was a two-lane that was very steep, with many switchbacks and hairpin curves. It was my kind of road and I was thoroughly enjoying it. The speed limit was fifty-five miles per hour, but there were few places that I felt safe at that speed. Most curves were marked with twenty- or forty-mile-per-hour safe speeds.

We were going uphill, approaching a curve marked forty miles per hour. As we started into the curve, a semi loaded with logs was coming down the hill at terrific speed, at least seventy miles per hour. I can only assume that the driver had been there before. He hit that curve at sixty. The trailer was piled very high with logs and leaned toward us at about fifteen degrees. We thought surely it would turn over. If it had, or if a chain had broken, it would have been "Katie bar the door!" We would surely have been killed. There was no place to go. It was a narrow road, with a guardrail on our right. If we had gone through the guardrail, it was a several hundred foot drop into a river. We decided we'd better stop at the next town and get more underwear.

Later, coming across U.S. 50 between Belpre and Athens, Ohio, we had another close call. The road was under construction, with a forty-five mile per hour speed limit. There was no passing for miles. Cars and trucks tend to bunch up behind the slowest vehicle (the one observing the speed limit). We were second in line in one of these bunches.

At one straight stretch, where we could see a mile ahead, another bunch approached from the opposite direction. The last vehicle in line began to pass all the others. It was dark and all we could see were headlights. It kept coming closer and it became apparent that it wasn't going to make it and a collision was about to take place.

There was a little wide place just then and we and the car ahead were able to get off the road as a semi roared past in our lane, narrowly avoiding a deadly head-on crash. It was a good thing we were getting close to home. We were out of underwear.

I've been wondering ever since what would make people take such risks. It doesn't make any sense to me. Death is so final. There's no recovering from death. Most people, if put in a position where their own deaths were possibilities, would run the other way if given the option; yet almost daily they take chances with their cars or trucks. It makes no sense.

I'm not talking about drinking drivers. That's a whole 'nother matter. I'm talking about sane, sensible people who use good judgment in other matters, yet become aggressive, rude, uncaring jerks when they're behind the wheel.

Several years ago, Walt Disney made a cartoon in which the character Goofy changed into a demon whenever he drove a car. He cursed and shook his fist at other drivers. He cut them off and sped away, just being a real jerk. When he got out of his car, he was his old sweet self. I have an acquaintance who is the same way. He is a real Casper Milquetoast until he gets behind the wheel. He weaves through traffic, ranting and raving, cutting other cars off. One day after such an episode, he had to stop at a traffic light. The driver behind him got out of his car, walked up to my friend's car, and through the open window, grabbed my friend's necktie, pulled his head out the window and gave him a knuckle sandwich. My friend didn't know why.

That might be part of the reason we're so rude on the road. Maybe we don't realize it. I kinda doubt that, though. We know when we're rude. I think part of it is that cars are so much better now. When we are in a good, fast car, we are anonymous. We are untouchable. We can do things and get away with them because we don't have a face-to-face encounter with other people. It's your car against my car, not you against me.

Most of us would avoid a confrontation with another person if we thought we'd get a knuckle sandwich. If we have a mishap with another car, the police will sort it out and we won't get involved personally because it's illegal for another person to hit us.

In the case of the big trucks, who's going to argue with them? Your car doesn't stand a chance against my big truck, so I'll do as I please. Truck drivers have a reputation for being big, tough guys, so we don't argue with them. Some are, some aren't, but a big machine is a great equalizer. I've known some truck drivers who were demons on the road but couldn't punch their way out of a paper bag. The only ones to challenge them were other truck drivers, and they belong to a sort of fraternity and stick together pretty well.

All of this leaves us at risk every time we drive. If we don't have a change of attitude soon, the highways can only get worse. State Route 93 South, where I live, has its share of accidents, which strangely are mostly one-vehicle wrecks. I have had several close encounters, however, caused by impatient people who passed in inappropriate places.

In the twenty-three years I've lived here, eighteen people have died between Ilesboro and Logan that I know of. Three near-death experiences in one week have made me extra cautious. I guess you have to assume that every car or truck is out to get you. That's a helluva way to live. It's also a helluva way to die.

Life in the Swamp — Part I
May 23, 1998

Whenever I get a chance to take a few days off in the summer, I head north. I like to get away from the heat and humidity.

A few weeks ago, my best friend, Marie, asked if I wanted to accompany her to South Carolina to visit her daughter who works as a tour guide at the Francis P. Beidler Forest.

I knew there would be no heat and humidity there so I jumped at the chance.

We left at about 7:30 a.m. last Saturday. We took the scenic route to Ravenswood, West Virginia and got on I-77. This road is fairly new and up to interstate standards, and we could move along at a good clip.

Somewhere along the line, and I have never been sure just where, it turns into the West Virginia Turnpike. This is the oldest part of the interstate system, and it shows. It is of concrete for the most part, and rough as a washboard. It's not broken up, it was just paved that way.

I surmise that it was built by the low bidder. In spite of this it is a magnificent road. What a challenge to build a road through the rugged Appalachian Mountains some thirty or forty years ago.

The road goes right down the valley where two ranges meet. There is almost no valley there. There is just enough room for a river in the bottom with none of the flood plain we ordinarily associate with valleys. They managed to squeeze the road beside the river most places but had to kick her out of the bed here and there. The road constantly curves back and forth, going around tongues of land that come down the mountains, first on this side, then on that.

The result is a series of vistas that are breathtaking. The mountains are so steep on either side that it seems almost impossible to climb them. No wonder it was 200 years before settlers were able to cross them into Ohio.

It was a nice drive. The traffic wasn't too bad until after noon, when the weekenders came out in force. There are no rest stops on that stretch except three plazas where they slow ya down long enough to nick you for a buck and a quarter at each of them.

West Virginia makes up for it by having a tremendous tourism center just at the border. They know you'll stop because you have a bladder ready to burst. They do a land-office business.

After we got into the Carolinas, the terrain became less mountainous. The steep grades flowed gently into the undulating hills of the Piedmont and then flatlands as we got onto the coastal plain.

We arrived at Beidler Forest just as the staff was sitting down to a Southern barbecue. It was not what we would expect a barbecue to be, but more like a picnic.

Marie's daughter, Jenny, has a staff housing facility that would pass for a trailer. It's located a mile and a half off the main road, which is made of sand, on the edge of Four Hole Swamp. The first order of the day was a canoe trip into the swamp. A real swamp is not the dark, dismal, scummy, foreboding, snake-infested place we see in the movies. It is dark and dismal and snake-infested, but not scummy and foreboding. In fact, it is quite pleasant. It's just a woods growing in water.

I was surprised that there was a current in the water. It's really a half-mile-wide river about a foot or so deep. There are deeper channels that flow until the late summer droughts, but most of the swamp dries up enough to walk through in the summer.

Our canoe trip was like a walk in the woods, sitting down. Thankfully, Jenny was well acquainted with the place. I was hopelessly lost in ten minutes. Everything looked alike. It felt as if we had passed the same trees dozens of times.

We entered the swamp from a "lake." A lake is anyplace that doesn't dry up in the summer. This one was the largest in the swamp. It's about a city block long and from fifty to seventy-five feet wide and perhaps eight feet deep. Two-thirds of the way upstream we made a right turn into the forest. Immediately, the atmosphere changed. As we became accustomed to the gloom we became aware that we were almost in a fantasy world. The atmosphere was almost ethereal. We moved silently along, the quiet disturbed only by the rippling of the water off our bows and the out-of-place booming of the damnable aluminum canoes as we banged off of trees and cypress "knees." (Canoes should be rubber to go into a place such as this.) The cypress knees were everywhere. They sprout up from the roots of the cypress trees. Their use to the tree is unknown to science, but it's generally agreed that at least one purpose is to help stabilize the root system and hold the tree in place in high winds.

Some of the cypress trees are well over a thousand years old. This has been confirmed by core drillings. (Core drillings are made by a special drill that makes a hole in the tree but leaves a core of wood that stays in the drill as it is removed. The age of the tree can be told by counting the annual rings left in the core.)

I was fascinated by the size of the trees. They are immense. Some are seven feet in diameter and at least one hundred feet tall. Most have had their tops broken off by hurricanes. Hurricane Hugo wreaked havoc on the trees of this area, which took a direct hit in 1989. Testimony to the strength of their root systems is the fact that only one in the swamp was uprooted.

Canoeing in the swamp is a challenge. There are so many broken tops and dead trees down in the water aside from the knees that there is very little room to maneuver. The turns are graded in two-point turns or three-point turns and so on, by the number of times you have to back up before you can get through. There are also lots of brown water snakes lying on floating logs and overhanging tree limbs that are hard to see. Jenny, who is a tour guide here, is quite adept at spotting them. We would have missed most of them had she not pointed them out.

We didn't feel threatened at all. Not one even moved as we passed. There are also lots of skinks. We saw one sitting motionless on a limb only inches from the head of a snake. Both were absolutely motion-less, the skink afraid of losing its life and the snake afraid of losing its lunch. When we came back an hour later, neither had moved. I don't know which one won.

The swamp is an almost magical place and we were sorry to see the trip end. Thanks to Jenny and the National Audubon Society which owns it and Francis P. Beidler who had the foresight to purchase 1,800 acres before it could be logged, we had a marvelous time. The forest is open to the public at a modest charge but reservations must be made for the canoe trip.

More next week ...

Life in the Swamp — Part II
May 30, 1998

Last week I wrote of my trip to Francis P. Beidler Forest in South Carolina and the canoe trip through a portion of Four Hole Swamp. Nobody seems to know why it's called Four Hole. The guides made up weird stories to tell the tourists so that they have something inter-esting to tell the folks back home. One story Jenny, daughter of my best friend Marie, tells that I like is that the original owners were very rich and had a very large and fancy outhouse and named the swamp after it. Makes sense to me.

The swamp is a fantastic place. It's just as I imagined the bayous of Louisiana would be. To get a better picture of the internal workings of a swamp, the owners and operators, who are the National Audubon Society, have built a boardwalk through it. It's a mile and a half loop built on stilts about two feet above the water. At least it was when we were there. The level fluctuates with the amount of rainfall, of course. This year has been a very wet one, some sixteen inches above normal. That's wet. Normally they have to discontinue canoe trips about mid-May, but this year they can go until close to mid-June.

The boardwalk itself is a piece of work. It's about three feet wide with four-by-four treated posts about every twelve feet. The posts extend high enough to support railings on either side. The floor is dead level, of course, or there would be places where it might dip into the water.

Every few hundred feet there is a place to sit and rest and just enjoy it. You almost feel as if you are in Jurassic Park, expecting to see dinosaurs, and you do occasionally! There is a side trail, also boarded, that leads to a small lake. We sat and rested and had a snack that we had brought for the occasion. We sat and looked and talked quietly, soaking in the grandeur of the place, when we noticed a floating log begin to move slowly. It came directly towards us, very slowly, leaving hardly a ripple. As it got closer, we could see a tail moving from side to side, propelling an alligator. He or she was about eight feet long and perhaps a foot and a half wide. When he got to within fifty feet of us, he just sank out of sight. There were a couple of heron nests in the trees near us and we surmised that he was waiting for one of the young, which were nearly fully grown, to fall out of the nest. A free meal is all that any self-respecting 'gator could hope for.

There were also lots of skinks, which look like tiny dinosaurs. They are a type of lizard. There were several kinds present, of different colors. The prettiest, to my notion, is the blue-tailed. He is almost invisibly camouflaged except for his brilliant blue tail. Why not camouflage the tail, too, while he's at it? The scientists that study these things say that it is a defense mechanism. A predator's attention is riveted on that pretty blue tail as he chases the skink. If he should catch up with the fleeing skink, he would naturally grab the tail, which breaks off while the rest of the skink escapes to grow a new tail. Now, that's pretty smart, I think.

It takes about two hours to mosey the length of the boardwalk and take in the sights. One nice thing, you can't get lost. There are lots of signs telling you the names of the trees and plants that you see. You get an education in spite of yourself. I saw trees that I've never seen or heard of and lots that grow right here in Hocking County.

The favorite, though, is the bald (or balled) cypress. (The only cypress I know of here are a patch at Lake Hope and one tree at the state forestry office on State Route 374.) I've said this before, I know, but it bears repeating, I think. It's the size and age of them that catches your attention. The ones on the boardwalk are even bigger than the ones on the canoe route. I suppose they built the walk so that you can see the biggest ones. That would make sense, I reckon. Nonetheless, it staggers the mind to stand beside and touch something that has stood there for at least a thousand years. It's something special. The only thing that can rival them for size would be the giant sequoias of California and the cedars of Washington and Oregon, and they're nearly all gone now.

Think back to what was happening 1,000 to 1,500 years ago. Some of these trees were growing in the times of the Roman Empire. These trees were here seven or eight hundred years before Columbus sailed the ocean blue. These trees were here when only the red man paddled his canoe among them in search of sustenance. Isn't it wonderful how much we've been able to destroy in less than a third of the life span of a tree? Thanks to the foresight of Mr. Beidler and the Audubon Society, we will be able to see these for a while. I'm sure that eventually we'll find a way to ruin these, too. A good dam upstream would do it.

The Four Hole Swamp is fragmented now. The Beidler Forest is only 1,800 acres. There are bits and pieces here and there, but in between it's farmland. In fact, just a half mile or so from Jenny's abode is a large tobacco farm. Nearby is a strawberry farm. The land is flat and apparently fertile even though it's mostly sand. The area around the forest is rural and agricultural in nature, but it's only a few miles to the interstate, and you know what that means.

Speaking of interstate, I had a wonderful trip home. We went down in Jenny's Explorer, which is a large and comfortable car. Marie was staying with Jenny a few days more and then they were going on a trip together, so I drove Jenny's other car home by myself. It's a Suzuki Samurai. A luxury car it ain't. It's somewhat akin to a baby buggy with a windup rubber band for a motor. On top of that, it was only running on three cylinders. I really had no hope of getting home without a major breakdown.

I started out slowly, with my fingers crossed. Once I got on the interstate, the minimum speed was forty-five so I had to speed up a bit. After an hour, when nothing had fallen off, I stepped her up to about fifty. The traffic got heavier as the day progressed so I kept going a little faster to keep from getting squashed.

By mid afternoon, I had my foot in the carburetor. It got up to sixty going downhill, but uphill I was going through the gears. I used to drive a truck, but the trucks today ain't like they used to be and neither are the drivers. They seemed especially resentful of someone driving a baby buggy when it's their God-given right to go eighty miles an hour on their roads. There were almost as many trucks on the road as cars.

I overtook exactly one truck on the whole trip. It was an old dump truck loaded with stone coming up a hill on the West Virginia turnpike. He was going fifteen and I was going seventeen. It made my day. Several times I thought I would be sucked up into the air cleaner of a huge diesel truck, but I managed to repel all challengers and made it home safe and sound, though slightly weary.

I pulled in home after dark, rolled up the driveway behind me and have been a recluse ever since. God bless Hocking County!

Getting There Isn't Half the Fun
December 27, 1999

For the past two or three years, my family has come to the Hocking Hills to spend Christmas Eve in my cabin and loved it.

But the memories of the good times were overshadowed by the memory of the lousy trip home in the dark. My son and family live in Wilmington, 120 miles away, and opted to stay overnight and proceed to Cleveland in the morning. My daughter and sons live in Lancaster and so it isn't much of a drive, but the rest of the in-laws and outlaws live in and around Delaware and so have a seventy-mile drive each way.

This year it was my turn. All were invited to my sister and her husband's home in Delaware. There is no good way to get there from here. The options are to go through or around Columbus. I usually go through, but there is so much construction going on that there are delays all over. To make things worse, I heard on the radio that there was a humongous wreck on I-71 that had traffic tied up for miles. I decided to take I-270 around, but which way? I seemed to remember that the east leg had some construction the last time I tried it. The west leg was it. I wanted to get a glimpse of my old stomping ground, Hilliard, anyway.

The trip around the outerbelt wasn't that bad in spite of heavy rain for the first forty miles. I could hardly believe my eyes when I got near Hilliard. Almost all the old landmarks were gone, replaced by monumental commercial buildings. The only way I could tell my approximate location was when I spotted the CompuServe building. A friend I went to high school with told me that he had sold eighty acres of his farm to the owners of the building. His farm was on Davidson Road, just north of Hilliard. Almost every speck of land for miles is covered with these monuments to commerce, clear up to and including Dublin. I was a stranger in my own homeland.

I had heard about construction on U.S. 23, which is the main route to Delaware. It's a nightmare in good conditions, so I was sure it would be thoroughly disgusting on Christmas Eve at rush hour. I opted for the Olentangy River Road. It has always been one of the prettiest roads in central Ohio and I looked forward to seeing how it had been treated. Except for the first mile or so through what is now Worthington Hills, it was mostly recognizable.

Most of the stately old farm houses I always admired were still standing. They were, for the most part, surrounded by new houses. Because of the price of land in that area, there were no "cheapies," though. There were plenty of condos, but most were tastefully done and the road was familiar. It hadn't been modernized. With a forty-five-mile-per-hour speed limit and light traffic, the trip was a pleasant one.

It was a dark, wet day, so the atmosphere was dismal. I felt sorry for the poor old river. It was squeezed between the road and a line of trees on the other side. It looked forlorn and melancholy, its dark waters capped with white foam that had escaped a sewage plant somewhere as it plunged off the rocks of the myriad riffles. The darkness of the day contributed to the darkness of the water, of course, but I couldn't help but remember the beauty of this river when I first knew it at the age of five or six, and how later, as a young man, I had tasted the pleasure of wading waist-deep in those same waters when they were fresh and clean, casting flies to black bass, rock bass and bluegills. It saddened me to see the once-proud beauty reduced to a ditch wending its way between rows of million-dollar houses and condos, carrying their waste to the sea. It has been declared a scenic river so that the actual river bed can't be altered or houses built closer than a specified distance, whatever that distance might be, but there are still too many, too close.

We never seem to do something to save a natural treasure until it's too late. I only hope that the people of Hocking County are taking notes. Our treasures are falling back in their battle against the onslaught of development pressure.

Anyway, I was soon in Delaware. I can no longer make a left turn onto my sister's street and had to go a half mile or so past, turn around and come back. I was the last to arrive and just in time to eat. We stuffed ourselves on a sumptuous dinner to which everyone contributed. The evening passed too quickly as my six-year-old granddaughter acted as Santa Claus, delivering all the presents from under the tree and reminding anyone who hadn't opened theirs in the right order to do so.

All too soon, it was time to make the return trip. After hugs and goodbyes, I went outside into a pouring rain and made a dash for the old pickup. Fortunately, the rain stopped soon and the trip home by the same route was uneventful. I actually saved fifteen minutes over what the trip usually takes, even though it was ten miles farther each way.

I think I'll use that route all the time now. By the time I arrived home, I was wrung out. One hundred and fifty miles, a big dinner and Santa Claus, all in a nine-hour period, is about all a fella oughta do in one day. Now I see why nobody wanted to come here this year.

All in all, it was a great day, well worth the effort, and I'm glad I went. I hope you all had as good a Christmas as I did and I wish you all a happy and prosperous new millennium!

Shoein' in the U.P.
March 18, 2000

One of the highlights of my year for the past several years has been a winter trip to our cabin in Michigan's Upper Peninsula, or U.P. as the locals call it. (The natives are affectionately called Yoopers.) Because of some medical problems, I haven't made the trip the last two years. My son and I scheduled the trip for the middle two weeks in February. We like to go at that time because the backbone of winter is usually broken by then. It usually doesn't get below minus twenty degrees and the snowfall is at peak depth.

As fate would have it, because of another medical problem, this time not serious but it had to be dealt with, I couldn't go at the appointed time. My son wanted to wait for me, but I persuaded him to take someone else and I would go later.

He called from camp and said that the weather was fine, twenty below and thirty inches of snow with more on the way. About that time, it turned warm here and we enjoyed seventy-degree weather. I felt my time to go snowshoeing was slipping away. It turned cold again and we had some snow here. I began to feel better.

It wasn't until the first week in March that I could get away. I invited a close friend to accompany me. Loading a liberal supply of clothes, food and lots of other stuff we probably wouldn't need, we started out about mid-morning. (Yes, I did remember the snowshoes, although I forgot a few essentials.) It's a fourteen-hour jump to the "Cozy Inn," a beer joint, the closest parking place to our cabin. It's a mile hike from there, and I didn't want to arrive after dark, so we opted for a Mom and Pop motel about a third of the way across the U.P.

The disconcerting thing that gnawed at our feelings was the complete absence of snow all the way up the lower part of Michigan. We traveled perhaps 200 miles west before we began to see some patches of snow beneath the forest canopy. It didn't look good. A blue sky and brilliant sun didn't help our feeling of unease. Neither did getting stopped for speeding. Luckily I have an honest face and an endearing manner, and the nice trooper let us go without a ticket, with the promise that I wouldn't go over fifty-five. I swore on my grandmother's bunions and kept an eye peeled for blue SUVs thereafter.

When we were within thirty or forty miles of camp, the snow depth increased to the point where we thought we might be OK. Since the cabin is a mile hike from the road and everything must be carried or dragged on a sled, we wanted snow. The gods who look after fools like me were smiling on us. There are three elderly gentlemen who, after a hearty breakfast at the Cozy, hike on snowshoes right past our place and keep the snow packed so that it doesn't melt as fast. We started up the trail pulling two sleds loaded with supplies. The trail was hard-packed and we didn't need snowshoes, so we left them in the truck. By the time we were about a third of the way, we regretted that move. As we got deeper into the woods, the snow was deeper and rotten, so that we broke through about every fourth or fifth step. Believe me, it really jars your backbone to fall through the crust and hit solid ground about a foot below. We used the shoes thereafter.

We found the cabin in good shape. My son had left it well-stocked with food and water and firewood. From there on it was delightful. For four days, the sky was the bluest of blue and the sun was magnificently warm. The thermometer rose a few degrees more every day until it topped out at sixty-six. We spent at least half our time hiking in the woods. It was a real challenge. It had rained the previous week, and with the warm days, the snow lay a foot or more deep in the shade, but in the sun the ground was bare. It meant put on the shoes for a hundred yards and then take 'em off for a hundred feet; then put 'em back on. It would have been easier if the snow were three or four feet deep as it usually is this time of year.

The U.P. depends heavily on snowmobilers to make it through the winters. Restaurants, bars, motels and gas stations can't survive the winters without them. This year, they were hurtin'. We took one day to drive out to the tip of the Kewanaw Peninsula, and most places were closed. The little restaurant where we usually eat was closed, as were all the others that we could find. We found a little general store that was open and had to pay seven bucks for a box of crackers and a small piece of cheese so that we wouldn't starve. They're hoping for a busy summer, but with the price of gas, I wouldn't count on it. I paid $1.70 a gallon. It cost nearly 200 bucks for gas alone.

The best day of the trip was the day before we had to leave. We hiked to a lake that is nearly two miles north of the cabin. It's a tough hike under good conditions, but the snow condition made it even worse. A couple of things made it more than worthwhile, though. First, we found a place where a moose had come out of a thicket and followed the same trail we were on. I don't know if he was a big moose or not, but he sure had big feet. We kept a sharp eye out for him. (One don't run fast on snowshoes, do one?) This was the trail that the old snowshoers followed daily, but they were smart enough to quit when things got tough.

We finally reached the lake about noon, drenched with sweat. What a sight it was. It's about a mile long and a half mile wide. No buildings are visible. The whole thing is owned by a well-to-do doctor, and I'm sure he has a cabin or mansion or something on it somewhere, but nothing is visible from our viewpoint. It's absolutely pristine. I envy him, but I'm grateful that he is keeping it as it is.

Most of the way around this lake, the forest comes right to the waterline, but the trail we were on ended 100 feet or so from a rock outcropping that stepped down to the water. It took a bit of scrambling to reach it. We could have never found a better place for lunch. We built a small fire at the water's edge and heated water for coffee and hot chocolate and took sandwiches, boiled eggs, cookies and candy from our packs and had a lunch to rival Planet Hollywood. They might have better food but not a better atmosphere. To sit and look across that snow-covered, frozen lake at the dark green balsam firs spearing the fantastically blue sky on the horizon is a sight I'll long remember.

The trip back to the cabin was also one to remember. Just across the beaver pond from the cabin, the trail leads up a steep rock formation, and the snow was deep there. It's a tough climb in snowshoes. I decided to walk at the edge of the pond to avoid it. All went well until the snow under my feet collapsed, and I found myself belly-down in two feet of snow and up to my thighs in icy water. The snowshoes went under the snow, and I couldn't get my feet out of the water. When I pushed my hands down to raise myself, they went in the snow up to my shoulders, and also into the water. My companion was able to jerk my shoes off and toss them where I could support my weight on them and get to a kneeling position on a little hummock of grass; I got my snowshoes back on and got back to solid ground. It's a good thing it wasn't twenty below. Ten minutes later we were drinking hot coffee in the cabin. What a wonderful day!

Ironically, after all that beautiful weather, the day we left dawned to snow and freezing rain. It wasn't a great drive back to the "Big Mac" bridge, but from there on it was fine, and we arrived home without mishap. All's well that goes well and ends well, as the saying goes.

Chapter 7
Personal Thoughts

Enjoying a Bit of Paradise
August 5, 1995

I am writing this from paradise, or at least as close to paradise as I've ever been. I'm sitting at the base of a waterfall, which is more like a series of chutes than an actual waterfall. Water is rushing past on both sides of me. The noise, though not deafening, makes conversation difficult.

The sky is the bluest blue I've ever seen. It makes the water in the lakes appear blue also. At closer inspection, it is coffee brown, typical of northern lakes. Low, white puffy clouds march toward me, propelled by a pleasant breeze. Almost at my feet, a mother loon is feeding two babies. She has dived at least 200 times since I arrived, each time returning with a small minnow in her beak. Apparently, the turbulent water from the falls makes a good hunting ground. The babies keep trying to dive, but their baby down is too fluffy to go under water. They must be satisfied to swim with their heads under water. Loons are born to the water and spend their entire lives on it. Their legs are so far back that they can hardly walk and they venture upon land only to nest, and that is on the water's edge.

I'm in Quetico Provincial Park in Ontario, Canada. It's 1,250 miles from Logan, just north of Minnesota. My companions and I entered the water in Minnesota and paddled across the border, going through Canadian customs on an island in the middle of Lake Saganaga and then into the park property. It's a minimum of fourteen miles paddling to an entry point. One must obtain permits and pay fees in advance.

The Quetico is about one million acres of wilderness with lakes numbering in the hundreds. Only seventy canoes are allowed at any one time, so people are spread pretty thin. You are allowed to go anywhere you want to provided you go through a predetermined entry point. Canoe is the only mode of travel. I doubt you could walk a mile in any direction without coming to another lake. We purchased maps of the area we wanted to travel and literally navigated from rock to rock with map on knee.

Most people travel in loop routes, returning to the starting point in a certain number of days. I prefer to find lakes off the beaten path and stay put several days at a time. I have stayed as long as two weeks without seeing another person. This is what the experience is all about. To be able to plan a trip, assemble all the supplies you will need, and be completely self-reliant for a period of time does wonders for the self esteem. The magnificent scenery and wildlife are a bonus.

There is a downside, however. For one, you must cope with millions of mosquitoes, flies and black flies. So much depends on the wind when you're dealing with insects. It's usually breezy during the day, so they aren't even around. When the wind drops toward dark, it's tent time.

It appears to be the law that the wind shall always blow in your face when paddling. The farther you have to go and the bigger the lake, the harder the wind shall blow. I've been going up there for nearly thirty years and have never broken that law.

Portages are the main barriers to having fun. These are the same ones used by the French Canadians in the fur trade 300 or so years ago. It gives one a sense of oneness with history to walk where historical figures have walked, to stumble over the same roots, to fall in the same lakes, to use the cuss words: Sacre Bleu!

You must make two trips, one with the canoe and another with your gear. There are outfitters who will rent you everything you need, and their canoes and gear are lighter than ours. I see some young bucks put on huge packs and the canoe on top and take off. I took pleasure in finding one such fellow collapsed at the top of the hill. It made me feel good to shoulder his pack and leave him panting on his knees.

In short, portages can be hell. Now there is a paradox: The price of living in paradise is suffering in hell.

We saw numerous eagles patrolling the lakes. One evening we decided to go for a twilight paddle. It doesn't get dark until almost 11 p.m. our time. As we rounded the end of our island, we encountered a moose swimming to our island. When she saw us she turned and swam right at us. Not having room in the canoe for a passenger, we did some fancy back paddling until she went back to her original course and landed in a little bay and began to eat water plants.

On our last evening, we cleared all portages so we could make a quick trip to the truck. We decided to camp on an island near the ranger station. We had just unloaded the canoe when we heard a rustling in the brush. Thinking it was a moose, we grabbed cameras and waited. We could see the alders swaying as it approached, whatever it was. To our amazement, out popped a bear. He looked at us and we looked at him. He turned and retraced his steps while we stood our ground. He then came around the other side of the bushes and came to within six or seven feet of us. He appeared in no way threatening, just curious, so we took a couple of pictures. The click of the cameras seemed to rattle him. Discretion being the better part of valor, he backed up and we backed up. We loaded the canoe and took off. As we went around the point, we saw him swimming to another island. I guess we showed him.

The thing that really bothers me is that down deep in my heart I know the wilderness cannot survive. If Quetico is still here in 100 years, I'll be greatly surprised. Man seems to have an innate desire to tame wilderness. If that were the only thing, there are enough dedicated people willing to protect it. But overshadowing everything we do is the biggest problem in the world today. There are just too damned many people. We are overwhelming this planet by sheer numbers.

In the olden days, we could count on plagues, wars and various diseases to keep us in check. Now, because of the wonders of science, we no longer die in childhood in the numbers we once did and we live longer. This is great. I don't want to go back, but we need to balance this by having fewer offspring.

At first glance, the Quetico doesn't have any valuable commodities — just rocks and trees. It was logged 100 years ago and made a full recovery, so it could be logged again, I suppose, and survive. But it can't stand the overwhelming crush of people. The one thing it has that people need is water. I can see that in the future we will run out of water and if it is politically expedient, the politicians will find a way to steal it and make it potable for the masses. We've seen it happen time after time.

Right now, the Canadian government is taking Indian lands in Northern Quebec to dam the Whale River to make electricity a thousand miles away from where it can be used, thus destroying a way of life for people who have lived there since there have been people in North America.

Unless we take steps to control our population, we will breed ourselves into extinction. Not a pretty prospect!

Passing Marks of the End of an Era
February 3, 1996

I heard this week of the passing of Loren Hansel. He and his brother, Claude, have been a fixture in these parts for as long as anyone can remember. Loren was about eighty-eight and Claude a couple of years older. Claude died about three years ago. Since then, it's been a rather lonely life for Loren. They lived together all their lives.

Theirs was a perfect example of the nineteenth century farm. All the fields were small and about the same size, just about what a man could handle with a team of horses. They always managed to get things done on time. Without the desire to get bigger and richer, they were able to get their planting, cultivating and harvesting done when it should be done. They seemed to have good crops despite bad weather.

Their endeavors were well diversified. If it was a bad year for one, it would be a good year for another. They raised Hereford beef cattle. I always enjoyed seeing them scattered over the hillside pasture or wading in the small crick that cut through it. Their farm is the thing that calendars are made of.

In addition, they raised chickens and sold eggs, and Loren kept about twenty hives of bees. Many are the neighbors who knocked on the door regularly to buy eggs or honey.

For many years, they attended the monthly meeting of the Hocking County Bee Keepers Association. I think that was their only social life. They always dressed in their Sunday suits. I think their suits and shoes are at least as old as I am. I guess they saw no need to squander money on something that was worn only two hours a month. Every fifty years was often enough to shop for a suit. I guess I can't argue with that.

The general impression was that they were a little tight with a buck. I don't think they were so much tight as thrifty. They had no aspirations to be anything but what they were — just hardworking farmers. They spent money on farm machinery when necessary, and took such good care of it that it lasted almost forever.

When I first moved here, there was some snickering among the neighbors about their tractor episode. It seems they had decided it was time to get a new tractor. After considerable debate and shopping, they decided on an Allis-Chalmers. It was duly purchased and delivered. Loren, though the youngest, was the boss and took over the new tractor, delegating the old one to Claude. Though Claude probably resented Loren taking charge, he rarely argued and did as he was told. Not this time, though! A dog fight ensued. Loren, recognizing that discretion was the better part of valor, retreated. The next day they went and bought another tractor exactly like the first. After that, they each had their own. His and his. And they never touched the other one.

Loren had a little plumbing business on the side. He mostly sold and installed well pumps, but occasionally did some residential repair. One fellow told me he had Loren repair some pipe in a rental house. He worked about three hours and charged him four dollars! Can you imagine that? He was still living in the distant past when the average man made a dollar a day. He was apologetic about charging a day's wages for an hour's work.

Neither Loren nor Claude ever married. Claude's farthest venture from home was when he was an Army cook in World War I. Rumor has it that Loren was sweet on his neighbor, Grace Harsh, who died a few years ago at about ninety-five years of age. They "kept company" for fifty years or so, but were reluctant to rush into anything.

The boys — and they were always known as the "Hansel boys" — had a beautiful barn that they were proud of. I was invited to view the inside once. It's a work of art. It has a rounded roof. Seen from the end, it looks almost like an arched cathedral window. It has a short section on the end of the rafters that makes an overhang. From there, it rises vertically two-thirds of the way, then curves back to the center. It is so steep that it would be impossible to climb it without scaffolding and ropes.

Inside, it is made of trusses bolted together at the top. There are no joists to get in the way of filling it with hay. The trusses are about thirty-five feet long. Loren told me that they ordered them from Sears-Roebuck and they came to Logan by railroad. They hauled them from Logan with tractors and wagons. The roof is sheeted with twelve-inch wide boards. I asked how they were able to nail on the boards and then shingle it since it was so steep. He told me they put the boards on from the inside while standing on scaffold boards suspended from the trusses, then shingled each board as they went, also from the inside. Pretty clever, I thought.

I'll miss seeing the boys as I go by. They were always working, except in the evening, when they sat on the front porch and waved as people passed. They had no living relatives that I know of, so I don't know what will happen to the farm. Nobody can buy a farm at today's prices and expect to pay for it farming, so I expect its farming days are over. It's too bad. A perfect example of what we love to remember as the "good old days" will pass from view before our eyes.

So long, boys. We'll miss you.

Inventing a History of Inventions
May 31, 1997

There have been more inventions in the last fifty years than any time in history. Some of them are mind boggling. Some are silly. Most are just improvements on existing inventions.

The automobile is an example of that. The new cars have so many gadgets that you need a degree in engineering to even drive one. Almost all are computer operated. You might not see one, but it's there somewhere. All of this is veneer. Peel that away and you still have four wheels, a transmission, an engine and a steering wheel — the basics. When you stop to think of it, that's just a series of improvements on the horse and buggy. The horse has been improved upon by adding the engine in its place. The four wheels are still there and the steering wheel replaces the driving lines. It didn't even have a transmission. To stop it, you hollered "Whoa!"

The greatest invention in recent history has to be the computer itself. It intrudes into almost every aspect of daily life. Everything from banks to libraries is computerized. It's really nice how humans no longer make mistakes. Everything can be blamed on computer errors. The mistakes in spelling in this column are all caused by computer error. Mistakes in your checking account are computer errors. Everybody is blameless and guilt-free. Life is so much easier for everyone.

I don't know which came first, the computer or the computer chip. I guess they had to have a computer before they needed a chip. Anyway, the invention of the chip has had a tremendous impact on our daily lives. It has allowed millions of Japanese to visit our shores and give us a little of our money back.

All of these things are truly great, but let's go back in time a little bit and check out some earlier inventions. For instance, who invented the first loaf of bread? Bread has come to be called the staff of life, but what did people eat before bread was invented? Scientists who study these things tell us that our earliest humans probably lived in trees at first and gradually became earthbound. They ate whatever they could find. Fruits, nuts, berries and seeds. Later, they learned to catch and kill game animals.

After roaming, eating things where they found them for millennia, came an invention that changed the way people lived. Probably the second invention, after the club, was the basket. It might have started as a skin bag, but it allowed people to take food home and save it. In order to do that, they had to make a home. It might have been a nest of leaves and twigs or a cave. Anyhow, it allowed people to stay in one place and bring sustenance home. They didn't have to be constantly on the move.

After a while, some smart aleck found out that wild plants could be brought near home and planted so they didn't have to go so far afield. The fruit of their labor could be harvested at home, and agriculture was born.

What about the bread? Well it probably took several thousand years for that to come about. What do you need to make bread? Fire, grain, a leavening agent and a cooking utensil. Early man didn't have fire except when it occurred naturally, lightning striking a tree or some such event. He learned how to keep it going and nurse it and even carry it eventually, but learning to light it was a long time coming.

Among the wild plants they ate were grasses that produced seeds in large quantities. One of those was probably an ancestor of wheat, which they eventually learned to propagate. I suppose they parched it in the fire at first and then later learned to pound it with rocks to make it easier to chew. This probably led to the discovery of flour, which is just finely-ground wheat. Someone spilled water on some flour and ruined it. It was thrown in or at the fire where some of it landed on a hot rock and cooked. Some inquisitive child might have eaten it and found it good and started a trend. Later a mixture of flour and water was left out too long and got moldy and sourdough came into being.

All this had to be cooked on a flat rock. We had to wait several thousand years for someone to invent iron smelting and make a loaf pan. That's a whole 'nother story. Like most great inventions the whole process is one accident after another.

Cheese was invented several thousand years later by a lonely goat herd. (It's incredible that we had to wait this long for a cheese sandwich.) He slept in caves in what was later to become Italy, I believe, as he took his herd from place to place, following the grass. One of the things he used for food was goat's milk, of course. He left a bowl of milk in one of the caves as he led the goats to another pasture. It was several weeks before he came that way again. He arrived late and in the rain. He went to bed hungry and in the morning, he found the bowl of milk, which by now was a solid mass. It probably didn't smell too good, either, but being famished, he gingerly tried it. To his surprise, it was good. He started leaving bowls of milk in every cave and started the cheese industry. Sad to say, he soon ran out of bowls and started stealing them from the townspeople. He was caught and executed, which saved him from a fate worse than death. You see, after eating nothing but cheese for three months, he was severely constipated and it was only a matter of time before he would have exploded. Lucky for us, he had told his brother how to make cheese or we might not have cheese today. There aren't really that many goats — or caves, either, for that matter. This proved to be a boon to pizza makers.

So, you see, most of the great inventions are the result of accidents. I wish I could accidentally invent a squirrel-proof bird feeder. I've been trying for years to invent one on purpose. It will take a very large accident to get one to work.

It Gives Me the Chills
June 14, 1997

Do you have a theme that keeps running through your life — something that keeps popping up over and over like a bad dream? I do, and it's something that I wish would go away.

It's refrigerators.

It seems there is always a refrigerator skulking in the background, waiting to jump out and surprise me.

We didn't even have a refrigerator when I was a kid. We had an icebox. That seems a rather mundane, inert object, but it managed to keep me in hot water, or, I should say, cold water. It had a pan underneath to catch the water from the melting ice. From the time I was about six years old, it was my job to empty that pan. The trouble was, I usually forgot to empty it until I stepped in that icy water as it ran across the kitchen floor. I remembered real quick if my dad was the one who stepped in it.

It wasn't until after World War II that refrigerators began to be common. The factories that made war materials were out of work when the war was over and began to cast around for something to make. During the war, almost no domestic goods were produced and people were hungry for labor-saving devices. Several big factories began making appliances.

At that time, I worked for a grain elevator in Hilliard that also had a hardware and appliance store. The owner was a wheeler-dealer who saw what was happening. He managed to make deals with several appliance manufacturers and soon we were getting refrigerators and freezers by the truckload.

Guess who got to deliver a lot of them? Right, little ol' me. I was young and strong and learned quickly and was soon doing the bulk of the deliveries with whatever help we could scrape up at the time. It was nothing to start out in the morning with ten or twelve appliances on my truck and deliver them all over hell's half acre.

That was before the invention of the refrigerator dolly that could go up and down steps relatively easily. We had to carry them. It seemed that most of the fridges went in second or third floor apartments and the freezers went in basements. The freezers were the worst because they were so big. Most of them went to farmers who wanted

179

enough room to store a cow and a couple of hogs, and all the garden surplus.

The appliances were made of steel in those days because it was cheap, I guess, and there was an overabundance of dolts like me who didn't balk at heavy things. Later, light-weight metal and plastic were used to make them much lighter. Also, new insulation was invented so that they could be made smaller and still have the same capacity inside.

It's a good thing, too, because since I always had a truck of some sort, I frequently got drafted to help friends and relatives move from house to house. I still do, occasionally. I had one brother-in-law and his wife who moved seven times the first two years they were married. It got so all I had to do was back the truck up to the door and whistle and their stuff marched out and climbed on the truck by itself.

When I moved to Hocking County, I sold almost everything I had but the refrigerator and freezer. They had to be stored temporarily, then moved again when the house was completed. The fridge gave out in a year or so and had to be disposed of and a new one was moved in to take its place. The freezer died shortly afterward and had to be removed.

When I moved to my present place, I lived in temporary quarters adjacent to the shop and moved the refrigerator in there. A couple of years later, I let a neighbor use my shop for two weeks while I went on a canoe trip to Canada. When I returned, I was nearly knocked down by the stench emanating from my kitchen. The friend had accidentally turned off the circuit breaker that ran the refrigerator and for two weeks the freezer compartment contents had been composting. In spite of all the cleaning and deodorizing I could do, that stench remains today. Even the mice won't go near it.

That should have been the end of my refrigerator exploits, but it was not to be. My friend, Jack, gave me an old gas refrigerator for my new house because I built it with a twelve-volt solar system and didn't have enough juice to run an electric one. Jack only weighs about ninety pounds soaking wet — and he hardly ever gets soaking wet — so you can guess how much fun I had with that one. I wrestled it in my house by myself when I got it home.

You would think that would be my last episode. I did. But it was not to be. When we built our cabin up in Michigan, it was in the wilderness and there was no thought of electricity there. A couple of ice chests worked fine.

Jack said, "We gotta get a refrigerator and I think I know where I can get one. My barber has a gas one we could get, I think." Sure enough, in a few weeks, his barber said we could have one if we went after it.

On the appointed day, my son came to help and we went to pick up Jack. He said it was in the Legion Hall in a nearby town and he had the key. We soon found the building, but the key wouldn't fit. We checked all the doors and windows and all were secured. We were debating over what would be the easiest way to break in when the barber showed up.

"What'n the hell ya doin' here, Jack?" were his first words.

"We're lookin' for that stupid refrigerator," was the reply.

"You idiot, it's two blocks down the street in the Masonic Hall."

We got away from there quick before the police came and went to the Masonic Hall. If you guessed it was on the street level, you guessed wrong. It was up the longest flight of steps I've ever seen. It was over a grocery store with fourteen-foot ceilings. Luckily, we had an appliance cart and my son is about the size I used to be. We got it down without incident and hauled it to Michigan.

There we had to haul it by trailer behind a quadrunner over a mile of wilderness trail studded with boulders and wrestle it into the cabin by brute strength and awkwardness. That, I hoped, would be my last time.

But you know there's more. A friend had an old "refer" that she suspected of running up her electric bill. She had it hauled away and used a little box like you'd use in a camper for a couple of months. It brought down the bill dramatically. My son thought his had gone bad and got a new one. When he moved the old one, he discovered it had some of his daughter's toys stuck in the works. When he cleaned it out, it worked perfectly. He gave it to my friend and brought it to my house. I delivered it last week.

It was on a trailer. The ground was wet from rain and I couldn't get it up to her house. We had to take it off the trailer and put it in the back of her daughter's four-wheel-drive Explorer. She got it up without incident and we took it in through a bedroom. When we finally got it into the kitchen, it was as big as the old one and she knew it would cost as much as the old one to run. She didn't want it. We had to take it back out, load it on the four-wheel-drive, then put it back on the trailer and take it to a storage shed and unload it again. Three moves in an hour.

Now this is positively, absolutely the last move of a refrigerator for me. I've been haunted all my life by those big square boxes and I positively, absolutely refuse to move another one! Unless, of course, I have to.

Charles Kuralt: A legend in His Own Time
July 12, 1997

A sad event occurred this week. I lost a good friend. Actually, we all did.

Charles Kuralt died. I never met him, but he always seemed like a friend to me. I felt that he was talking directly to me when he spoke. I tried to never miss his TV program, "Sunday Morning."

His rich deep voice was soothing to the ear. He spoke slowly and distinctly with the cadence of a poet reciting his own poems aloud. He was, of course, because he wrote his own lines. He was a writer before he was a television personality. His way with words was unique. Would that I had his gift.

Charles — somehow, it never seemed right to call him "Charlie," and no one ever did, to my knowledge — got his start in broadcasting as a war correspondent during the Vietnam war. He had a knack for feeling out the human side of the conflict rather than the violent, bloody side. His reports made us feel as though there were people there, rather than just machines of destruction.

For several years before his last assignment as host to "Sunday Morning," Kuralt traveled the country in a motor home, searching out quiet and unusual people and places that would be of interest to his audience. These aired several times a week on the CBS Evening News. You would think that eventually he would have found his way to Hocking County, wouldn't you?

Truth is, he did. I didn't learn about it until a year or so later. Carter Holiday, a good friend of mine and a potter at the time, told me that he had met Charles when he went to interview old Dwight Stump, the only indigenous basket maker in the area. I don't know if that ever made the news or not. I never saw it or heard from anyone who did. Carter directed Kuralt to my place, but he had commitments elsewhere and didn't have time — maybe next time through. I guess there wasn't a next time. That would have been the highlight of my humble career if he had showed up. It would have been particularly exciting if his motor home had smashed through my rickety old bridge. I think that then he would have had something to write home about.

I had mixed feelings when it was announced that the "On the Road" shows would be discontinued and he would host "Sunday Morning." I enjoyed "On the Road," but the segments were only a few minutes long and I hoped that an hour and a half and a studio would make a better venue. It did. His homey style made us enjoy things that we might not have watched otherwise.

Kuralt's appearance has been described as "rumpled," and I think it was a good description. "Lumpy" might also fit. He was rather chubby and either couldn't or didn't bother to find clothes that fit well. I'm sure some expensive tailor could have made him look better, but he, in effect, said, "Here I am, this is me, please accept me as I am."

I did — bow tie, wrinkled collar and all. I like a man who is comfortable with himself. It also made me comfortable. He perched on a stool on a bare stage with no props to hide behind and talked to us as friend to friend.

The other morning at breakfast, when I heard the news that he had died, I felt like I had been hit with a brick. Tears ran down my cheeks and into my cereal bowl. It was almost as if my brother had died. I'm not often affected that way and I was surprised at my reaction.

When he left the Sunday show a couple of years ago, I didn't understand why he would quit when he was at the top of his game. They replayed his farewell speech on the evening news last night and I think now I understand. He seemed to know that this was "goodbye" and not merely "so long." He knew then that it was over and he wanted to enjoy what time he had left. There were vague rumors in the last few months that he was going back on the road and small segments would appear on news programs occasionally, but they never materialized. I'm sure he knew that they never would.

It's a shame that such a voice is forever stilled, especially at such a young age. He was only sixty-two. I guess the old adage that the good die young holds true.

Goodbye, Charles. I, for one, will miss you. I wish you could send us tapes of your new adventure. I'm sure you'll enjoy it to the fullest.

Fallin' in Love Again
July 26, 1997

The first time I fell in love, I was just six years old.

There was this beautiful little girl I adored. She was my age. I saw her only at the movie theater a few blocks from home. I went almost every Saturday or Sunday in my early years and it was the highlight of my week when I saw her. Her name was Shirley Temple.

She could sing cute little songs like "On the Good Ship Lollipop" and tap dance with the likes of Arthur Treacher and Bill "Bojangles" Robinson. She was terrific. I courted her there until I, and she, were twelve years old. She never really responded to my advances but I'm sure she knew that even though I had other sweethearts, she was my "main squeeze," as they say. I just couldn't take my eyes off her. She had pretty blonde hair that hung in ringlets, and wonderful dimples that appeared when she smiled and sparkling blue eyes. She had me hooked.

As I got a little older, another love came along. Her name was Judy Garland. She sang like an angel. She made picture after picture and stayed twelve years old for about five years. I caught up to and passed her by the time I was twelve. I still loved Shirley, but Judy gradually became the one. I hoped they wouldn't both appear on the same day. I was lucky. Even though there was almost always a double feature, they never were on together. I would have been terribly embarrassed if they had started fighting over me.

When I was twelve, we moved to the country, far from a picture show. The only movies we saw were free, put on by the fire department. They were shown on a couple of sheets sewn together to make a screen, which was hung from the water tower in front of the jail in beautiful downtown Hilliard. These films were very old. They were made before Shirley and Judy were born. We could count on missing about ten minutes of sound every time a train went through town. We sat on the curb or on the street. Some people brought lawn chairs, but we couldn't afford them.

Later, when I was in high school, one of my pals got a Model A. (For you under sixty, a Model A was a Ford car that supplanted the Model T.) He was a few months older than I and got his driver's license the summer I was fifteen. My mother let me go with him and some of our friends. I was surprised that she would let me go to downtown Columbus without adult supervision. I'd tell her what we did, which was stop at Tony's Coney Island for a hot dog and a coke or Gene's for a hamburger and a milkshake. She knew my friends and didn't worry. She said boys were no trouble. It was girls you had to watch. They could come home with a little surprise under their aprons.

I fell in love again. This time with Lana Turner. Boy, was she built! She really knew how to wear a sweater. There was also Alice Faye. She wasn't as pretty as Lana, but when she looked at me, I felt that she liked me for myself and not just for my money.

June Allyson was the sweetest one. She was so cute and cuddly and had a cute little lisp. (I can't believe she's on television now, pushing diapers for those with weak kidneys.) She always played the part of the sweet, loyal lady waiting for her lover to return from the war. I hoped she would come to me while he was gone, but she never did.

On the way home from these shows, we would critique them with such profound statements as "Boy! That Betty Grable sure has got a body!" The plot didn't matter much.

After the war, I fell again, this time for Doris Day. She must have made fifty movies and remained a virgin on the verge through forty-nine of them. I think she was married to Rock Hudson in one of them. She was to me the ultimate, unattainable doll. I wished that somehow I would be the one that finally got her. She was soft and gentle and totally luscious. I dreamed of her.

Some leading ladies like Bette Davis and Joan Crawford did nothing for me, although they were great actresses. They just didn't have what it takes to turn a young man on.

With the advent of television, movies weren't so popular for a while. I did see a few. I fell madly for Audrey Hepburn. Her elegance simply overwhelmed me. She was the epitome of elegance. She was so graceful. Even though she died several years ago in her sixties, I see her occasionally in an old movie on TV and she's still a beautiful thirty-five.

Julie Andrews stole my heart in the sixties. Her voice made her look beautiful even if she wasn't a raving beauty. She was, and still is, graceful and lively.

It seems as I look back at the movies that I judged a show not by the plot, but by how soon and how hard I fell in love with the leading lady. I think the last movie I saw was "Pretty Woman," starring Julia Roberts. When I saw her on TV, my first thought was that she's really sort of homely, but before that movie was over, I was completely in love with her, and she was a hooker at that. It's hard for me to believe, but that must have been a good movie, or she is a good actress.

It's a good thing that "Baywatch" wasn't a movie when I was in high school or I would have walked to Hollywood just to get a look at those dolls. I saw a piece about them on TV the other night. What a bunch of absolutely gorgeous young ladies — and I do mean young! They all look alike and all look about nineteen. They also have great swimsuit designers.

I hope I don't come across as a dirty old man. I am old, but when I get too old to take notice of a beautiful woman, you can start shoveling dirt in my face.

Soap Box
August 16, 1997

If you were to ask a hundred people to vote "yea" or "nay" on the statement, "The government is run by a bunch of idiots," you would get a whole lot more "yeas" than "nays."

When we speak of "government," we usually mean the federal government. Why do we mistrust government so? I can't say for sure. We all have different reasons, I suppose.

One reason, I think, is that we have no voice in the government. Even though we have a democratic system, with duly-elected representatives, we really have no voice. How many of us actually know a senator or representative? Outside of county or state party bigwigs, I'll wager almost nobody does. If it weren't for TV, most of us wouldn't know who they are. Then the best-known are more apt to be recognized for being in some sort of scandal. We have no contact with them.

The government is like a headless centipede with legs reaching into every facet of our daily lives. There are countless agencies scattered all over the country which are not in touch with Washington. Part of this is our fault. We don't vote when we can. We seem to show more interest in a school board election than important national elections. The country is just too big and there are too many people for us to get interested in distant issues. Every county and small town has at least one.

The original concept of the Constitution — giving specific powers to federal government, with all else controlled by the states — seems to have been changed, bit by bit, piece by piece, to the government controlling everything but what they can't fund, and that returns to the states. They keep nibbling away at us until we wake to find ourselves gone.

I wish that our founding fathers could have foreseen this and put into the Constitution a provision that all laws would expire in one or two years unless reexamined and voted on again. Once a law is passed, it's there forever unless Congress adds to it. I don't recall one ever being dropped, only reinforced.

The state government is a little less intrusive, but we still have very little say in it. Where does our representative live? Most of us couldn't answer that. I couldn't, except that one of them, State Sen. Nancy Chiles Dix, writes in The Logan Daily News. She's from Hebron, in Licking County, which is fairly close. Before that our rep was from Hillsboro, which is a "fur piece." We never saw him except at election time.

Thank God for local government. Most of us know our county commissioners or town council members and mayors. We can make our feelings known to them at about any time. Their meetings are open to the public and we can corral them in the hardware store or on a street corner. We might not change their minds, but at least they will hear us. This is the cornerstone of democracy. If we can deal on this level, we can feel good about the part of government that we live closest to.

I didn't start out to make a speech on a soap box. I just heard something on the news the other night that really rankled me. That's what I wanted to write about. The other stuff is just a preface.

One of the magazine shows, "Dateline NBC" or "20/20," I think, had a segment on the FDA (Federal Drug Administration), which was refusing to approve an experimental drug used in the treatment of Lou Gehrig's Disease because it wasn't helping enough people to warrant its existence. That might be true, but what about those who are being helped?

I have a friend who has that disease. (For those of you who are unfamiliar with it, it is a disease that causes the muscles to atrophy. One by one, the muscles shrivel and become useless. Eventually, the patient is left a useless mass, unable to move. It's extremely painful in the later stages. Death is inevitable.) My friend has had this disease for four or five years. He was still able to work some, but was failing when this drug, and I don't know the name of it, came on the market. His doctor suggested he try it, and it worked. The progress of the disease was arrested and he, for the first time, had hope. This is no cure. He knows that. But research into a cure is going on, and perhaps with the help of this drug, he could hold on long enough that they might find a cure.

But no. The great gods in Washington said that since it isn't helping a lot of people, it will help no people. Now there's democracy in action. What would it hurt for a few people to take a drug that could save their lives?

This brings to mind the plight of cancer patients who are dying and can get relief from pain only from smoking marijuana. The Food and Drug Administration says no. Marijuana is addictive and can't be used by anyone legally. Who cares if a dying man gets addicted? He's going to die, anyway. Why not let him die in peace even if he is addicted? He will surely quit smoking when he dies, unless, of course, he's shoveling coal in the hereafter. Then it's the devil's problem.

The same thing happened a few years ago. There was a harmless product called Laetrile made from peach pits or something like that. Some people were advocating it be used as a cure for cancer. Some doctors thought it was hogwash and maybe it was, but those that were taking it swore that it helped. The government refused to legalize it in this country because it was thought that people would use it instead of getting proper treatment. The people I heard from said they were taking it as a last resort because there was no treatment in their cases.

The substance was available in Mexico so people either smuggled it into the U.S. or moved to Mexico. I would assume that they are all dead by now. They would have died anyhow, if it didn't work, but at least they died knowing that they tried something, rather than just giving up. I don't know where the feds get the idea that we must be protected from ourselves — that we don't have the brains to look after ourselves. A lot of us don't, I'm sure, but that should be our business, not Uncle Sam's.

Anyhow, I hope you'll forgive me for speechifying. I just had to get that off my chest. I wish Ol' Will Rogers were still here. He made a career out of criticizing the government, and he did it in such a charming manner that they loved him for it. (It didn't change anything, though.)

Army Daze
September 6, 1997

The other evening I meandered through the woods to visit my long-time friend and neighbor John Brenneman, who is recovering from a recent heart attack. He's doing nicely, I might add. He was driving near Logan the night of the attack when he noticed the symptoms and drove immediately to Hocking Valley Community Hospital.

Thanks to quick emergency care by the staff and a helicopter to take him to Columbus, he didn't sustain the damage that might have occurred otherwise.

Anyway, as we sat on his veranda and watched a beautiful sunset, we debated whether the clouds were pinkish orange or orangish pink. As the light faded we were visited by a couple of does and fawns. John put out some corn and they fed contentedly. We watched and talked in the deepening twilight and suddenly they were gone. We listened to the quiet, punctuated by an occasional truck on the highway a quarter mile away. We wondered how a kid driving by could hear after being confined in his (or her) car with radio speakers the size of refrigerators in the back. We could feel the vibrations before we could hear the thump, thump, thump of bass notes.

We talked on into the darkness of cabbages and kings and other important things. One subject always brought up another and we whiled away another delightful hour. It's so seldom that either of us has had time for socializing in the past several years that we just haven't talked this way for a long time. I think we'll do it more often now. Life has a habit of slipping away, leaving small things undone.

During the course of these discussions, John said something that reminded me of several incidents that happened while I was in the Army during World War II. John enjoyed them and suggested I write them down.

Now I'm not a war hero. In fact, I wasn't even crazy about going into the service. I had lived with this war for years before I was old enough to serve and it didn't seem very glamorous to me. Coming home from a long visit in a GI casket left a lot of things undone. When my time came I went without protest and tried hard to be the best soldier I could be, but the day they dropped the bomb on Hiroshima, I gave a huge sigh of relief. I was doing my duty, attacking a 100-pound sack of potatoes with an M1 potato peeler, when the news came over the radio. I was the hero of the day when I shouted the news to my weary compatriots as they returned from a fifteen-mile hike, footsore and dragging. They came alive again when they heard my tale. Supper was a boisterous affair. They didn't even complain about the eyes I had left in some of the potatoes.

We all thought that training would be canceled and we would go home the next week. In truth, it was another year before we got those walking papers. We had to continue our basic training to the end. It was hard to get serious about destroying an enemy that was already destroyed. If we had known what we know now, that we won the military war but lost the economic war, we would have gladly climbed on the next boat to Japan.

I was shipped from training in Texas to Camp Roberts in California, there to be a trainer instead of a trainee. It was sort of like graduating from high school one week and being a high school teacher the next. I wasn't too secure in that position. As each company graduated, it was not replaced. As the men with longer service were discharged, they were not replaced either. As you can imagine, the place began to shrink.

Soon I was a platoon sergeant. As the veterans were discharged, I climbed the ladder by attrition. I was top dog over a gang of pups. I was platoon sergeant although officially I was still a private.

It became apparent that this was the last group to go through training. The rumor mill worked overtime. It had the camp closing soon. Morale fell as the experienced men left and we "wet behind the ears" guys tried to maintain control. Training became minimal. On one training exercise the wheels fell off.

We were to do a compass course. The lieutenant in charge said, "This course will take forty-five minutes to complete. You have three hours to finish. I don't want to see a single man back here sooner than that."

Who could resist a situation like that? The troops dispersed into the countryside and took cover. This was rolling country and very dry. The hills were barren but all the ravines and draws had stunted trees which provided at least minimal cover. In five minutes not a man was visible. Most threw down packs and rifles and just goofed off. Several groups played cards or shot craps. It was an assignment to remember.

This was also the day the commanding general decided to inspect the troops. He came zooming over the hill in his jeep with driver, his general's two-star flag waving. The troops, seeing his approach, did what any self-respecting gang would do. They scattered like a covey of quail when a fox jumped them. The general, rising to the occasion, rounded them up with his jeep like a cowboy rounding up strays.

After ascertaining the company to which they belonged, he chewed them out and went to have a discussion with the company commander, who should have been in the field with his troops. The captain, first sergeant and company clerk were all busily engaged with official business. They all sat, feet on desks, reading comic books and didn't see him approach, and therefore didn't snap to attention as required by military code. This didn't make the general happy.

After the required chewing out, he went to battalion headquarters to register his discontent with basically the same results. He was not a happy camper. We at the bottom of the pyramid fared better than those at the top. Up there were bigger butts to chew.

After that, things went down hill in a hurry. The trainees were shipped out and soon there was no one left but instructors.

The commanding general, seeing his kingdom melting away, saw that he had to do something. After all, this was a training camp. He had to train somebody. He sent out an order that everyone in camp would start basic training all over again. That brought cheers of joy from all hands. All but a couple anyhow. A friend, Bill Granch, and I were discussing the situation that evening when Bill said, "If they think I've gone through basic and fought oversees for three years just to take basic all over again, they've got another thing coming."

"What are you going to do?" I replied, "Go AWOL?"

"Just during the day," was his answer. "Right after breakfast, I'm headin' for the hills. Wanta come with me?"

After considering the proposal long and hard for about fifteen seconds, I said, "Deal me in."

And so the die was cast. The next day after breakfast we picked up what we could swipe for lunch at the mess hall, swung past the barracks where we had stashed a deck of cards, some books and magazines, and embarked on a two-week vacation, coming home each afternoon for supper and a warm bed. It was a delightful time. Just to while away the carefree days in leisure was a luxury I've seldom seen since. It started me on my life of civil disobedience with a twist. I don't protest and raise Cain over unjust situations, I just ignore them. It works for me.

Holiday Fights Off Gray November's Gloomy Melody
November 15, 1997

Oh, it's a long, long time
From May to December
But the days grow short
When you reach September.

That is the first verse of "The September Song," a very popular song of some thirty or so years ago. Whoever wrote it, and I should know but I've forgotten, apparently never spent an autumn in Ohio. If he had it would have been called "The November Song."

I seem to forget from year to year just how lousy the weather can be in November. September is usually just an extension of summer and October is delightful, but when November arrives, it's like pulling a gray curtain over the world. The sun takes a vacation and the cold wind substitutes for it. Winters are for the most part unpleasant, but we expect that.

When we are coasting through a beautiful October, it's a slap in the face when we suddenly see the end of the colorful leaves, sunny days and chilly nights. We know it's coming, but we're never quite ready for it. Suddenly, we are forced to check the weatherstripping on windows and doors. Pipes that are subject to freezing must be insulated. We should have done that in September, but it was just too nice to worry about that stuff. There's plenty of time. We still have October to enjoy. Well, surprise, surprise. It's over. It's judgment day.

I thought a month ago that I was ready for winter. I have the woodshed full and enough propane to last until January. The weather-stripping is still good from last year. There is enough sawdust on the septic tank to keep the drain from freezing. All is in readiness.

Uh-oh. I forgot to put a new heat tape on the well-pipe. I didn't check the pipes under the cabin or replace the Styrofoam panels on the utility room door that two little rugrats tore off in July. I'd better check my supply of heat lamps. They are sometimes hard to find during a prolonged cold snap in winter. I guess I'm not as ready as I thought.

That's the only saving grace of November. It serves as a reminder of what's coming before conditions are really dangerous. Unpleasant as November is, it's not really dangerous.

When I was a kid on the farm, November was taken seriously. The wheat had better be growing and green or there would be no crop next July. Any corn that wasn't husked by now would most likely have to wait until the ground was frozen. To take a team or a tractor and wagon into a muddy field would do a lot of damage to the wheat. Usually, by mid-November, it was too late.

November was butchering month. The weather was cold enough to keep the meat from spoiling before it was cooled. It was a cruel blow to lose the winter's meat supply because the weather suddenly turned warm. That seldom happened in November. It was a good feeling to have a beef hanging in the upground cellar and a hog in the smokehouse. This was before the advent of the home freezer. A lot of farms didn't even have electricity. It's hard to believe so much has changed in just fifty years.

The one bright spot in November was, and is yet, Thanksgiving. I liked Thanksgiving more than Christmas and I guess I still do. For one thing, I suppose, it's not mandatory to go shopping for gifts. The retailers have found a way around the snow. They start the big push for Christmas shopping at Halloween and by Thanksgiving we are so brainwashed that some people jump up from Thanksgiving dinner and work off the overstuffed feeling at the malls — Christmas shopping.

At home on the farm the day was for visiting or hosting friends and family. We had a meal that the pilgrims would have envied. The fun was not all in the eating, however. My mother was a great cook and loved a get-together or a party. She and we kids spent several days getting ready. She would make pies and cakes a day or two ahead. She also made an English plum pudding just as her mother had done when she was at home in her native England. She made two a year, the other for Christmas. She made them a year in advance. The one she made this year would be wrapped in cloth and boiled. She then hung it in the attic and took down the one from last year and we'd eat that one this year. I know it sounds a bit bizarre, but I have never tasted anything as good. Mom would take off the cloth and wrap the pudding in a new one. She put it on to boil about midway through the meal and it was served piping hot with a special sauce (also hot). Magnifico!

We hardly ever had turkey because there was no place near to buy the young poults to raise. We had home-grown rooster and roast beef, along with potatoes, turnips, peas, carrots, green beans and beets, all from the garden. With the main part of the meal came Yorkshire pudding, which is not a dessert. It's not even sweet. It's made of flour and eggs and the grease from roast beef. It is served with gravy. I've never had it anywhere else except once in Yorkshire and it was lousy.

When dinner was over the women folks did the dishes while the men talked. Of course, the women talked, too; they talked so much they didn't realize they were working. At least that's what the men said. When dinner settled a bit, the men would go rabbit hunting. I think it was mostly to get away from the chatter of the women and the kids.

As wonderful as those days were, we can't go back. They have to be filed away in our memories, to be pulled out and reviewed upon occasion. We must go forward with life. When I look out, I still see gray November. That much hasn't changed. I've managed to get through seventy or so Novembers, and I'm good for another twenty at least. November makes us appreciate the rest of the year. I'm really looking forward to March.

Catching up with Ann
August 22, 1998

My daughter called a couple of weeks ago to say that Ann was coming for a week or so. I was happy to hear that. It's been eighteen years since I saw her last.

Our first meeting was in, I think, 1970. We (my wife, son and daughter) went down to the bus station to pick her up. We were early, and we waited a little nervously. Would we recognize her? Would she like us? We had corresponded with her and she had sent her picture, but it was only a small front face shot. All of a sudden there she was, a small dark-haired girl in the shortest skirt I'd ever seen except on a cheerleader. (It was the style at home, she said.)

She came up to us smiling and holding out her hand, loaded down with luggage. She was obviously nervous but trying to be bold. I'll give her credit, she handled the situation better than I could have. She had just flown into New York the day before and been put on a bus with several other foreign students and a chaperone for the trip to Columbus. She had come from Cardiff, Wales, to live with us for a year.

We had been approached several months earlier about hosting a foreign student through our daughter's senior year of high school. We had a couple of interviews with AFS officials, and they came to our home to check it and us out. They approved us in the end. We signed papers accepting the responsibilities and attended some training sessions so we would know what to expect.

I should mention that AFS stands for American Field Service. That is an organization formed by a group of ambulance drivers who served in World War I. After the war they wanted to continue to serve. This was their way of trying to bring peace to the world after the terrible things they had seen in the war. They thought that if the young people could get to know and like each other they would be less likely to kill each other when they were adults. A noble endeavor, I think you will agree.

Anyway, that evening was the beginning of a year that changed all our lives for the better. There were hugs all around. That wasn't easy for me because I was raised without touching another person unless it was to pop 'em one. It took a lot of getting used to, but eventually I came to accept it as a fact of life. I must admit I rather enjoy it now.

We took Ann into our home and our hearts. Soon she was a member of the family. She enriched our lives in ways we hadn't thought of. We had to take her to various meetings where she was the speaker of the evening and we learned to mingle with students from other lands, so that we learned more of other countries and their customs.

When the end of the year was near, we had to think about giving her up. That was the hardest part of all. We dreaded the day when she would leave, but it finally came. We had to load her and all her belongings in the old station wagon and take her to Boardman, Ohio, which is in the Akron area, as I recall, and put her on one of several buses with many other AFSers. They were to tour the eastern part of the country for two weeks before flying home. The departure was heart-breaking and we all cried. We followed the buses for several miles, hoping she would jump off and we would have her back, but it didn't happen, and we reluctantly turned toward home.

At the same time Ann was touring east, more buses were coming here from the west. We hosted them in our homes. We had students from Japan, Nigeria, Germany, Spain, France and many other countries staying in our community, so we were hosting Ann by proxy.

After Ann returned home, we waited anxiously for letters. My wife and I laid plans to visit her the next summer, but alas, the best laid plans of mice and men oft are gone awry. A few months before we were to go my wife died. I was despondent for a while and decided not to go. After a few months, time began to heal the wounds and the kids and I decided to go anyway. I'm glad we did. We had a wonderful time. We stayed with Ann and her parents for a week and they took us to see the sights by bus and chauffeured car. The second week I rented a car and the kids and I went sight-seeing in England. After a few days of touring, we looked up some of my mother's relatives. They were getting old and it was enlightening to see how they lived, mostly in the past. They are all gone now.

The third week, I rented a van and we toured Wales with Ann and her parents. It was a delightful week, but soon it was over. We left castles and pubs and Ann and her family and flew home, rather morosely I guess. Why do so many good times end in sadness?

Ann and her husband and two boys came to visit my daughter and her husband and two boys a few years ago and it was good to see her again. Because we lived so far apart, I didn't get to see much of her.

And now she has returned for a short visit. It was wonderful to hug her again. We sat on my porch and talked and caught up on each other's lives amid a rush of hummingbirds. We talked of cabbages and kings and other important things and then she was gone again. I saw her for an hour or so last Sunday as I went to my daughter's for brunch. I took her a wind chime with a hummingbird on it to remember the Hocking Hills and me by. Then we parted again. It was especially sad for me because I know I'll probably never see her again. Such is life in the fast lane.

Birthday Book Inspires Ideas
March 13, 1999

A nice thing about this winter's miserable weather has been that I've had time to read. Actually, I've always had time to read, but didn't. I guess it has more to do with advancing age and growing indolence than the weather. I find that the older I get, the less guilty I feel about not working in lousy weather. Usually, I just went ahead and worked regardless of the weather. I just cussed under my breath. Now I sit in my easy chair and cuss the weather and open a book.

Since October I've read thirty-some books. These have been mostly Zane Grey cowboy novels. I'm hooked on them. By today's standards they are sorta hokey. The hero is always the hardest ridin', straightest shootin', honest-est feller you ever seen, and the heroine is the purtiest, sweetest, bluest- (violet, golden, green) eyed little gal in all the West. They are always at odds and don't get together until the last page. He never thinks he's good enough for her and she thinks he's too arrogant (crude, dishonest, unfaithful, ignorant, etc.) for her until at last she sees the light.

In spite of this, Grey weaves a pretty good story, with many a novel twist and surprise. Most of his stories take place in the desert southwest. He spends page after page on description of the landscape, the sky and weather. I truly enjoy them.

Those wilderness areas remained intact until the 1940s and '50s when the National Park Service decided to "open them up" so that they would be accessible to anyone with a car. Now they are covered with blacktop roads, parking lots and people. Lots and lots of people. You have seen films on TV news programs showing the crowds and traffic jams in Yellowstone and Yosemite.

I was out there in 1968 and thought they were crowded then, but they are at least ten times worse now. We are faced with the question of which is better, to reduce wilderness to shopping malls so that everyone can "enjoy" it or keep the wilderness so that only those willing to endure the wilderness adventure can enjoy it.

It's too late to do anything about the developed ones. They are already overwhelmed and beaten half to death. But surely we can save some places so that some people can walk and camp as the early pioneers did. I have found the Quetico Provincial Park in Ontario,

Canada to be an example of what a wilderness park should be. It's accessible only by canoe.

All this came to my consciousness while reading a book my daughter gave me for my birthday. It's not a Zane Grey, but takes place in the same area that several of Grey's books did.

The book is titled "Desert Solitaire" by Edward Abbey. He was a strange and brilliant "hippy" who served as a summer park ranger in Arches National Monument near Moab, Utah, for three seasons, starting about 1957.

He loved the desert and even the climate. I was there and found the landscape absolutely enchanting but the climate unbearable. It was 105 degrees at 11 a.m. and by mid-afternoon we had to leave. It was so hot I thought we would die before we again attained the cool mountains.

Anyhow, he reveled in it and hated to leave when Labor Day came. He tells of several of his trips and adventures on his days off. He hiked into the canyon country in which one could easily get lost. In fact, he did get lost, but had the guts to keep on looking and/or climbing until he saved himself.

One trip he made with an old friend was almost the ultimate adventure. They went 150 miles down the Colorado River in two little discount store rubber rafts. The Glen Canyon Dam was under construction and that stretch of the river would soon be lost forever. He describes the most magnificent canyons and waterfalls, which are now under 300 feet of water. He tells of a sign put up a few years later on one of the canyon walls that says, "Water ski in a clockwise manner. Let's all have fun together." This in a spot that was only accessible to people who had the fortitude to battle that river for two weeks in a rubber raft. This is progress? He calls this "industrial tourism." He was very bitter. Who can blame him?

As I read the book, I began to think of our situation here in Hocking County. We are 200 years too late to preserve the wilderness, but we still have the wonderful state parks. Even there, progress is sneaking up on us. There is a wheel chair trail at Ash Cave. I guess we couldn't deny access to handicapped people in all conscience, but it's the start of "development."

When the Department of Natural Areas and Preserves took over

Conkle's Hollow from the parks system, I remember reading in The Logan Daily News that it would remain forever "natural." No improvements would be made to make it more easily accessible. It wasn't long until a set of wooden steps appeared, replacing the rugged trail to the rim. My next visit I found a viewing platform above the falls. The last time I found board walks so that "hikers" wouldn't get their feet wet. What next? An elevator and electric train so hikers won't have to hike?

A year or so ago, a flood washed out several bridges at Old Man's Cave. They haven't been replaced yet. The Division of Parks' engineering department is "studying" the situation. Their solution is to close parts of the trail. I remember it before there were any bridges. Getting your feet wet was part of the adventure. There's more to a hike than just sight-seeing.

I want to say that Steve Bennett, the park manager, and his crew are a dedicated group of hard-working people and I'm not finding fault with them. The same for Mark Howe of natural areas. They are doing the best they can with what they have. The problems lie with the politics of state government. Every election brings new leadership and a change of direction. 'Twas ever thus.

This all brings us to think where we want to go with tourism. I'm surely not knocking tourism. I make my living from tourism. If it weren't for tourism I'd be beating my brains out in some dead-end job. With tourism I can beat my brains out any way I want to. I was one of those crazy guys and gals who met every week for a couple of years to forge a disparate bunch of people into a cohesive, coherent organization known today as the Hocking County Tourism Association.

My point is we have to be careful that the tail doesn't wag the dog. We wanted to make a place where local people could make a living on their own places without having to move away to a city and work in an office or factory. We did that. The cabin industry is an example. There were a few people who had an extra bedroom or a small weekend cabin that could be rented to tourists. Not only would they make a bit of change, but the people could stay an extra day or two and spend some money. Thousands of tourists have been coming here for years to go to the parks, but with no place to stay, they went back home in the afternoon without spending any money except for a bottle of pop or an ice cream cone.

Soon, people, I among them, started building cabins on their places. They caught on and more and more were built. Now there are about 110 cabin operators. The trouble is people are now moving here just to build cabins and now it is no longer a local thing. Land is being gobbled up and divided at an alarming rate. If we don't wake up and establish some sort of control over development, everything we came here to enjoy will be ruined.

This country has been exploited forever. First it was the forests that fell, then iron, coal, oil, gas and clay. The good earth has managed to recover from most of the damage over the years but might now face damage from which it could never recover. That is the development of the land. We are faced with too many people cutting the land into too many plots and building too many houses. Better roads and better cars have made it a shorter trip from Columbus. We are now a bedroom for Columbus.

It behooves us to exercise some control over how this land is used. It's inevitable that a Disneyland-type of development will occur somewhere around the parks. It could happen without our knowing in advance. The Nazarene Church managed to buy 3,000 acres without the general public being aware of it. I hope the county commissioners and others will take some action to protect our most valuable asset. I'll even let 'em read my birthday book. If it got a clod like me stirred up, think what it could do to some really intelligent people.

Talking About Cancer
June 26, 1999

There's something about the word "cancer" that scares us. It's so mysterious. It sneaks up on us and takes us by surprise. Whenever we learn someone we know has it, we don't know what to say, so we don't say anything and feel guilty about it. For that reason, I told only my closest friends when I found out that I had it. I didn't want people to avoid me or feel guilty.

I've never been really sick since childhood. I've been mangled a few times, but my constitution is such that I throw off diseases pretty well. Since I've been sixty-five or so, I've taken better care of myself than I used to. I go to the doctor regularly and get checked and tested yearly. Last fall, the doctor told me that my PSA test showed elevated numbers and I had better see a urologist. (I'm not sure what PSA stands for, but the P stands for prostate. The PSA test is simply a blood test for prostate cancer. It takes only a few minutes and is relatively painless. It's not completely accurate but it gives an indication if something is amiss.)

Anyway I went to see this feller and he did his thing with the finger and said, "There is a lump on your prostate that would indicate that something isn't as it should be. What do you want to do about it?"

"Well," I said, "what can I do about it?"

"You can have a biopsy or you can do nothing," was his reply.

I thought to myself, "I guess there isn't much choice. It will certainly not cure itself if it is cancer and eventually I'll have to have a biopsy."

"I'll have the biopsy."

"That's what I would do," the doc said. "I'll make an appointment for you."

On the appointed day, I arrived on time, as is my practice, and after the usual forty-five-minute wait, was ushered into a small room and ordered to take my pants off. That always starts off an interview with a bang. The nurse draped a sheet over part of my bare bottom, and the doc sat on a stool in front of a TV screen, which he said guided him by ultrasound.

I got a glance at a contraption. It looked like a foot-long piece of a pitchfork handle with an eyeball about the size of a bowling ball attached to the end. Before I had time to break and run, he shoved that thing where the sun don't shine.

"This might be a little uncomfortable," he said, "but it only takes a few minutes." There was a clicking noise and I felt a little pricking sensation. "There's one, now we only have five more," the doc allowed. In a few minutes it was over and he up and walked out, leaving me panting on the table like a just-bred sow.

The nurse said, "You can get your pants on now," and left.

I thought, "I waited forty-five minutes to get in here. They can wait on me to get out." An appointment was made for a week hence to get the results.

I was let into an exam room the following week, and after a moderate wait, the doctor came in with a folder, which he proceeded to open. "Um, yeah, well, it seems that you have prostate cancer. What would you like to do about it?"

"What are my options?" I asked.

"Well, since I'm a surgeon, I would naturally like to remove the prostate, but you could also have radiation or chemotherapy, or you could do nothing."

I wasn't really prepared for this. I've been too healthy to give in to anything so easily. I told the doctor that I would explore the possibilities and take whatever action I deemed the best, but removal would be on the bottom of the list. I don't think he liked that too well, but he didn't object.

I went right home and called my brother-in-law in Washington, D.C., who had gone through the same thing two years previously. He told me about a new procedure that he had tried and it worked well. Two years later he was apparently cancer-free. It sounded good, but I hated that 400-mile drive and trying to get around in a strange, big city.

This procedure involved implanting radioactive palladium seeds directly into the prostate. I called the James Cancer Hospital and they said they had nearly the same procedure, but they were guided by ultrasound, while the one in Washington was guided by a CAT scan.

I also checked into radiation therapy. This meant a trip to Lancaster five days a week for seven weeks. This wasn't too attractive since I thought I'd probably get killed on the highway before that was over. After a few more calls to Washington, I opted for that procedure and made an appointment for two weeks later.

The procedure was a two-day affair. I went in the day before the actual work and got an exam, a shot and a prescription. It took about an hour. The next day, I arrived at 9 a.m. and was prepped. I won't go into details about that, except to say forget about dignity. It was about like any hospital procedure. The doctor had his own little hospital with all kinds of electronic gadgets. He has his own staff, including a urologist, anesthesiologist and several nurses. I was taken into the operating room about 10 a.m. and given a spinal anesthetic. After that I felt nothing below the waist.

I was placed on a CAT scan table. The actual operation consisted of placing hollow needles into my prostate from the rear, thirty-three of them to be exact. After each row, I was scanned to see if they were placed correctly. When all were in place, the seeds were implanted through the needles and scanned again. When all was deemed correct, the needles were removed and it was over. I never felt any pain. I was put into a recovery room until the anesthetic wore off and I left the office about noon.

We stopped on the way back to my sister and brother-in-law's house to pick up some prescriptions, and that was it. Saturday, I drove the 400 miles home without difficulty. I stopped every couple of hours to rest and exercise. The only discomfort was a burning sensation during urination. A prescription eased that considerably. This continued for about a month. Each day things got better, until three months later, I'm nearly back to normal.

Last week I had my three-month PSA test and got the results yesterday. I was astounded to find that the numbers had dropped from 7.6 to 0.1. Talk about happy! I'm basically cancer-free. I can't say I'm cured, but my future looks bright. I have to have a PSA every three months for life, probably because cancer could recur, but I've been given new hope.

As I said in the beginning, I don't like to talk about these things, as a rule, but I'm going public in the hope that all men over fifty will get a yearly PSA and take control of their health. Early detection is the key. There are no early symptoms that you can sort out from just growing older. When the PSA numbers exceed three or four, you should take some action. Under two is normal. I had a friend who died a horrible death because the cancer was not detected until it had started to spread throughout his body.

In my case, it was caught early and treated early, and therefore, I have been spared. I don't mean to imply that this whole thing was completely worry-free, because I spent a rather uncomfortable month, but compared to months of wasting away in and out of hospitals knowing you are going to die in the near future, it was a romp in the park. Please keep tabs on this highly curable cancer and save yourself and your family much grief.

Weddings: Not My Strong Suit
October 30, 1999

Weddings have never been my strong suit. In fact, you could say without exaggeration, I hate 'em. I'll do anything to avoid attending one, including telling monstrous lies, but this time it was unavoidable.

My sister's only son was getting married a couple of weeks ago, and there was no getting out of it.

She's been in ill health the last couple of years and in fact was back in the hospital three days after the wedding for a lung operation. She sure didn't need any flack from the family curmudgeon, so I meekly submitted. I was a couple of weeks late returning the reservation, but they apparently made allowances for old age and didn't complain.

Surveying my vast wardrobe, I discovered to my surprise that I didn't have anything that would circumnavigate my waistline. Them doughnuts have sure been sneakin' up on me. There was naught for it — I had to get some pants and a new sport coat. My sister dropped a hint that my usual attire, baggy jeans with glue spots and a black T-shirt with bleach stains, wouldn't cut it this time.

I like a trip to a clothing store just about as much as a wedding. Armed with most of the cash I'd hidden in the mattress for my retirement, I ventured forth to a haberdashery. They must have seen me coming. It was sale day and the first thing I saw was a rack of sport coats just inside the door — twenty-five percent off discount. I found one just shy of circus tent size and I said, "I'll take it."

I was out the door so fast that I was halfway home before I remembered I hadn't gotten any pants. I stopped at a department store and went straight to the work clothes department and found a pair of uniform pants that had a stretch band in the waist and I was set. They were for farmers and just the right color so that cow manure splattered on them wouldn't show. They went well with the coat, which looked like it was splattered with cow manure.

I still didn't have a shirt that fit. I rooted around in the back of the closet and found one I'd worn to the last wedding I'd gone to — my daughter's twenty-some years ago. It almost fit, but I couldn't get the neck buttoned. After much deliberating, I decided on the obvious solution. I took the scissors and cut the back of the collar. It buttoned fine. I decided to not get a haircut so that my hair would hang down and cover the collar. A dash of white paint on the back of my neck, and I'm cool. It worked so well and saved me thirty bucks to boot. Sometimes I'm so clever that I astound myself.

That left the present. I didn't know whether to get them a toaster or an alarm clock. I eventually went down to the shop and slapped some boards together. I called it a "Fassig Original." (I didn't tell them what it was, but I think they'll use it for a footstool. At least I heard them say that they wouldn't put their muddy boots on that thing.)

The next chore was getting there. My sister and her husband live in Virginia. She reserved rooms in a hotel in Maryland and the wedding was in Pennsylvania, so it promised to be a fun thing. My son got some computerized maps from the Internet. They claimed that it was 396 miles to the hotel and would take six hours and four minutes. I thought, "Heck, I don't care if it takes six hours and ten minutes."

I left home about 10:30 on Friday morning. Six hours and four minutes later I crossed the line from West Virginia into Maryland. Up to this point it was a beautiful drive. The fall colors were superb, the road was wonderful and the traffic was light. Then everything went to hell. The closer I got to the Washington-Baltimore mess, the heavier the traffic was. You can imagine the beltway on a Friday night. It was three lanes, bumper to bumper at seventy miles per hour. Here's one hillbilly who wished he was back home cutting firewood.

It was flat dark when I hit Baltimore. I had to find a turnoff and was trying to go as slowly as I could without getting killed when suddenly traffic stopped. Holy cow, what a scramble! After about ten minutes, we began to creep forward a few feet at a time. Three EMS trucks, a fire truck and several police cars went screaming by on the right berm with inches to spare. I could see their lights flashing about a mile ahead. Finally, I got abreast of the scene just as they were extracting a couple of bodies from a three-car pileup. I don't know if they were dead or not, but they weren't dancing a jig.

Ten more minutes and I was at the Holiday Inn, a five-story edifice that sorta looked like a jail. I went in and checked with the jailer — I mean room clerk — and was assigned Room 532 and given a "key" that was like a credit card, only it didn't have any numbers on it. I was to stick it in a slot in the door and it would open, he said. The same key would open the outside door and the elevator. When I tried the fifth floor, it wouldn't work. Someone else got on and punched four and up we went. I got off at four and lugged my bag up the fire escape to find the key wouldn't open 532.

After nearly breaking off the door knob, I looked at the paper the clerk gave me. It said 352, not 532. It turned out that the fifth floor was the executive floor and it takes a special key to get on that floor. I'm glad some executive and his secretary weren't in that room!

I didn't know where the rest of my kinfolk were, so I started back down, after a bathroom break, to find out which rooms they were in, when I heard someone shout, "Grandpa!" My grandson had been looking through the peephole in the door hoping to spot a friendly face. The desk clerk wouldn't tell anyone which room anyone else was it. It was like a jail and we were all in different cells. We left my daughter's door open and eventually they all showed up. It turned out we were all in adjacent rooms.

The next morning we all had breakfast together and it was like old home week.

About 1 p.m. we gathered for the forty-mile drive to the church. We had good directions and only missed two turns. The church was a pretty little old Catholic country church in a pretty little old country town. There was a good crowd, about equally divided between elderly farmer types and young yuppies. There were no fights. The church was filled to capacity. The music was provided by a timid young lady with a timid little voice that was pleasant but hard to hear and an elderly gentleman with a booming baritone voice that rattled the windows. When they sang a duet, it reminded me of a fight between a Chihuahua and a great Dane, but not unpleasantly.

The priest was a jolly, good-natured gentleman who kept everyone smiling for an hour and a half. I shifted from cheek to cheek, but I kept smiling. It was my first Catholic wedding, and I have to say that when he got through with them, they were married. It was luverly.

After the ceremony, it was back to the hotel for a two-hour wait for the reception. It was held at a ritzy country club not far from the hotel. I was a little out of my element, but I managed to hold my paunch in check until we could eat. They held us captive there by serving just a little dab every once in a while. It was nice to sit around and meet people and chat about nothing in particular. And then something hit the fan. They had hired a D.J. to play music for two hours. He didn't. He turned the volume up way past the point that it could be called music. All conversation was impossible. I entertained myself by watching the ceiling tiles flutter in rhythm with the beat and trying to guess when they would come flying out. There was some attempt by some brave souls to dance. It wasn't totally unpleasant; there were some beautiful young ladies to watch. None asked me to dance. Maybe it was the garlic salad dressing I spilled in my lap.

At last it was over and we went back to the hotel for a shower and rest. I went to bed early and by 6 a.m. I had checked out and was heading the wrong way on the freeway. A three-mile detour got me on the right track and six hours and four minutes later I was home. Never did my hovel look so good.

Chapter 8
Nature Notes

Living the Wild Life in Hocking County
August 26, 1995

Ever since I've been able to read adventure books, I've wanted to live in a cabin in the wilderness of Alaska or the Yukon. I've wanted to pit myself against Mother Nature and her creatures — the strong, silent hero of hundreds of adventures, storms and blizzards and the attacks of bears, cougars and wolves. It all sounded so romantic.

At last I'm able to live that dream. It's scaled down a bit, though. I'm in the wilderness of Hocking County. The adversaries are still blizzards and storms, but in lieu of bears, cougars and wolves, I'm matching wits with deer, coyotes and 'coons, and an occasional vicious chipmunk.

I tried for several years to have a garden. The first year the deer, 'coons and groundhogs ate it. The next year I spent about a hundred bucks to put a barbed wire fence five feet high around it — the 'coons went under it. Then I put chicken wire three feet high around the bottom. Did you know 'coons can climb?

The following year I took edge trimmings from the saw mill, which are about an inch square and eight feet long, and wove them into the barbed wire, standing on end about four inches apart. It looked like a Vietnamese prison camp. My friends called in the "vegetable gulag." I knew nothing could get in there.

Wrong!

The next spring, I spent another hundred bucks on an electric fence. That kept them out. I worked diligently and had a wonderful garden. The night before the sweet corn was ready to pick, the stockade was breached and morning light showed not one edible thing left. It looked like a herd of buffalo had spent a week there.

Two hundred bucks down the tube and nothing to show for it. I've found that it's easier to cultivate friends than a garden. I get plenty of fresh vegetables from neighbors by just whining about my bad luck. I don't know how they keep the deer out, and I don't care.

I now feed the deer corn at my feeders. I get more satisfaction watching them than I did having the garden. I have several does that come regularly. It gives me a special thrill when they bring their fawns in to meet me.

A special bonus is all the other critters that come to clean up after the deer. There are a dozen or so gray squirrels that entertain me with their acrobatic prowess daily. They also offer the challenge of keeping them out of the bird feeders. They chewed several holes in my screened-in porch to get at the feed buckets. I have to keep them in the living room now.

Three times this week I've see a young coyote. So far he hasn't bothered anything, but you can bet if I had sheep or chickens he'd be right after them.

Wild turkeys come to the feeders occasionally in the summer. Yesterday, two hens with an uncountable flock of young ones were cleaning the drive. When snow is on the ground they are here almost constantly. So far, they have posed no threat to my being.

Then there's Oscar. Oscar is one of the smartest, most persistent 'coons I've ever run across. He's also very precocious. He doesn't sneak around in the dark stealing food (not much, anyhow). He just walks up to the door about supper time, stands on his hind legs, bangs on the door and in the 'coon language (I haven't been able to teach him English yet) says, "How about a handout, Bub."

I respond by tossing him a couple of slices of bread and a hot dog or two. He loves hot dogs. I call him Oscar after Oscar Meyer hot dogs. I can't afford Oscar Meyer, so he gets some cheap brand, but he hasn't complained.

Last week he threw me a curve. As I tossed him his supper, three little heads stuck through the lattice from under the porch. Oscar is a mother. More mouths to feed.

Oscar is not only curious, but athletic. He enlarged the squirrel holes and made a mess out of the porch until I put hardware cloth over the screen. Now he's turned his attention to the humming bird feeders. They hung on wooden brackets on the posts between my windows. I found the feeders on the ground one morning, two of them broken. I thought a buck deer might have torn them down with his antlers. I bought two new ones and they were down the next morning. It was then I noticed the muddy paw prints on the window. Determined not to be outwitted by a 'coon, I got some chain and hung the feeders from the gutter board between the posts where a 'coon could not reach them.

I was awakened about 2 a.m. by a thump on the window. There was Oscar sitting on one of the brackets, trying to reach the feeder. He couldn't quite make it. He climbed down and up the next one just as easy as if it were a ladder with the same results. Up the third one. This time he was able to just tick it with one finger (if that's what you call them) and the feeder moved just a fraction. As it swung back he hit it a little harder and then the third time he whopped it a good one. It swung away smartly and back into his waiting arms. He hung onto the bracket with his back feet, the feeder with his front and was trying to gnaw off the little plastic flower so he could get at the sugar water when I spoiled his game.

Next day, I took down the brackets and the feeders haven't been touched since.

The thrill of one small victory doesn't offset years of the agony of defeat, but at last I've got one check mark on my side. Considering my success rate, it's a good thing we don't have cougars and bears.

The Roads of Spring

April 6, 1996

The conditions of our roads this time of year are atrocious.

I don't mean the potholes and soft spots. We can expect and accept that. The township trustees take their work seriously and do the best they can with what they've got. The county engineer does a marvelous job. Our county roads and bridges are as good as anyone's. As far as I'm concerned, Bill Shaw has a job for life.

What I'm talking about is trash. The roadsides are deep in litter and it doesn't need to be that way. There is no excuse for anyone throwing trash out of a car. It shows lack of manners and consideration for others. I think it takes a trashy person to litter. The trash shows up now because the vegetation is dead from the winter. Later the grass and weeds (wildflowers) will grow up to cover most of it, but right now it looks like hell. The amount of litter seems to be in direct relation to the distance to the closest fast food place or carry-out and how long it takes to eat or drink the products sold there. Since we have a convenience store or fast food place on every road in or out of Logan, all routes are covered.

For some reason, some roads are worse than others. I take a short cut to the west side of town over Sauer Kraut Road several times a week. The amount of litter there is disgusting. If I lived there, I think I would be out there with a shotgun, or at least binoculars and pencil and pad, taking license numbers. There is a farmer there whose cows must eat barrels of paper a year. It might save a little feed, but I doubt if the cows grow much on styrofoam and plastic.

The Adopt-a-Highway program of the Ohio Department of Transportation (ODOT) has helped a lot on state highways. In fact, a group I belong to, the Hocking Hills Activities Association, cleans two miles of highway four times a year. We were all set to clean two miles of a county road, Big Pine, until we found out that we would have to buy a $100 insurance policy to protect the county in case of an accident. Needless to say, paying a hundred bucks to pick up someone else's garbage didn't set well with our members, so the project was abandoned. If the county would change their policy, I'm sure a lot of people would be willing to help clean our roadsides. Until then, it would help if we all cleaned up in front of our own places.

I did just that this week with the following results:

• Thirty-five aluminum cans. These were about equally divided between beer and pop.

• Eleven plastic pop bottles, two of which were two liters. The strange thing about drinkers of pop from screw top bottles, they almost always replace the cap before they throw the bottle away. Only one of the eleven didn't have a cap. It must be nice to be a neat litterer. Sorta like a giant shrimp. I believe that's an oxymoron, or at least a moron.

• Sixteen glass beer bottles. It's nice to know glass is making a comeback. More work for Anchor-Hocking. Four of these also had caps. Are pop drinkers spreading this habit to beer drinkers or are they becoming beer drinkers?

• Eight glass juice or pop bottles. All had caps. I'm beginning to see a trend here.

• One peanut butter jar. A disgruntled picnicker, perhaps?

• Ten McDonald's large drink or milkshake paper cups, and one from SuperAmerica. They really got a break today.

• Eleven styrofoam coffee cups, most with lids. Two were McDonald's, one SuperAmerica, the rest anonymous. I always thought McDonald's coffee wasn't all that good. The trashers may agree.

• One sack of bagels. I don't know what that's all about.

• One foam food tray. Maybe Chinese food is beginning to compete.

• Three lottery cards. No winners.

• Three aluminum pie plates. No forks or knives. Must be finger food.

• One valentine candy box. The candy was gone so someone made some points.

• Six pieces of bumper and grill from a car wreck. The driver probably didn't want them.

• Two flares left by the highway patrol after the car wreck.

• One mangled highway sign left after the car wreck.

• One 300-pound piece of concrete left by ODOT after repairing guardrail after the car wreck. They probably didn't want it, either.

• One mangled hub cap left after different car wreck. Not much

213

good. Driver probably didn't want it.

• Twenty-five potato chip and pretzel bags. McDonald's should take note here. A new trend seems to be developing. A six pack and a bag of chips is replacing the Big Mac and fries. I didn't find a single burger box or French fry container.

• Three milk jugs. No explanation here.

• One towel. Beats me.

• One pack of cigarettes. Give 'em credit. They're trying to quit.

• Eight empty cigarette packs. They didn't make it.

• One Skoal box. They're still trying.

• One box of percussion caps for a muzzleloading gun. I couldn't understand why someone would throw away thirty-six caps until I tried to open the box. It took fifteen minutes. If it had been me, I would have found another kind of box.

• Two quart plastic oil cans. They couldn't have poured oil in a car while driving. Do you suppose they drank it?

• One five-foot long carton. Probably just too big to fit comfortably in the front seat.

• One yogurt cup. I always liked healthy litterers.

• A mascara brush. This one is a mystery to me. It must have been a lady on the way to a hot date or a cross-dresser trying to hide the evidence.

• Lastly, a plastic bag full of miscellaneous papers and trash. Must have been the competition.

This adventure took me about an hour and a half. It was not hard work, but it galled me to have to take that time out of my day to pick up other people's trash that shouldn't have been there in the first place. It shows me that people have no pride. I'm proud of Hocking County and want others to feel the same. I believe that most of the perpetrators are local. I've seen piles of fast food containers in the morning at places to pull off the road. They weren't there the day before. Tourists would be in their motels, cabins or camps at night, not running the roads eating.

Those of you who are doing this — and you know who you are — take pride in your home county and dispose of your trash properly.

Ah, Springtime

April 27, 1996

Last Sunday was the day for which I've been waiting for months. The first day of spring. The calendar said that was weeks ago, but it wasn't until Sunday that it really felt like spring. We've had some really warm days in the last week or so, but nothing was growing, nothing was blooming. Ah, but this day Mother Nature awoke, stretched and smiled.

I had a flashback to grade school. Dear, sweet Miss Zitt, our music teacher, would smile and say, "On a lovely spring day like this, children, let's sing the spring song," and we'd sing:

'Tis springtime,
'Tis springtime,
Cold winter is past.
Warm breezes are blowing
And May's here at last.
The birds are returning
Their song fills the air,
'Tis springtime
'Tis springtime,
'Tis springtime, so fair.

I don't know how old Miss Zitt was, but I thought she was about ninety-five. She had white hair done up in a bun and those old ladies' black shoes. She was the only teacher I had who wasn't a grump.

Spring also brings back memories of Nelson Eddy and Jeanette McDonald face-to-face, inches apart, singing at the top of their lungs, "Ah, love is so sweet in the springtime!"

I often wondered why they weren't hearing-impaired, or as we used to say, "Deaf as a door post."

As I looked out my windows at the woods, I couldn't see many signs of spring. In fact, I couldn't see much of anything but a film of winter's grime. I had to break down and wash the windows. What a difference! There was a green mist dusting the tree tops and there were faint patches of color on the forest floor. I had to have a closer look. After downing a couple of Advil for my aching knees and grabbing my binoculars and hiking stick, I went for an excursion in the woods. To my surprise, the wild cherries were out in almost full leaf. The soft

215

maple already had set seed. It won't be long until they're helicoptering far and wide. The sugar maples are breaking buds and show a good bit of green, the same with the oaks. The sassafras are poking their chartreuse leaves from the buds.

Underfoot, thousands of spring beauties are in full bloom. They are among the earliest bloomers; their delicate pink blossoms appear to be almost shy, in spite of their numbers, and take comfort in each others' presence. Interspersed among them are small patches of hepatica, their blooms open wide for all to see, not at all shy. Most are snowy white but some show a hint of pink. Overlooked, at first, are large numbers of may apples, their leaves struggling to push aside the leaf cover, some wearing leaf hats like jaunty French berets.

My main interest this trip, however, was dogwood. It has taken a beating the last few years. About three years ago, we had nearly forty-below-zero temperatures, which killed some of them and weakened the rest. This allowed a fungus disease to get started. Many have died since. Last winter, I looked for some red berries to decorate for Christmas and couldn't find any at all. Neither did I see any buds for this year's blossoms. In fact, most of the trees I found were dead. I was gratified to find some live ones this year, but they were not healthy. There were no buds showing, so there will be almost no blossoms this spring. I despair for their survival. How can it be spring without dogwood? I looked first on the south-facing slope. When I crossed the ravine to the north-facing slope, I didn't find a single live tree in perhaps five acres.

One must remember that dogwood is a pioneer species, meaning that they are among the first trees to grow on open ground. They protect and partially shade the forest trees until they can get established. Eventually, the forest trees outgrow the dogwoods. They prefer open areas with lots of sun. They are pretty well shade intolerant and when they are fully shaded, they die, their job done. My woods was logged twenty-two years ago and the dogwoods came on strong. The woods are well established now. Perhaps this is part of the natural cycle. Time will tell, I guess, but I'll miss them for a while. Nature will take care of things if we leave her alone. Somewhere there is bound to be a disease-resistant tree that will survive to have seeds that will be spread by the birds to repopulate the area.

Speaking of birds, it's about time for the hummingbirds to return. The last two years, they have returned on April 4. It's been too cold this year. There have been no flowers to support them.

I hope they didn't start out at the usual time and starve along the way. It's amazing that they can find their way back to the same spot. Last year, I was looking out the window when a hummer came to the exact spot where a feeder hung last year. It hovered for a moment then went to the place where the other feeder was. I hurried and filled a feeder and hung it up. Within minutes he was happily feeding. I'm certain he had been here the summer before.

If the hummers are late, the juncos left early. May 5 is their usual date of departure. It must mean an early spring for the north country. Juncos nest from northern Michigan northward to Canada, and just visit us in the winter because of our tropical climate.

So natures' wheel keeps turning and we can but observe. I'm glad because each new season brings something new, even if we've seen it scores of times before. Viva la spring!

A Crawl in the Woods
August 24, 1996

Since I live in the woods, I observe what's going on fairly frequently. I'm usually looking around or up in the trees as I walk, and don't pay much attention to the ground, except in the winter when I'm keeping an eye peeled for tracks. Last evening, for some reason, I decided to take a closer look.

I took my magnifying glass and a notebook and went for a stroll. From walking height, the eye doesn't pick up many details and I soon found myself on my knees and then on my belly.

My first stop was under a silver maple tree not far from the house. It's in an area where I frequently drive my tractor (when I have one of them running). The earth is hard-packed clay and not much grows there, but what does is more visible. I was looking at some moss. There are several different kinds. Some are like little Christmas trees less than an inch high. Some resemble a bunch of broccoli in color and shape. They are only one-eighth to one-fourth of an inch high with leaves about one thirty-second of an inch in diameter. Others are like tiny ferns. One looked like a fern leaf that was growing flat on a rock, apparently attached by rootlets on the back. The details were visible only because of the glass. Without it, I would have missed most of them.

While engrossed in these things, I became aware of something falling from the tree. It was light in weight, whatever it was, because it made very little noise. I listened intently and watched closely until finally I saw and heard something hit the ground. I retrieved it carefully. It was just a blob of something black. Under the glass it became a thing of beauty. It was made up of six little tubular pieces of a soft substance, laid side by side in a circular pattern and stuck together at the ends. They looked like little Japanese lanterns. When I tore one open, it looked like the pulp of chewed leaves. It could be only one thing — caterpillar droppings. They are absolutely unique. I found several trees with the same thing under them. I never did see the critter that made them. He has to have a six-barreled rectum with glue jets to make a thing like that. I'm looking forward to meeting him one day.

After I got up into the woods a little more where it was shady, I found more toadstools. There were four or five different shapes and colors. It's odd that fungi are the buzzards of the plant world, yet all are susceptible to being eaten by one thing or another. Some had insect holes in them, others were attacked by squirrels and mice.

In a sunny spot I found Queen Anne's lace, which is not particularly pretty to my way of thinking. A close look under the glass revealed hundreds of tiny flowers, about one-sixteenth of an inch across. They resemble dogwood blooms and are just beautiful.

It's only August and tree leaves are falling already. Most that fall this early have been damaged by insects and are full of holes, though they are turning color.

When I moved away from the tractor road and into the thicker woods, I noticed that not much was growing. The bigger trees put down a thick carpet of leaves that act as a mulch to keep things from sprouting. The heavier canopy also cuts down on the available light to further inhibit growth. The most prominent plants in these areas were minuscule maple trees. Some were no doubt several years old and only an inch or two high. They will patiently wait until a tree is cut or blown down, letting light in, then they'll grow like crazy.

An old stump presented a pretty picture. It had been riddled by carpenter ants, leaving intricate patterns in the wood. The outside had several kinds of lichens and mosses growing on it. A very artistic piece. By the way, lichens are not a single plant but a combination of algae and fungi living in what's called a symbiotic relationship. That means each contributes something and neither could live without the other. The algae collects the food and the fungus collects the water and each holds them in place for the benefit of them both.

The forest duff contains, under the fallen leaves, the skeletons of last year's leaves and fine hair roots of millions of trees and plants, all mixed together. Buried in this mixture, I found mouse- and squirrel-chewed hickory nuts and acorns. There were also fungi, some as small as the head of a pin, some quite large. I also found several small toads, some no bigger than my little fingernail.

Also significant is what I didn't find. I never saw that first ant. Usually the forest floor and tree trunks are crawling with ants. Not so now. I don't know if it's just too late in the season or if something has killed them off. I will investigate that further. There are no bees, either. A couple of different tracheal mites have infected the bees all over the county. They usually don't winter over unless treated with antibiotics in the fall. The wild ones are doomed.

It was not bad at all crawling on my hands and knees. In fact, it was quite pleasant except for one incident. I found myself nose-to-nose with a pile of horse manure. It's funny-looking stuff, too, when viewed from three inches through a magnifier. I had forgotten that I'd given Dick Erb and his wife, Sandy, permission to ride my trails. They surely got my attention.

When it got too dark to see well, I was astonished to find I was only about twenty-five yards from my house. You don't hike very fast with your nose on the ground. It was a pleasant hour made even better when I emerged from the dark woods and was greeted by a new moon. How lucky we are to live in a place like this.

A Thanksgiving Ode to Mother Nature
November 16, 1996

One day, when I was six or seven years old, I came home from school for lunch to find a surprise. My mother said I wouldn't have to go to school in the afternoon. We were going to see the circus parade.

The circus had come to town and they always had a parade through the streets of downtown Columbus. I was shocked. I was made to attend school if my head was falling off. This didn't fit the pattern. I didn't object, however, and accepted it like a man.

There was a quite of bit of discussion between my parents, and after a while the parade fell by the wayside. A picnic emerged to take its place. I still didn't object. It seemed to me that either one beat going back to school on such a beautiful spring day. I couldn't understand why my dad wasn't going to work. It wasn't until several weeks later that I comprehended that he had lost his job that morning and didn't have work to go to. This was in 1933 or 1934 in the depths of the Great Depression and losing one's job was commonplace. I just didn't realize what was happening.

Anyway, a picnic it was. Mom packed a lunch and asked our neighbor, Mrs. Glass, to go along. I was glad of that. She was funny and cussed like a sailor. Besides, my dad was less confrontational when someone else was along. Most people didn't know he was a closet tyrant.

We hopped in the old flivver and drove to one of my dad's fishin' holes on Big Walnut Creek near Port Columbus Airport. It was a gorgeous day in May. The sky was gloriously blue and the sun was warm. Mom spread a blanket with the oilcloth tablecloth from the kitchen in the middle. She put the peanut butter and jelly sandwiches, pickles, cheese and potato salad on the oilcloth and we all knelt around and ate. There was lemonade to drink. Never had a meal tasted better. After eating our fill, we just sort of laid back on the cool grass and inhaled the scent of the earth flavored with the smell of millions of violets that bloomed all around us. They were white, yellow and blue. Under the trees, spring beauties bloomed in profusion, accented by the deep blue of phlox. I reveled in the beauty of the moment. I think on that day were planted the seeds of my love of the earth. I had been fishing with my dad for a couple of years, but it usually wasn't a very happy experience because I never could please him. Here, with Mrs. Glass to run interference and my sisters to keep his attention elsewhere, I was in another world.

We caught crawdads and minnows in the shallows and found a gar fish that had been trapped in a pool when excess rain had raised the water level. We ran through the grass and rolled 'midst the flowers. Never was there such a day. I hated to go home. When we finally left, I was hooked on the outdoors.

That brings me to the purpose of this piece. I still am hooked on the outdoors, and with Thanksgiving Day just around the corner I want to express my gratitude to Mother Earth for making my life such a joy. Every morning when I leave the house, usually to feed the deer patiently waiting at the old stump, I inhale a lungful of the woodsy smell of pure air and say to myself, "What did I do to deserve this?"

Most of the year, the air is filled with bird song. The sweetness of the wood thrush song could not be improved upon by any of man's noises. The tufted titmouse has a note so pure that it almost brings tears at its perfection. The haunting call of the whippoorwill at dusk is of another world. Each has a quality of its own that can't be improved. If only man could accept things as they are and not always try to improve them to their detriment. The natives of America considered themselves part of nature, subject to her whims, and not above nature, bound to control her.

Anyhow, to get back to my premise, I'm thankful that I can live here in a fairly natural part of Ohio's most natural county. Things are changing rapidly and I'm afraid for our future. I'm afraid we'll be overrun by crowds of people who don't respect the place as we do. Already, there are hundreds of new houses. Each new house means a smaller piece of land for more people. This area has been exploited time after time and has always recovered when left alone. This time, I'm not so sure.

Meantime, I'll stick to my domain and guard her borders against invasion and be thankful for the opportunity to live as I choose and for all my friends who make life easier.

Spring, at Last
May 10, 1997

This has been a busy week here in the backwoods. Spring has finally sprung, I hope. After weeks of cold weather that put spring on hold, it just couldn't be held any longer. Spring is bustin' out all over!

The dogwoods finally bloomed. I was surprised at how many did bloom. The last two years they have been very sparse. Last year I could count on my left hand (and I only have four fingers on that hand) the number of trees with blossoms on my place. This year I can see eleven from my vantage point on the porch.

This is one of the few evenings that it's been warm enough to sit out after supper, so I'm taking advantage of the gorgeous evening. Right now, I'm being serenaded by that most beautiful singer of all, the wood thrush. I only hear one at the moment but soon there will be enough for a chorus. I love to hear them sing. I know it's spring when I hear their concert.

The night I hear the whippoorwill, I'll know that summer is nigh. They have been on the decline in the last few years. Ten years ago, I heard them every night and they sang for hours. Now, it's a special evening when one sings nearby. I don't know what the reason is. It surely isn't a shortage of bugs to eat. We have an adequate supply of those. I suppose it has something to do with their wintering grounds. My book says they winter in South Carolina and farther south. There's a big influx of people there, so I suppose that their home is being destroyed for human housing, just like here.

I've walked (or hobbled) the woods several times in the past couple of weeks and I'm amazed at the amount of wildflowers in bloom. The cold weather held the early ones back and they are all blooming at once now. There's hardly room to walk without stepping on them. The dry hilltops are covered with spring beauties and cutleaf toothwort while the woods along the streams are full of trilliums, violets (blue, white and yellow) and purple phlox. There is also a yellow strawflower-type plant about eighteen inches high that I can't identify.

The wildflowers have never been as plentiful as they are this year. I even saw some fire pinks this week. They don't usually bloom until a little later. They are certainly the reddest of the wildflowers.

Speaking of red, last Monday I was treated to the sight of a scarlet tanager in a tree just a few feet from my porch. They are absolutely the reddest of the birds that inhabit these woods. A cardinal pales by comparison. I usually only catch a fleeting glimpse once or twice during the summer, but this one wanted to show off for some reason. He sat on a tree limb and preened and posed for a good ten minutes. With his red body and black wings and tail, he was truly a sight to behold.

On May 2, as I was eating lunch, I noticed a female hummingbird hovering in the exact spot that a feeder has hung for the last several years. I stopped in mid-bite and hurriedly filled a feeder and hung it up. Within a few minutes, she was back. The males usually return first, followed by the females a week or so later. Another female came the next day. Now there are at least three males bickering with each other. The last two years, they came April 4. I guess this spring has everything out of kilter.

I have to concede, the squirrels have bested me again. I've tried all kinds of feeders for the birds, but I have been thwarted at every turn by those little gray bandits. I finally made a feeder out of a two-foot long piece of stove pipe. I thought at least I wouldn't have to fill it so often. It holds about two gallons. At first, the squirrels couldn't figure out how to get into it, but the woodpeckers wasted most of the seed and the squirrels cleaned it up off the ground. I put a four-inch band of half-inch hardware cloth around the bottom that covered the holes. That made the holes smaller so the woodpeckers couldn't throw out so much feed.

Things went along pretty well for about a year until some smart-alecky bushy-tail figured out the secret. He hangs upside down and slides down the pipe, catching the wire with his back feet. He then raises up and takes a seed, heads down and eats it, then raises up for another. He can do this for half an hour. Now he has taught another one to do it. There's an almost overwhelming temptation to blow 'em away with the old twelve bore, but heck, if they want it that bad, why not let 'em have it? They are at least entertaining.

Last Saturday, I happened to look out the front window of the shop just as a female goshawk landed in a tree just outside. She has been sitting on eggs in their nest for at least three weeks that I know of. I've been watching her daily through binoculars. I never saw her leave, but the male came near now and then. He is always very vocal. This day, she sat for a few minutes, fluffed up her feathers and shook. Her body language said, "It's sure nice to get out of that damned house for a change!"

Just then, a blue jay dived at her head and she took flight back to the nest. I hurried outside to watch just as the male left the nest, screaming loudly. The female seized something and started to tear it into little pieces and stuck her head down in the nest. I knew she had to be feeding her chicks or whatever they're called. I don't know what unfortunate individual volunteered to be the first meal, but I'm sure the young are grateful. The next several days, she sat on the nest again, then yesterday the feeding ritual took place again. I surmise that maybe only one egg hatched at first and the second a few days later.

My book doesn't say how many they have but I don't think the nest would hold more than three. They grow fast and large. Today there was much coming and going as the male brought food and she met him several feet from the nest and brought the prey in to feed them.

This morning, I saw a thrilling sight. I heard the male screaming from high over the hill across the road. I looked just in time to see him approach. He folded his wings into tight curves and dived like a rocket. He was dropping fast. He made a curve at the edge of the woods and shot upward without moving a feather, it seemed. He spread his wings and tail and dropped lightly as a feather on the limb beside the female. They talked briefly and she took the offering and went back to the nest to feed the young. I'll bet most people have never seen this.

I ain't got much learnin', but after living twenty-three years here in the woods, I think I've learned a thing or two a lot them college perfessors don't know. I just ain't learned how to outwit a squirrel, but I'm workin' on it!

Change Is in the Air
August 30, 1997

This has certainly been an unusual year weather wise. I guess you knew that. After a mostly mild winter, we had a wetter and cooler summer. There were several floods during a period when most small streams are dry. I had to replace the gravel approach to my bridge two mornings in a row last week. Old habits die hard.

Now we are in a transitional period — summer winding down but not quite fall. During a walk in the woods yesterday, I was surprised to see how many leaves had fallen. It's much too early for most trees to lose their leaves, but the maples are shedding a lot. The gums always start at this time of year. They have turned red and many have fallen. The buckeyes will probably be next.

I think the hummingbirds are getting ready to leave soon. They have been hitting my feeders rather heavily the last couple of weeks. I counted (or estimated — you can't really count them when they are numerous) between fifteen and eighteen at one time. They seem to be building up their bodies for their long journey south. They usually leave in early September. They have certainly been on a binge lately. I have three feeders that hold about a quart each, and I have to fill them every third day. That adds up to a lot of sugar.

There seems to be a dramatic increase in the number of hummers in recent years. I can remember seeing only one or two when I was a boy. Nobody fed them then and I suspect the fact that almost everybody does now has affected the population. It sure has made it easier for them to make a living. A minute at the feeder nets them more food than an hour of foraging. I don't know if we're doing them any favors. I hardly ever see one at a flower anymore. After several generations have been raised at feeders, they might have forgotten how to feed at flowers. If the feeders suddenly disappeared, a lot of them might starve.

Some species of wildlife have taken a beating lately. Two of my favorite sounds are no longer heard in my immediate area. It's been two years since I heard a whippoorwill, and even longer since I heard a ruffed grouse drumming. It's a shame. They were part of what makes Appalachia what it is. It's hard to say what is the cause of their demise. The countryside still has adequate cover for their existence and I'm sure there are plenty of insects for the whippoorwills. There must be some other reason they have gone. Some theorize that the whippoorwills' wintering grounds, which are in central and northern South America, have been disturbed or destroyed. I'm inclined to agree with that.

As for the grouse, I don't know. They have been on the decline for several years. They require a lot of room so they can remain undisturbed, especially at nesting time. It might be that there are just too many people here now. Part of the trouble might be the recent influx of goshawks. They are moving in from their original home in northern Canada, where their main diet is ruffed grouse. Nature is on a reorganization spree, shifting habitats around. At any rate, I miss them.

The quail have never recovered since they were wiped out in the fierce winter of 1977-78, despite efforts to restock them. Releasing pen-raised birds won't do the trick. The instincts are there, but survival skills must be learned from parents if they are to make it. ODNR will have to capture wild coveys and release them here just as they did the turkeys if we are ever to hear that beautiful clear song again. The tone is so pure that it almost brings tears to my eyes with its perfection.

Mother nature is an opportunist and will fill any empty space with something. Speaking of turkeys reminds me of their success story. They have taken off like wildfire. They have filled the void left by the grouse tenfold. Maybe that is a contributing factor to the disappearance of the grouse. They do overlap somewhat in their diet and roosting and nesting habits. I don't know if anyone is studying this phenomenon or not but it would be interesting to find out.

The problem is that all nature is intertwined in ways that we can't even imagine. When a species is eliminated, who knows what the implications are?

There are some obvious things that we notice, but it might be years before we know how they affects us personally. Honeybees are a case in point. I used to keep bees here and they were everywhere doing their job of pollinating plants — not just flowers, but garden, farm and orchard crops as well. An almost microscopic mite has invaded the trachea of honeybees, killing them during the winter.

There are treatments beekeepers can use to help, but at least half the hives still don't make it. The wild swarms that inhabit hollow trees in the woods get no treatment, and so none that I am aware of survive. I haven't seen a honeybee in at least three years. So how are the plants getting pollinated?

By the same method that they used before the honeybee was imported from Europe by early colonists. They thrived in an alien land because they had no natural enemies here. Now the other bees that we thought of as nuisances have their old jobs back and are doing all right, thank you. Bumble bees and yellow jackets are the main ones, but there are dozens of others. Don't forget the wind. I was afraid there wouldn't be any blackberries this year even though there were more blossoms than I've ever seen. Somehow there was a bumper crop.

I know it's futile to worry about such things. The whole planet is being overrun by a relatively new species — homo sapiens. I won't live to see the end result and I hope my grandchildren won't, but I'm afraid it is inevitable if we don't learn to control our own population. I've seen dramatic changes in the twenty-three years I've lived here. What will another hundred do? I certainly hope we wake up to what's happening before it's too late.

Man's Best Friend Can Be a Predatory Fiend
October 25, 1997

The nights are alive here in the woods. Not my personal night life, but the wildlife is active in the dark.

I hear all sorts of rustling in the dry leaves. The deer sound like people walking. Their cadence is about the same speed as a person's.

I sleep in a screen house in the woods in the warmer months, so I'm attuned to the creatures of the night. I hear 'coons chattering and chirruping and occasionally fighting. There is the squeaking of mice rummaging in the leaves and the hooting of the owls. There are three kinds of owls that make their homes here: the barred owl, the great horned and the screech owl. Screech owls have been scarce in the last few years.

They call back and forth and sometimes they fight. I also hear coyotes howl once in a while. There are always dogs barking. I pay little attention to them.

Things quiet down as dawn breaks. When I get up to start my day, the night creatures are just ending theirs. The first thing I hear as I awake is the putt-putt-putt of an oil well from somewhere over the hills. That is soon drowned by the traffic, first a hum, then a roar. It seems we can't escape the ubiquitous trucks. Then the dogs, the ones that slept a little during the night, start their symphony.

Last Friday morning, as I prepared my cabin for new guests, I noticed a turkey vulture (or buzzard, if you will) land on a low tree branch just out back. I see them circling daily as they ride the thermals effortlessly, but I have never seen one land in the woods. I watched him for about ten minutes. He just sat there, looking around patiently. At last he sailed off the branch a few feet and apparently landed in a small side ravine just above the crick.

I knew there had to be something dead there. Their only occupation is soaring the skies looking for carrion. (I have often thought that I would be willing to live on dead animals if I could soar through the boundless skies as they do. I rarely eat anything alive anyhow.) Now this was at eight o'clock in the morning and there were no buzzards there the day before. There were thick trees overhead, so the ground wasn't visible from the air, so how did he find it, whatever it was? I've heard that they can smell death from amazing distances and now I believe it's true. It is truly an amazing feat to find a freshly dead body from several hundred feet in the air from where it couldn't be seen.

I determined to find out what was there. I had a sinking feeling that I knew, but hoped that I was wrong. I wasn't. I walked back toward the area. As I turned into the ravine, three more vultures took the air. There, sprawled grotesquely on her back, was a large doe. She hadn't been dead long. The earth was torn up in a circle around her. She still had blood seeping from dozens of wounds. Her abdomen was ripped open and her entrails were spilled out onto the forest floor. I found strips of skin and hair lying about. These were about a foot and a half long and three inches wide. I turned her over and her back and haunches were nearly stripped bare and large mouthfuls of flesh torn from her hams. There were more strips of skin under her.

All this indicated to me that there could be but one creature that would do a thing like this. Dogs! Not wild dogs that kill to eat, but someone's pets that were now home sleeping in their master's kitchen. Outside of the chunks torn from the hindquarters, nothing was missing. Whatever did this wasn't hungry! They did it purely for the thrill of the chase.

What got me was that all of this was done while she was still alive. Can you imagine the sheer terror and pain this poor defenseless creature must have endured? How would it feel to be surrounded by vicious animals, snarling and barking, unable to run any longer, and have your skin torn off and your guts ripped out while you watched? I don't think I would enjoy it, would you? The only other animal that has ever made a practice of this kind of cruelty is the human race.

Wolves, bears, mountain lions or coyotes go for the throat and kill as quickly as possible. There is no evidence that they enjoy killing. They do it because they must to live. The dogs don't have to kill to live. They are well fed, well rested and sheltered. The kill for sport, just like their masters.

I would bet if these dogs were caught in the act and taken to their homes, their owners would swear that their dogs couldn't have done it. The never hurt anything in their lives. Dogs are so gentle and kind and affectionate you just couldn't believe that they are capable of killing.

This isn't the first time I've seen this happen. About four or five years ago, I heard dogs making a commotion down in the crick. I figured they had run a groundhog to ground so I didn't respond right away. When they kept it up for a while, I got curious. When I looked over the bank, I was sickened by what I saw. Two dogs had a doe down in the water and were tearing at her back end. Huge chunks of flesh had been torn from her haunches. These were not large, vicious man-eating dogs. One was a small beagle and the other was a medium-sized German shepherd. I yelled at them and they ran off. I tried to help the doe out of the water. She couldn't walk very well. It was then I noticed that her front foot had been chewed off. I figured she was doomed. I went some distance and watched. She managed to hobble a few yards on three legs and lay down in some tall grass where she all but disappeared. I was sure that she would die a horribly painful death, so I called the game warden to put her out of her misery, which he did.

He told me that this was much more common than one would think. Most people wouldn't think that a beagle could catch a deer, but it can. The thing is, it doesn't do it alone. There are always two or more. The pack mentality kicks in when there are more than one. They will do things collectively that they wouldn't do alone. Most people think that deer can run too fast for a dog to catch them. Actually, they can, but they can only run short distances at that speed and then they must rest. A dog, especially one that is well fed and rested, can run for hours and wear a deer down until it is exhausted. When that time comes, the deer is helpless. Then the dogs have their fun.

I'm sickened by this episode. I'm begging people to keep their dogs home. If they could see what I have seen, they would. I guess they will have to see it to believe it. I would invite anyone to come see, but those marvelous garbage disposals of the air have all but cleaned up the woods in three days time. There were as many as twenty at a time at the feast. All that remains are the hooves and a few bones and hair.

I miss that old girl. She's all I had left of a herd that once numbered about ten. Several have been shot by hunters and at least four have been killed by cars and trucks this summer on about a hundred yards of highway out front. I put out feed and only the birds and chipmunks eat it. It's kinda lonely out here now without those sweet, gentle friends.

Bringing Out the Beast in Us All
March 28, 1998

Have you ever noticed that people attribute human traits to animals?

It seems to be just a natural thing to do. When you stop and think about it, it's an act of utter arrogance on our part. We are assuming that people are the smartest, strongest, most thinking, most caring beings in the world.

I guess in some ways that is true, but many of these critters were on this earth millions of years before man appeared and did very well, thank you. Maybe they have assigned some of their traits to us. Some of us are bull-headed, while others are as stubborn as a mule. I'll bet you know someone who is grouchy as a bear or can run like a deer. We all know people who are strong as an ox or even smell like a horse. I had a friend who drank like a fish, or at least people said he did. I never really saw a fish drink, so I don't know for sure.

I've heard that crows hold kangaroo court. I've never heard of kangaroos holding kangaroo court, however. Wolves are said to be evil man-eaters though there has never been a verified case of that happening and only one or two instances of wolves even attacking a man. How many cases are there of men attacking men? There are certainly plenty of instances of men eating men. Which one is evil?

The early Indians, and I suppose the contemporary ones too, believed that all creatures had a spirit just as humans do. In fact, even inanimate objects had a spirit. Most of them worshiped animals and felt as one with them. Many believed that bears and wolves and others were their brothers. That's only natural, I suppose, because they lived close to the earth and the animals. Most of us don't live that way anymore, so we must think as we do out of habit.

Surely, we've all talked to dogs as though they understood every word. I have a friend who thinks of her dog as her offspring. She says things like, "Just a minute, Sweetheart, Mommy'll get your din-din," or, "Come on, Sweety, help Mommy feed the horses." She also feeds deer and has them all named for their habits or physical appearance. There's Momma, Bossie, Scar Baby, Bucky and so on.

Different people see animals in different ways. My neighbor John Brenneman and I share the same deer and turkeys. There is a buck that had one antler shot off the first day of doe season and a turkey that limps. He calls the buck "One Horn" and the turkey "Chester" after the stiff-legged deputy on the TV series "Gunsmoke." Isn't that ridiculous, for a grown man to give silly names like that to wild animals? Besides, the buck's name is "Lefty" because the right antler is missing and the turkey's name is "Hopalong" after "Hopalong Cassidy." I suppose he should be called "Ed" — he walks just like I do.

Another animal that most people think of as evil — or at least as a devious character — is the snake. People seem to give it human characteristics such as wickedness and hatefulness. The poor critters are guilty only of being snakes. They do what snakes do and apparently what some humans do — sneak around and kill things. Think about it. What would you do if you had no arms or legs and had to slither around on your belly to catch some four-legged varmint for supper. I don't think you'd be dancing around playing a guitar. You would hide and ambush your supper.

The aversion we have to snakes goes back to Adam and Eve in the Garden of Eden. Evidently snakes could talk then. The serpent talked Eve into eating an apple and that started all our troubles. No wonder we don't like snakes.

Skunks don't get much affection from humans, but we attribute some human traits to them, too. If you've ever seen Walt Disney's "Bambi," you can't help but love the sweet little bashful friend of Bambi's, Flower. He's so cute! Or if you're too young to have seen that, I'll bet you've seen Pepe LePew on the Saturday morning cartoons. Now, he's not a bit bashful. He is the epitome of the ladies man. (In my youth, he would have been called a "gay blade," but that has all changed now.)

The cartoons are fertile grounds for humanizing animals. Some of them portray the animals as villains, and we can see the possibility of the animal having these traits — for example, the Tasmanian Devil. In truth, he is about the size of a small dog with a bad temper and never ate a tree in his life. Other times the critters are given personalities just opposite their real-life personality. Tom and Jerry come to mind. The tiny mouse always outwits the big ol' bad cat, and we love it. We love to root for the underdog even if the underdog is a mouse. (What is an underdog, anyway? I never did understand where that phrase came from.)

I guess we'll never know why we do what we do, but it's been around for a long time and I suppose it will never change, unless we run out of animals (and that could happen sooner than we think). The good die young and the "evil" ones will be the last to go. It's something to think about, anyhow.

Why Can't I Find Mushrooms?

April 25, 1998

This has been an odd spring. After a mild winter we are spoiled. We keep expecting spring to be mild too.

It is, upon occasion, but then after a day or two it slams us between the eyes with a blast that leaves us wondering what happened.

I think you'll have to agree that this past Sunday was just absolutely lousy. It rained almost all day. Not a rain that would keep us inside doing inside jobs like working on income taxes or cleaning, but a soft mist that nevertheless left us soaked after a while.

A walk in the woods was not all that pleasant. The wildflowers don't show up as well on a gloomy day as when the sun shines. The mushrooms evidently don't show up either. I didn't find a single one.

I'll have to admit that I'm one who doesn't live to hunt mushrooms. It's a good thing too, because I rarely find any. I wish just once I could find a whole mess of them so that when somebody asks, "Ja' find any mushrooms yet?" I could say, "Yeah, I got a few."

I don't know why everyone I meet asks that. I think the ones who have found some want to show off and ask about it so they can say, "I found a sack full last week." They don't say how big the sack was. Just for the record, so you don't have to ask me, "No, I ain't found no damned mushrooms!"

This evening, an hour before dark, I took a tour through the woods to see what I could see. There are very few wildflowers bloomin' in the deep woods. They are concentrated mostly around the edges where they can get more light. The trilliums seem to like the shady glens. Down in the ravine, near the little nameless brook that feeds Scott's Crick beside my FEMA Memorial Bridge, there are dozens of them, along with yellow, white and blue violets, hepatica and bloodroot. Purple and white phlox bloom just a few feet up the side of the ravine where a little more sun can reach. They are so beautiful.

As I wandered up the ridge toward my neighbor's place there was almost nothing blooming on the ground, but overhead the trees were exploding into new leaves.

The red maples were almost through blooming, but the smaller twigs in the treetops were adding a touch of red to the bright, light green of the poplar and hickory leaves. (I think I might have hit on the reason I don't find mushrooms. I'm usually looking up at the tree-tops. The 'shrooms don't grow up there.)

I eventually found myself at John's lake. It is always a gorgeous jade green, except after a storm that leaves it muddy for a time. I wonder if that's why it's called Jade Lake. It's just like a jewel mounted in a setting of green hills.

The dark pines on the other side were reflected upside down perfectly in the still water, like a brooding painting. A stray shaft of sunlight escaped from the cloudy sky and landed a few feet away. It painted the shoreline a marvelous pinkish hue. Bright red splatches caught my attention. What a surprise!

Several dozen fire pinks were blooming there in a patch about ten feet across. They are certainly early this year. I don't expect to see them until well into May. They are absolutely the reddest red in the flower world, I think. The only thing redder that I can think of in the natural world is the elusive scarlet tanager. It's rare to see more than just a flash of them and they're gone.

As I wandered back toward home, I spotted John clearing the winter's hoard of leaves from the ditch along his driveway and decided to go over and chat with him. By the time I had moseyed that far, stopping to inspect things of interest along the way, he was sitting on his back porch taking his shoes off, his day's toil at an end.

I sat down on the top step and we had a nice half-hour talk. We talked of cabbages and kings and other important things.

While we were chatting, a pair of wild geese flew over, talking as they flew, as they always do.

I've often wondered what they are saying. After much conjecture, we decided it goes something like this. She is saying, "Don't fly so fast. Don't fly so high. Look out for those trees. Are you sure this is the way to Aunt Martha's?" And he's replying, "Yes dear. Yes dear."

John said, "Just stop and look around. I'll bet some people would pay a million bucks just to be able to sit in a beautiful setting like this and talk to good friends."

I had to agree. Even though neither of us can be considered well off financially, we wouldn't trade places with anybody. There are not many places more beautiful than this and we've each built our environment to our own tastes. What more could we want?

Just as important as the place where we find ourselves are the friends we have made. John and I have been friends for nearly thirty years and we seldom ask anything of each other, but we are secure in knowing that we can and it will be given without question. That's what real friendship is, and I consider it a treasure beyond price.

Let Nature Run Its Course
June 6, 1998

It finally feels like summer. After a mild winter and a spell of cold spring and hot spring, summer seems to have settled in at last.

And yet the weatherman this evening predicted that it would be more like fall the rest of the week. What are ya gonna do? We'll just have to take what comes and make the best of it.

That's what put mankind on top of the heap. Adaptability. Man has managed to prosper wherever he has ended up. We have colonized every part of the earth. We've not only been everywhere, but managed to make it our own. No matter how inhospitable a place is, man has been there, done that. Everywhere on earth there are some animals that survive and thrive there, but only man is everywhere. Kinda scary, ain't it? What's left? Outer space and under the sea, and we're working on them.

What brought all this to mind was an incident that happened last Sunday. I'll grant you that the thought process took me around Robin Hood's barn to get to this point, but when you get into old age you think a lot. Why don't we think in our youth? Don't ask me.

Anyhow, last Sunday a friend called to ask me something. A neighbor had seen a very small fawn standing by the road for the better part of two days. The neighbor was almost in a panic. She was sure that the baby's mother was dead and she didn't know what to do. She wanted to help but didn't know how. What should she do? Since it was Sunday, there was no answer at Ohio Department of Natural Resources' Division of Wildlife and there was no one to ask, so she asked me.

Without being there and knowing all the facts, I wasn't much help, either. I had heard of someone near Athens who was licensed to rehabilitate hawks and such, but didn't know her name. My friend

235

made some inquiries and was able to locate the lady. She said she would come in immediately. When she got there, they couldn't find the fawn so the whole thing was moot. We don't know if the doe came back or someone stopped and picked up the fawn or if it were set upon by dogs or what, so there was a lot of anxiety about nothing.

My personal opinion is that we shouldn't interfere in these situations. I know it's hard not to help something so sweet and lovable as a fawn. It would be easier if they were covered with scales and breathed fire. It seems cruel to leave a baby alone to fend for itself, but nature is cruel. It's the survival of the fittest. It always has been and always will be.

Let's conjecture on what would have happened if they had caught that fawn. First off, they would have to feed it soon. But what? What do baby deer eat? Milk, for one thing. But what is deer milk like? It's probably similar to cow's milk as it comes from the cow, with either more or less butterfat and more or less of this or that. If it's not pretty close, it will sicken a baby and give it scours (diarrhea) and it will die in a day or two. Not a happy way to go.

If it should make it past that hurdle, where do you keep it? In the house would not be an option for most of us. Most people anymore don't have barns or fenced-in areas except the back yard. We don't want it in Mama's flowers. We don't want it doing its job on the sidewalk. We end up prevailing on a friendly farmer to save this poor baby. Chances are the farmer would like to get rid of most of the deer anyway.

Well, suppose we find a place to keep it. What then? It must have room to move around a bit. After all, it's a wild animal. It's not fair to keep it confined. We find a pasture in which to keep it. How do we keep it in? A deer, even one not full grown, can jump a standard farm fence with ease. The first thing you know it's in the woods again. That's what we wanted, right? The thing is, it's not fully wild. We couldn't teach it the things its mother could and it wouldn't have the skills to survive in the wild. It wouldn't know the best things to eat, where are the best places to hide, what are the things to stay away from, how to get through a bad winter. It would be imprinted on humans. That might be OK for a while. Most humans wouldn't hurt it, but come hunting season most humans in the woods are carrying

236

guns. Guess what will happen to a deer that doesn't run at the sight.

I know for a fact that we are not doing wildlife any favors when we try to tame them. I have had deer at my doorstep for several years and I confess that I like having them here so I have fed them. They became partly tame and accepted me as part of the landscape. I was flattered when I met them in the woods and they didn't run. A couple of years ago, during hunting season, I saw them down by the crick one afternoon and spoke to them. They stopped and talked a bit, then wandered on. They followed the stream toward a neighbor's place. Within four or five minutes, five shots rang out and I never saw them again. Three generations were wiped out at once. Four does that I considered my pets were gone forever because I interfered with their lives. I don't think I did them any favors. Had I left them alone they might have had better lives.

So to get back to my story, I called the Athens office of ODNR and talked to the wildlife man. His response was almost identical to my thoughts. He said he had sent questionnaires to the natural resources divisions of all fifty states asking what their policy is on like situations. Of the twenty-five or thirty replies received, the overwhelming majority agreed. To add to that, he said that the only way you can legally keep a wild animal is to buy a hunting license and shoot it in season or have a license to rehab orphaned or injured animals under state supervision. Otherwise you are subject to fine or imprisonment.

That sounds pretty clear to me. There is such an establishment in Nelsonville. Though I don't know the name of it, I believe that it is operated by or in conjunction with Hocking College. A few phone calls would find it for you if you should find yourself in that situation.

Finding "orphaned" animals this time of year is quite common. Most are not orphaned. Rabbits, for instance, scratch a little hole in a field or lawn and line it with hair and leave their babies in it.

To avoid leading predators to the nest, they don't go near it all day and go sit over it at night so the babies can suckle.

Young birds fall or fly out of the nest and the parents raise a ruckus. Most people feel that they have to help and try to put them back in the nest. They jump right out again and the people start calling the authorities or TV stations for help and that doesn't help. What we have to realize is that nature works that way. If only one out of five survives, that is enough to keep the population stable. If one out of several thousand fish reach adulthood, that is enough. We must let nature work its wonders. If we want to help wildlife, let's concentrate on saving habitat for them and keeping the waters clean for them. They will make it if we let them.

I told you I had to go around Robin Hood's barn to get here, didn't I? I hope you'll forgive me for preaching the gospel of common sense, but sometimes I just can't help myself.

Observations Made During a Stroll in the Woods
June 20, 1998

We've had some rainy weather for the last couple of weeks that has kept me close to home. I'm not so sweet that I'll melt if I get wet, but I still prefer to stay dry if I can. This past Sunday morning was just gorgeous, so I decided to let my housecleaning go for a while and take a stroll. (I used to hike, but now I stroll.)

Though everything was dripping and the ground was damp, there's not much growing on the ground in the deep woods, so my feet stayed fairly dry. I started at about 7:30 a.m., while the sun was still struggling to climb over the hills. The air was pleasantly cool and a faint breeze dried the sweat that started to pop out on my brow before I got to the top of the first hill. The sky was a deep blue and a few puffy white clouds sailed majestically overhead. It was a morning to make you glad just to be here.

The birds were happy to have a sunny day, too. They sang their hearts out. My favorite singer, the wood thrush, put on a concert to gladden the heart. They are the most beautiful singers of all, in my opinion. I almost never see one, but they serenade me daily. Somewhere, high in the treetops, a scarlet tanager sang harmony. I didn't see him either, but his robin-like song was unmistakable. I wish I could have seen him. They are among the most beautiful of birds. They are the reddest of reds. All the body is red but the wings and tail, which are jet black. I'm sort of glad they are secretive. It makes every sighting an event. It would be a shame if they were so common that we didn't pay any attention to them.

As I walked the dry ridge tops where the oaks and hickories grow, I noticed several white oaks were dead. There were three in a cluster, about ten feet apart, that had died. I don't know what could have killed them, but I do know that the roots will graft themselves together and some diseases can be transmitted that way, so I deduced that's probably what happened. I saw a couple more on another ridge that were isolated, so that might be something different. I'll have to check into that. There are always trees dying in the woods, but these were fairly young trees that should have been growing vigorously and not dying of old age. 'Tis a puzzlement!

I had crossed over onto the Hocking Valley Ranch by now and I came across isolated fields of grass that were very wet and soon my feet were gurgling in my shoes. One of my favorite parts of the ranch is what they call the "high pasture." From there, you have a nice view — down the valley, through which Zeigler Road runs. The grass had gone to seed and was waist high. I love to see it that way, a sea of grass — amber waves of grain and all that. I took about three steps into it and decided that I would soon be wet to my chubby little buttocks, so I gingerly backed out to save it for another day.

There were plenty of tracks of deer and an occasional 'coon. The horse manure on the trails had been scattered, the work of wild turkeys retrieving the undigested grain from the meadow muffins. One animal's waste is another animal's breakfast. Nothing is wasted in nature. Everything is recycled.

By the time I had climbed to the highest ridge, the sun had finally made it over the hilltops. It didn't penetrate the woods very much, but here and there a stray ray of sunshine found its way through the thick foliage. One shone directly on a spider web that was strung across the trail, illuminating it like a spotlight on the face of the lead actor in a Broadway play. It was magnificent. The web was perfect. The symmetry was perfect. The lighting was perfect. The sun made the web glow as though it were an icicle on a sunny winter day.

How can we comprehend that a tiny insect can create such a work of art on the first try with no parent to teach him how? It's inborn that he knows this. We call it instinct. Why do we higher creatures have to spend a lifetime learning to do things that others know at birth? The only instinct that humans have is to suckle. It ain't fair.

While the spider might know how to build a perfect web, he doesn't know where to build it. He knows only to find tree limbs or something, spaced about right. He has no idea if it's a good or bad place to catch insects and therefore whether he prospers or starves is purely up to chance. I guess that might level the field somewhat.

During the past couple of weeks, I've heard a lot of screaming up in the treetops that tells me the goshawks have hatched another brood. They didn't use their nest of last year, but opted to move farther from the road. I've seen them about a mile west of here all fall and winter. It's strange that they came back to a few hundred feet of the old home place to raise their young'ns. I still haven't seen the fledglings, but I hear them all day, every day. It's kind of comforting to know some very wild things can manage to survive here.

It was a wonderful walk Sunday morning, but the best thing was that I was able to do it at all. For the past couple of years, I've been able to hobble around where I had to go but didn't feel like walking just for fun. Since I've had my arthritic knee replaced, I haven't been up to one hundred percent. Then last December I sprained my ankle and it just wouldn't heal. Just in the last month I've been able to walk on it. I also was taking a prescription for high blood pressure that did a good job on the pressure but left me short of breath. I had to stop and blow like an old broke-winded workhorse every fifty feet. I finally figured that out and changed medicine.

At last I can walk again and life seems worth living. I intend to do more and more walking and regain my old vigor. I used to walk my city friends half to death. I intend to do it again!

Humming a Little Bird's Happy Song
July 11, 1998

I sit on my screened-in porch almost every day and watch the world go by — at least the natural world.

I'm entertained by deer, turkeys, squirrels, chipmunks and birds. The most entertaining of the birds are the hummingbirds. They zip in and out like bullets and stop like they've hit a stone wall. They can maneuver quicker than a flash.

I love to watch their aerial show. They are feisty little mites. They fight and squabble constantly. There always seems to be one that will lay in wait until another comes to feed and then ambush the newcomer. The funny thing is that it's not always the same one. They change off occasionally. Sometimes it's a female in charge but mostly a male. I think there must be a referee that makes them spend time in the penalty box if they get too aggressive.

They are also very bold, or at least tolerant. I had a guest in my cabin last week who really wanted to get closeup pictures. He sat about fifteen feet from the feeder with a long lens and had trouble trying to hold it still enough to get a clear picture without a tripod.

"Why don't you get closer with a closeup lens?" I asked. (He had a ton of camera equipment.)

"I don't want to scare 'em," he said.

"Watch."

I went up to within six inches of the feeder and stood very still. Within two minutes, they were buzzing around my head as if I weren't there. One even hovered about three inches from my nose and looked me in the eye. The man snapped a great picture. I left him alone, then, to go back to work. I wasn't more than fifty feet away before he was beside the feeder, camera plastered against his eye. He told me later that some came right up and stared into the lens and he had some real closeups.

Hummers seem to be a fairly recent phenomenon. I can only remember seeing four or five in my entire life until I moved to Hocking County, and then it was rare to see one. It was only after I saw several at a neighbor's feeder that I realized they were more common. I put up a feeder about ten years ago and I would see one every now and then. By summer's end, there were a half dozen or so. Every year I see more, which I guess are the young ones and their young. They now empty a quart feeder every two days. I thought that was a lot until I talked to a lady who lives in Vinton County who has about forty or fifty come to her feeder. She has a gallon-size feeder that they empty every day. That's a lot of sugar. I use about fifteen pounds a summer. She must have to buy it by the barrel.

I saw a program on PBS about hummers a couple of years ago.

There was a house somewhere in Arizona that had fifty feeders hanging from the eaves and they all had to be filled twice a day. I think that's a little extreme. They estimated that there were about 5,000 birds there. I have trouble counting eight because they move so quickly. It's like trying to count a swarm of bees.

I had been reading whatever I could find about hummers for some time, and it wasn't much. For Father's Day, my daughter and my grandsons brought me a book called "Treasury of Classic Nature Tales." It is a book of excerpts from works of authors including Henry David Thoreau, John Muir, John James Audubon, John Burroughs and many other more modern authors. It's a rather large book, some 500 pages.

The book is edited by Roger Caras, who is an animal activist. I'm sure you've seen him on television. Coincidentally, he included one of his own. He wrote a lengthy treatise on migrations of several species, among them the ruby-throated hummingbirds, the only species found in Ohio. It's quite amazing that a creature can fly so far and so fast.

He states that a ruby-throat weighs only one-eighth of an ounce. During late summer they eat heavily and lay on fat. That fat is equal in weight to a postage stamp. They fly at about fifty miles an hour, stopping only occasionally for a sip of nectar when they migrate. They stop to refuel for a day or two on the coast of the Gulf of Mexico. Just where depends on the route that's been genetically implanted throughout millions of years. They fly 500 miles over water to the Yucatan Peninsula in Mexico and then disperse over the jungle, some as far as Central and South America. Now, that's truly a Herculean task. My butt gets tired just driving 500 miles with rest stops. Can you imagine what it would be like to have nowhere to stop or die if you did?

Hummers have such a high metabolism rate that they would starve if they didn't eat for twelve hours. To overcome this, they actually hibernate every night. Their heartbeat and respiration slow to about one third normal and return to normal in the morning.

I've noticed that the birds give way when challenged by a bee or wasp at the feeder. I think that they could kill a bee if they tried, but when you think about it, the risk is too great for them. They are so tiny that the amount of venom would be several thousand times stronger than it would be if injected into a human adult.

Hummingbirds line their nests with spider webs. I guess some spiders object to seeing their day's work destroyed in a moment. A friend who's fed hummers for years told me that he found a bird wrapped in spider web and almost unconscious. It apparently had been bitten by a spider after getting entangled in the web. He took it in the house and carefully cut away the web. The bird couldn't move its wings but could cling to a perch. He managed to get a few drops of sugar water into its beak with a very small syringe. He did this every few minutes for several days.

When he got up on about the fourth day, the bird was flying about the kitchen. He opened the door and the bird went outside to the feeder, apparently none the worse for the experience. The man felt great!

It's nice to know that at least one wild thing is prospering from man's activities. If it would help, I'd gladly put up a whippoorwill feeder. If there was money to be made, you can bet someone would be raising flies to sell.

The Advent of Autumn and Other Seasonal Thoughts
August 15, 1998

Do you get the feeling that summer is almost over? I do. It's only mid-August and leaves are falling already.

The other day when we had the first breeze in weeks, the leaves came down like snow here in the woods. Even maples and poplars are shedding. The gums are bright red. They are usually the first to turn, but it seems a little early. The sourwoods are getting a purple tinge to them. The walnuts are yellowing a bit, too.

This is all too soon for me. I want summer to cool off a bit but linger on for a couple of months yet. An old Kentuckian I used to work with summed it up beautifully when he said, "It makes ya wonder whur yer summer's wages went, don't it?"

I suppose El Niño will get the blame for all this. We didn't really have much winter last year, and a wet spring that made things grow like crazy. Now it's so dry that most trees and plants are under stress.

Except for two rainfalls of about a half inch each, we haven't had a good rain here for about six weeks. Things always seem to balance out in the end, and I look for a wet fall and a cold winter with lots of snow. I don't have anything to indicate this but the law of averages, and that's not very scientific. It's usually not far off, though.

I took a little drive this evening and was taken aback by the number of Eastern tent caterpillar webs I saw. I knew that there was a heavy infestation, but there were literally millions of them. The sun lighted the webs from behind and made them glow like fluorescent lights. It was quite attractive in spite of the damage they are doing. Nature is beautiful even when she hurts.

It's unusual for these critters to appear so numerous in the fall. They usually come in the spring with a big infestation and then a minor one in the fall. In the spring they seem to prefer wild cherry trees and they can strip every leaf off a tree in a few days. Once they leave the tree, new leaves appear and the tree seems none the worse, though a little slow to fruit. I don't know how this fall onslaught will affect them. Maybe not at all. We'll see, come spring, I reckon. It appears they are attacking just about any tree regardless of species — even walnut, which doesn't taste good to most insects. A very cold winter will help control them next year, though it will be hard on the woodpile.

Speaking of the woodpile, it's about time to get started laying in the winter's supply. I have three or four trees that have either died or blown down since this time last year. They will just about get me through the winter. It's really too hot to cut wood right now, but it takes about three months to get new wood dry enough to burn, so the time is not far off. I have some left from last year because of the mild winter. That will help.

I do hope that we get a soaking rain soon. As dry as it is, there will be considerable potential for forest fires if it doesn't rain soon. The crick is dry except for a few pools. The 'coons and kingfishers are having a ball with minnows trapped there. We need it for the corn and beans to mature as well. It's crucial that corn get moisture in August to fill out the ears. Corn has grown so well this year. It just shot up after a rain-delayed planting. It would be a shame to have the crop reduced for lack of rain now.

That reminds me of a story told by Bob Burns, a homespun comedian on the radio back in the 1930s. He called himself "The Arkansas Traveler." Come to think of it, I probably told this before. Well what the heck, you've probably forgotten it anyway.

It seems back home in Arkansas they had a terrible dry hot spell just as the corn was ripening. Bob had planted a field of popcorn right next to the barn. (You can see it coming, can't you?) Well it got so hot one day the popcorn popped right off the ears. It was about six inches deep on the ground. Bob's old mule (mules are always old) saw that and thought it it was snow and laid down and froze to death. Now that's hot!

I had a wonderful thing happen in front of my driveway today. The Ohio Department of Transportation finished the bridge they've been working on for six or seven weeks. They took away the barriers and signs and orange barrels and turned off the traffic lights. The silence is deafening. For weeks cars and trucks have been stopping and starting right in front of my drive, twenty-four hours a day. The brakes on a lot of the big trucks squeaked as they stopped and they shifted gears about twenty times as they drove off. Some of the hot-rod pickups had modified mufflers or no mufflers and roared away like they were in a tractor pull. Some people waited on the lights, which seemed to take a half hour to change, and others who were behind them got impatient and started blowing their horns. Lots of shouting back and forth. Ah! Blessed quiet.

Now I can hear the katydids and tree frogs. I like them better. I heard a screech-owl tonight — the first one in a couple of years. I guess he is glad for the quiet too. I've heard coyotes howling very early in the morning. They seem to call just as it's starting to get light. They'll howl maybe five or six times and that's it. I know they can be pests, but I sorta like to hear 'em. I'm glad there is enough wildness left that they can live here, at least a few of 'em.

The Pond
April 24, 1999

At last, it seems that lazy Ol' Spring is awakening and starting to raise its drowsy head. After such a mild winter it feels as though spring is taking a long time to get goin'. We have a rain or storm about every other day now. If we could get some warm nights now things would really pop.

The service berry trees have put on a grand display this year — the best I've seen in recent years. The dogwoods are just beginning to open. They've lingered in limbo this year for a long time. By next week they should be in full bloom. The red buds are out in all their glory now. I don't think I've ever seen them prettier.

I was out in the bottoms this evening and all the little early wild flowers are at their peak. The violets are, though shy, at their loveliest. You have to look for them in the grass. The same is true of the Star of Bethlehem and spring beauties. The spring beauties show up well in the deep woods where there is no underbrush, but you have to look for them in the pasture. I haven't had horses for several years and I think that's the reason the small flowers are doing so well. I guess the horses ate 'em before. I even found some dog-toothed violets, or trout lilies as some people call them. They used to be plentiful, but mighty scarce of late.

The hepatica is blooming along the crick where it's shady. It's so delicate that it won't take much trampling. The same is true of trilliums. There was a sizable patch near my rental cabin, but I could find only four plants there today.

All this spring talk gets me in a fishing mood. I've always wanted a house on a lake or river, but it never worked out. Last fall I got to thinkin' that it would be easier to build a lake next to the house than to buy land with a lake and then build a house. Sorta makes sense when you think about it. Well, I decided to build a pond where I could see it from the house and just grab a pole and walk out there when I wanted to fish.

I got started digging in mid-October when it was cool enough to exert myself without over-heating. (One smells so when one perspires, you know.) In only a few days, I had a pond excavated. It wasn't really large, but adequate. Fall being the dry season, I had to wait some time for it to fill. Meantime, I scoured the neighborhood for some aquatic plants to plant around the perimeter to give fish and wildlife some cover. I was just sure that deer would come to drink, and ducks and geese would nest there, and foxes and 'coons would appear to raid the nests for eggs and ducklings and goslings. It was all so exciting.

At last the rains came and it filled to the brim. I installed the greenery in appropriate places and sat back to await action. Nothing happened right away, as it was November and too cold for rapid growth. It soon froze over and I dreamed of having all my friends over for a skating party while I made hot chocolate over a roaring fire. But alas, it never got cold enough to freeze solid enough for winter fun, though I did see signs that a 'coon had tried it and fallen through the thin ice, and that was fun.

At last the ice melted and things began to happen. The cattail is a foot high and I saw some sort of a water bug in there today. I called the wildlife people for advice on how to stock it and they said that since it was only three by five feet it would support exactly one blue gill to eat bugs that fell in and one very small catfish to vacuum the bottom. At last I have a fish pond. I think I will add a couple of gold-fish, though, so that I can at least see something. I did so want a bass boat, but I guess that's out since there won't be any bass. I'll also can-cel my water skiing lessons. I wouldn't want to injure my blue gill. It seems cruel to have one fish all alone. Maybe I'll get two blue gills and they can talk about how ugly the catfish is. I'll have to make sure they are both the same gender or they might over-populate the pond, and over-population causes a lot of problems, ya know. I guess I could feed them a little bit to make sure they don't starve.

What about the ducks and geese, though? I suppose the catfish will get used to eating goose poop. Will the 'coons eat all the eggs? It would be nice if one of each hatched, then I could get a little airplane and show them how to migrate south in the fall the way Disney did on TV last Sunday. Oh, this pond is going to be so much fun, and educational, too. I don't know why I didn't think of it years ago. I think I'll have to start a journal and write down everything that hap-pens. Soon I'll be able to write true nature stories and then maybe some books. I'll make lots of money and buy some land with a lake on it and build a new house so I can see the lake and write more stories and books and make more money. You know, this might be the smartest thing I ever did.

Nature's Mysteries
July 24, 1999

A couple of nights ago, I rode my four-wheeler through the woods to visit my friend and neighbor, John Brenneman. We passed a pleasant hour on his veranda, iced tea in hand, watching and talking to the deer that came for their evening snack. We talked of old times and new times and solved most of the world's problems with our innate wisdom.

Among the subjects discussed was the drought, of course, and the effect it could be having on our wells. It's especially critical this year with all the new homes being built by city folks. A good many of them have swimming pools, too.

Another subject was the increased traffic down on the highway. There was scarcely a moment free of the noise of passing cars and trucks. We could remember twenty-five years ago when we were newly-moved city folks, and there were only about a third of the cars that there are now. That's progress, I guess.

Another interesting part of the evening was the trip over. I found hundreds, perhaps thousands, of leaf bundles, for want of a better name, on the ground. These were green, though dry, and not the brown ones we've become used to seeing hanging on trees. The brown ones were damaged by the recent seventeen-year locust infestation.

It was in the gloaming and I couldn't see them well enough to tell how the green branches had been severed from the trees. I gathered up a few of them to take home and scrutinize more closely with a magnifying glass. Each "bundle" consisted of a main stem about three-sixteenths of an inch in diameter with several smaller limbs branching off from it. Each held about six to twelve leaves and most were white oak and a few were maple. There were none of the brown ones on the trees, and very few on the ground. Very strange.

My first thought when I saw them was that friend Dick Erb, who rides his horses through the woods, had been trimming the branches as he does periodically. I don't blame him; it's a real nuisance to have your hat knocked off while you're on horseback. It ain't easy to climb back up on them long-legged varmints every few minutes. I went back the next morning for more evidence, and I did find a few larger branches with a smooth cut on the ends. Either Dick had been trimming or the beavers learned to climb trees. It was a coincidence that both events took place at about the same time.

Upon close examination with the glass I noticed that every one of the branches was broken off at almost exactly the same diameter, three-sixteenths of an inch. Each break left a ragged end on the branch. I noticed that each branch had several small slits at the break-off point and several more at about one-inch intervals. Most of these slits had a small pin-hole about in the center. Some also had a groove starting at the hole and progressing along the branch for about an inch. I cut open several of these splits and couldn't find an egg or larva in any of them. They might have been there but were too small to see. It soon became obvious that these splits were caused by the female locust, or periodical cicada as they are more properly called, in which to lay eggs.

The mystery is, why didn't these leaves turn brown like the rest of them did, and why were they almost the same size? If you take a green oak twig and bend it, you can form it into a loop and it won't break. I tried that with dozens of these twigs and they broke as easily as a kitchen match. The slits not only weakened the branches, but allowed them to dry out so they would break more easily.

Could it be that this is a method that has evolved over the millennia to get the larvae quickly and safely to the ground? The branches float slowly to the ground like a parachute, transporting the larva in a few seconds to where it can enter the soil and start the cycle all over again. If larvae had to climb down, they would be subject to predation by birds and other insects. If they fell or jumped out of sixty- to eighty-foot-high trees, something else might happen to them. Who knows?

Why didn't the leaves turn brown? Maybe they would have, given time, but were visited by the late hatchers and hadn't had time to turn before a freak wind broke them off. I can't reach any of the brown leaves to know their condition, so I can't speculate on that part of the mystery. I might get to some of them one of these days. I did try to further this scientific research by saving a dozen or so of the twigs in a Tupperware box. If any should hatch out, I will see them. I suspect they are already gone.

John and I also talked about the disappearance of the whippoor-wills and owls. We haven't heard a whippoorwill or a screech owl in two or three years. They seem to have vanished. We both heard barred owls in the spring, but none lately. Talk about coincidence. John called the next morning to say that he had heard a barred owl within an hour after I had left.

Another strange phenomenon is the sudden proliferation of hum-mingbirds. I had a smaller number than usual this spring, and after a few weeks, that number dropped off to about half. In the last three weeks or so I've had at least four times as many. There are at least six at the feeders at any given time. They drink a little more than a quart of sugar water a day. I'm well into my third five-pound bag of sugar. I'm guessing that the drought has caused the flowers to finish bloom-ing early, leaving them unable to get food naturally, and they are tak-ing advantage of my hospitality.

Another mystery, to me at least, is where do frogs come from? My little pond, which is right outside my porch, is inhabited by six or eight frogs of varying sizes and colors. They all found their way here by themselves. The pond is at least 800 feet from the nearest water, which is Scott's Crick, not well-known for its amphibian population. John's lake is probably a good healthy quarter of a mile as the crow flies; and to my knowledge, frogs don't fly. Now that had to take a lot of three-foot jumps to get here. I'll bet they wore blisters and bruises on their bellies. Why would a frog go uphill looking for water, any-how?

Oh, well, I guess some things have to be mysteries. Life would be dull if we knew all the answers, wouldn't it?

Eager Beavers
June 24, 2000

Man in his wisdom has managed to eliminate most of the nuisances that have bugged him ever since the first white man set foot on this continent. The natives considered all creatures, including themselves, equal parts of the whole scheme of things and learned to live with them.

We have extirpated, so far, the buffalo, elk, bear, wolf, mountain lion, deer, wild turkey and beaver from the Ohio country. Some of these, when given a chance, have made a comeback. Without predators to keep them in balance, some are coming back with a vengeance. When I was a kid there were virtually no deer in Ohio except a few along the Pennsylvania border. I never saw one until about 1960.

After many failed attempts to bring the turkey back, ODNR finally was able to get some started. Now they are everywhere in great numbers. They tried turning domesticated turkeys loose in the woods at first. The foxes were grateful. The turkeys had all their brains bred out and were too dumb to take care of themselves, and were promptly eaten.

Next they tried pen-raised wild turkeys hatched in incubators. These had the instinct, but without mothers to teach them the tricks of the trade, they too failed. Finally someone had a brainstorm. They imported trapped wild birds from states that did have wild ones and turned them loose. They knew how to court, nest and raise a brood, and they did. From these some were trapped and transplanted to other parts of the state and now they're off and running. For some reason unknown to me, the grouse in this area have nearly disappeared in the last ten years. I wish ODNR would do the same for them. I miss hearing them drum on a log.

The same strategy has worked on the deer. A few were imported from West Virginia and Pennsylvania and you can see what happened then. A hundred years ago there were almost no woodlands left in Hocking County. They had all been cut to satisfy the enormous appetite of the iron furnaces. They gobbled up two acres of woods a day each, and there were five or six furnaces in the county at one time. It wasn't until the discovery that coal could do just as well as wood that they quit making charcoal. Then the forests began to come back and the deer with them.

The problem we have now with the deer population is that the balance of nature has been destroyed. There are no predators except man and his machines to keep them in check. If it weren't for the automobiles and roads good enough to let them go fast, we'd be up to our hips in deer. A few wolves and mountain lions would help, but few of us would go for that, I think.

Most of the wild animals are content just to live and increase. They have no agenda, save to eat and not be eaten. The main exception is the beaver. Their lives are lived for a purpose. Their lives are spent trying to stop water from flowing. They can't stand the sound of running water. (It's been rumored that the founder of the Corps of Engineers was mothered by a beaver. Since the corps' inception its main purpose has been to stop water from running.)

Beavers are compelled by some deep mysterious force to build a dam wherever possible. They have accomplished some wonderful feats. It's claimed by some that they are responsible for most of our farmland here in hill country. They dam the small streams and make ponds. These ponds fill up with silt washed down from above. The beavers move up or downstream and build new dams and start the process all over again. Eventually, after thousands of years, these become meadows and finally forests. The beavers cut the trees and build more dams atop the old and raise the whole valley another four to six feet.

This went on for thousands or even millions of years until guess what! The white man came! And you know what happened. He found out that beaver fur could be made into hats and killed millions of beavers for that purpose. The beaver was also responsible for much of the exploration of this country. The trappers would kill every beaver in an area and move on, ever westward, eventually to the Rocky Mountains. The beaver was all but wiped out just for the sake of a hat style.

The beaver hat went out of style, the forests grew back, and the predators were eliminated so the beaver started to make a comeback in just the last thirty years or so. I for one was happy to at last see a real live beaver. There was no such thing in Ohio when I grew up. The first that I know of took up residence in the bottom lands near Lake Hope.

I was thrilled to see several dams and ponds. It wasn't long until the dams flooded the state highway that bounded the ponds, and the battle was on. Beaver absolutely won't give up. They must be removed or killed to stop them. The road is still there so I guess one or the other method was used. I suspect the latter.

In recent years they have become a real nuisance in some areas. We take a different approach than the Indians did. They didn't own land as we do. If a beaver flooded an area or cut down trees, that was OK. They belonged to the beaver as much as to the Indians. To the white man, those are my trees that the beaver cut and my land that he flooded, and therefore he must die.

I know several instances where there is conflict between landowners and beavers. One person I know in Athens County has two ponds that are being used and a new one built by beavers. At first it was wonderful. Then they cut down some potentially valuable trees. Next, they kept plugging up the overflow on one of the ponds, threatening to wash out the dam. It was cleaned out every morning and plugged every night. The latest event was when a large culvert was plugged, and during a heavy rain, the drive was washed out completely, cutting machinery access to the rest of the farm.

My neighbor John has an even more perplexing problem. He has been bothered by beavers from time to time. They cut some nice-sized poplars, one of which fell into his pond. They didn't eat much of it, just started cutting another one. He was able to salvage some of them so no real harm was done, but it would be nice if the beavers would let them grow a little more. A month ago they cut down a pine tree that fell across three canoes. Again, no real harm, but it's beginning to be a nuisance.

The real trouble began when John noticed that the water was higher on the dock than it had ever been. A closer inspection revealed that no water was coming out of the overflow. As I said before, beavers can't stand the sound of running water. They had undertaken to stop it and filled the pipe with sticks, mud and rocks. Now this isn't just any ordinary pipe flowing horizontally. It's about two feet in diameter and goes straight down behind the dam about twenty feet and makes a right angle turn for another twenty or thirty feet and into a small crick. Lord knows how long those beavers have been working on that, but I'll bet they plugged it a whole lot quicker than John will unplug it. To make matters worse, they drowned in the pipe and did nothing to improve the air quality. It's my opinion that it will take a crane with some sort of a grab bucket on it. All that I've ever seen are much too big to fit in that pipe. Something will have to be made to fit the pipe. Good luck, John.

I restate my case. Wild animals are fine as long as they don't interfere with man's possessions. As poet Bobby Burns said long ago, "The best laid plans of mice and men aft are gang a glae." When that pond was built, there weren't any beavers to plan against. They'll know better next time.

BACKWOODS MUSINGS

To order

This book from the publisher you may
Call: 1-740-385-7618 or E-mail: mimi@eurekanet.com

Or:
Send $12.95 plus $3.00 (for shipping and handling)
By Check, Money Order, Visa or Master Card

To:
The Backwoods Publishing Company
P.O. Box 1053
Logan, Ohio 43138

Ship Publication To:

Name: _____

Address: _____

City: _____ ST: _____ Zip: _____

Telephone: _____

Credit Card number: _____

Expiration date: _____

Gift From: _____